MW00463820

Paul of
Tarsus

Paul of
Tarsus

T. R. GLOVER

HENDRICKSON
PUBLISHERS

PAUL OF TARSUS
T. R. Glover

Hendrickson Publishers, Inc.
P. O. Box 3473
Peabody, Massachusetts 01961-3473

ISBN 1-56563-728-3

Reprinted from the first edition, originally published by the Student
Christian Movement, London, 1925.

First Printing—Novtember 2002

Printed in the United States of America

JOSEPHO LARMOR

EQUITI SOCIO AMICO

CUIUS ME LAEVUM MITIS SAPIENTIA REXIT

CUIUS AMICITIA VITA BENIGNA FUIT

It was at Simla in August 1916 that the lines of this book were laid, but for myself it is chiefly associated with America—with classes in a summer session at the University of Chicago in 1920; with lectures on the Earl Foundation in the Pacific School of Religion, at Berkeley, California, in October 1923; and again with the Carew lectures in the December of that year in Hartford Theological Seminary in Connecticut; and lectures on the Dowse Foundation in Cambridge, Massachusetts. To write down these names is to recall the kindness of friends and to think of days in pleasant places, not to be remembered without happiness. Nor does this exhaust the tale of my indebtedness. For my friend, the Reverend George William Harte, of Tyndale Chapel, Bristol—another place of indelibly happy memories—made the indexes for me, and my daughter, Elizabeth, read my proofs. It has been well said that the Latin for " modern daughter " is *in loco parentis*.

St John's College
6th May 1925

CONTENTS

PAUL OF TARSUS

INTRODUCTION

" HE is certainly one of the great figures in Greek literature." So says Mr Gilbert Murray; [1] and whether one judge the great writers by the number of their readers age after age, or of those whose minds they shape and whose lives they guide, whether we measure them by their gift of transcending their disciples and commentators, and suggesting perpetually new avenues of thought and experience to be explored, or whether we apply to them the test not merely of knowing what to say, but how to say it, Paul stands among the greatest of the Greeks. It might surprise him to find himself so placed ; they too might be surprised ; but who of them, apart from Homer and Plato, has had so wide and so long an influence, who has opened up more of the real world to men, whose words have lived more in the hearts of their readers ?

He is no easy author. Homer is simpler, and Plato's thought is plainer to follow. Paul can be simple and direct, but when he soars, it is into another region of beauty than Plato knew, and with wings uneven. A bilingual man pays for his gifts, and the Semite who thinks in Greek never quite forgets Jerusalem and the speech of Canaan; his genitives accumulate, his threads break, and it is in losing his way that he arrives. In any case a man who, like the Greek Odysseus, has seen in the spiritual world so many cities of men and learnt their mind, who has

[1] Gilbert Murray, *Four Stages in Greek Religion*, p. 146.

A   1

wrestled with so many religious vocabularies, will not
be easy to follow. It is remarkable that Jesus was, in
a sense, a man of one locality, Paul a man of all the
world; the one might have been expected to show
marks of race and place and time, and he does not;
the other, who should, one would guess, be the easier
to understand, is incomparably harder. Everywhere
men understand Jesus at once, though they do not
quickly exhaust his mind. Paul baffles the reader with
his wealth of suggestion, the temporal and the per-
manent are so involved in his mind and in his speech.
It is treasure in earthen vessels, as he suggests; but,
as in the greatest artists, it is hard to take the treasure
from the vessel. Style is thought, and Paul's style
perplexes the attentive reader, partly because Paul
does not attend to it, partly because in him as in his
gospel, Jew and Greek, barbarian and Scythian, are
one. However well we may know the elements, genius
has the power, as Browning saw:

> Out of three sounds to make
> Not a fourth sound but a star;

and for most minds such transcendental alchemy is
impossible.

But his chief difficulty for us of to-day is not in
the vessel but in the treasure. While he accumulates
height and depth and half spiritualizes them, while he
insists on the mystery of Christ, we, trained in another
age, and sharing its limitations as well as its emanci-
pations, hesitate and are uncertain; we have not his
experience, or we have it only in part, and, pupils of
a scientific school, we mistrust ourselves, our experience,
and our vocabulary. He comes upon us with the
splendid air of one who has found his freedom and
can speak it in a language without drawbacks; and
such language of such men inevitably makes our age
uncomfortable in its uncertainty.

Yet, like Plato, he remains to charm and to challenge.

He has the same gift of interesting men in himself, without intending it, without quite knowing it. He shares also with Plato a progressive habit, which leaves his thoughts here undeveloped, there superseded, while he sweeps on into a new plane of intuition or vision; he is so keen on the last discovery that he forgets the old, and is too eager altogether to care about reconciling them. In another sense, all his life is given to this task of reconciliation, yet he never overtakes it; revelation comes too quickly for tradition and inheritance to be wholly re-interpreted. In the midst of the process comes a spasm, and the work is wrecked; things are left more ill-adjusted than they were before. The old, the half-developed, and the overpowering fresh gain lie there together; and the man is too exultant in his new knowledge to notice that he is inconsistent, or to care. After all Paul and Plato had this in common; neither sought to develop a Paulinism or a Platonism; they both pursued Truth; and to keep abreast of Truth leaves a man little time to be consistent with himself, and little wish for it. Hence any Paulinism or any Platonism, if correct and consistent, will so far misrepresent Paul and Plato.[1] The only -ism that will represent either of them is a habit of mind, a temper, an attitude to life, a faith in God and in what God does. Results will be wrong, however carefully drawn; the man must be known; his failures, his false starts, his entanglements will be more illuminating than another's achievements, for they will reveal him. It is a wise saying:

Errare mehercule malo cum Platone quam cum istis vera sentire.[2]

---

[1] Cf. F. G. Peabody, *The Apostle Paul and the Modern World*, p. 109; " Consistency is the last of virtues that Paul would claim."
[2] Cicero, *Tusculans*, i. 17, 39.

CHAPTER I

TARSUS

I

WHEN Paul told Claudius Lysias that he was a Tarsian, "a citizen of no mean city"—a city "not inconspicuous"—he was not speaking idly. Legend said it was founded by one of the Argives, who, with Triptolemos, sought Io, when she was turned into a cow.[1] Xenophon had been there some four centuries or so before Paul's day, and found the palace of a Cilician King Syennesis. The Greek mercenaries of Cyrus signalized their stay first by looting in the city, and then by a mutiny which Clearchus and Cyrus settled by a 50 per cent. rise in pay.[2] Antiochus Epiphanes, it is inferred, settled Jews as colonists there in 171 B.C.[3] The place had a name for a famous Stoic school; and visitors from other Greek regions of the Mediterranean found a pleasing conservatism in Tarsus, as Chicago people perhaps do still in Boston.[4] Modern travellers speak of the scenery round Tarsus as magnificent; and it is remarked that Paul never alluded to it. Neither did Xenophon, apart from its bearing on military affairs. The ancients were not apt to expatiate, without provocation, upon scenery. An episode recurs to the reader of Plato, where Socrates is taken to a pleasant spot outside Athens—to hear a speech read;[5] and when his guide tells Socrates that he speaks of the

[1] Strabo, c. 673; Dio Chrysostom, *Oration*, xxxiii. 41.
[2] *Anabasis*, i. 2, 23, 26; iii. 1-21.
[3] W. M. Ramsay, *Cities of St Paul*, p. 181.
[4] Dio Chrysostom, *Oration*, xxxiii., § 48 f.
[5] Plato, *Phaedrus*, 230, B-E.

place like a stranger, he owns that he is a stranger, trees and flowers cannot teach him, men can ; so he stays with men in the city. Gratuitous description of scenery in prose was a trick of the rhetorical school ; and what survives of such attempts makes the reader content that there is so little.

If we follow Socrates' example and ask what men had to teach in the city, we learn that long before the Roman times Tarsus was a centre of Greek culture.[1] Strabo, who wrote or compiled his geography about the Christian Era, says that the Tarsians had an enthusiasm for philosophy, and for education generally, that out-went Athenians and Alexandrians or any other citizens of what we should call university towns ; nearly all the students in Tarsus are natives, strangers rarely come, but the Tarsians go abroad to study, and they are rather apt to stay abroad when they have got their education.   In other such places, Alexandria excepted, the students are strangers, and the natives rarely study either in their own universities or anywhere else— which suggests modern Cambridge and Oxford, while Tarsus is perhaps more like Aberdeen.   Strabo speaks of Stoic studies flourishing, and mentions by name five eminent Stoics, one a friend of Marcus Cato, another of Caesar ; he adds the names of a great Academic (the tutor of Augustus' nephew Marcellus), and of others, all men of Tarsus ; " Rome is full of them and of Alexandrians." [2]

Tarsus was a " free city " from Antony's time ; it paid no tribute, and it had self-government.[3] Dio Chrysostom [4] speaks of the workers in sailcloth at Tarsus, and of their repute for being many in number and disorderly in ways, and their uneasy position in the city, of which however they are not full citizens ;

---

[1] Mommsen, *Provinces of Roman Empire*, Vol. ii. p. 122.

[2] Strabo, cc. 673-675. Cf. Walden, *Universities of Ancient Greece*, p. 70 ; Holm, *Greek History*, iv. p. 447.

[3] Appian, *B.C.*, v. 7.   [4] *Oration*, xxxiv. 21-23.

and he urges the concession of full rights to them. Readers of the Acts will recall that Paul in his day worked at the trade; and the suggestion is easy that Aquila and Priscilla may have been Tarsians themselves (Acts xviii. 3).[1] The river Cydnus, Strabo tells us, flows through the city, hard by the young men's gymnasium—a cool and headlong stream. With one last scene on this river recalled to mind, we may pass from the " not inconspicuous city " to its most famous citizen. It was here that Cleopatra came to meet Antony " sailing up the river Cydnus, in a barge with gilded stern and outspread sails of purple, while oars of silver beat time to the music of flutes and fifes and harps. She herself lay at full length under a canopy of gold, dressed like Venus in a picture, and beautiful boys, like painted Cupids, stood on each side to fan her. Her maids were attired like Sea Nymphs and Graces, some steering at the rudder, some working at the ropes." So Plutarch; and English readers will know where to turn for a more splendid version drawn, like so much else, by our greatest dramatist from Plutarch.[2]

That Paul's family, or at least his father, enjoyed Roman citizenship, he tells us himself, when he informs Claudius Lysias that he was " born free." How the citizenship was gained, whether for services rendered or for money, or on the manumission of an enslaved ancestor, we do not know. Paul says more of the Jewish traditions of the family; they were Benjamites as he twice tells us (Phil. iii. 5 ; Rom. xi. 1), Hebrews of of the Hebrews; and it has been an easy and profitless conjecture that he owed his Hebrew name Saul to memories of the tribe's one king. The social and financial position of the family has been much discussed, and we cannot quite escape it ; but the fact that Paul

---

[1] See Varro, *de Re Rustica*, ii. 11, 12, on the cloth, *cilicium*.
[2] Plutarch, *Life of Antony*, c. 25. *Antony and Cleopatra*, Act II. sc. ii.

at one time worked at a trade has to be ruled out as evidence. It appears that it was usual for a young Jew to learn a trade; at least the rabbis are quoted as inculcating this upon parents.[1] It has been conjectured that Paul's father may have been concerned with the sale of the fabric in the markets of the East. Travel seems to have come naturally to Paul, but that cannot be pressed as an argument. He alludes to his " kin "—Junia and Lucius bearing Roman names, and others Greek; [2] and the list in which they appear is now in his Epistle to the Romans, whatever may be the value of guesses as to how it came there. But with a people, who shifted about the world as the Jews have done since Alexander the Great, there is no telling where these " kin " belonged. A nephew lived, or at one time resided, in Jerusalem (Acts xxiii. 16). It was common for Jews, then as now, to have Gentile names, which sometimes suggest their own. Thus Joshua might be Hellenized as Jesus, or transformed into Jason or Justus.[3] A Roman citizen took a Roman name, as the satirist reminds us in his sardonic picture of the change of Dama into Marcus,[4] to the great improvement of his character. But however the name Paullus came to the family whom we are now considering, Paul inherited the name, and, as we shall see, a good deal of the Roman with it.

It has been pointed out that, while Jesus was conspicuously a man of fields and country towns, Paul, as plainly, in allusion, metaphor, and illustration, shows that he is a man of the city, and, further, that he had been a boy there.[5] If we trace back his metaphors to

---

[1] Conybeare and Howson, *St Paul*, vol. i. p. 51.

[2] Romans xvi. 7, 11, 21. See pp. 58, 179.

[3] Cf. Acts xvii. 6; Rom. xvi. 21; Col. iv. 11; Joseph Justus, Acts i. 23.

[4] Persius, 5, 79. See Deissmann, *Bible Studies*, p. 314; Ramsay, *Paul*, pp. 81-88.

[5] Deissmann, *St Paul*, pp. 74, 75.

their first appearance in his mind, we shall see the boy on his way through the streets of Tarsus stopping to watch the builders at the new house—how the wise master-builder (*architecton*) draws the cords and lays the foundation and another builds on it, and how sometimes the work of the latter has to be taken down and done over again; and the boy hears that the man's wages are reduced for his bad work (1 Cor. iii. 10). Or a wrong-headed labourer breaks brickwork down and has to rebuild it (Gal. ii. 18). Later in life he has many hints of the scene, disguised in our English version by the rather obsolete word *edify*. He has the boy's interest in shops—none the less that in the Orient there were no huge plate-glass windows, no departmental stores with hordes of shop-girls, but that barter prevailed, and all the shops of a kind were in a row and more or less open, as they are in the bazars of Smyrna or Calcutta to-day. Here are the butchers (1 Cor. x. 25) with the perplexities that grow for a boy about the distinctions between *Kosher* and other meat, and the carcases of pagan sacrifice; there again are other traders, huckstering, wheedling, and bargaining, illustrating everything that led the Greek to his contempt for " shop-keeping " (*kapeleuo*). Paul later on repudiates that style of procedure in recommending the word of God; it does not need tricks; give it sunlight and sincerity and God looking on, and it will do (2 Cor. ii. 17). It is noted, further, that he uses metaphors of debt, and of the market, and " calculates." [1]

Slaves no doubt abounded, as they did not in Galilee, though Tarsus certainly must have had much fewer than Rome; and Paul, like other boys in Greek and Hellenistic towns, probably got his first conceptions of the world's variety of races from the sorrowful figures of slaves. He does not allude to the slave-market, but he must have seen it; and he does

---

[1] Ramsay, *St Paul*, p. 286.

speak of the branded slave (Gal. vi. 17). One can imagine the small boy's bright interest in recognizing one of the Greek letters he was learning on the side of a man's brow, and how indelible would be the memory of his first discovery of the cruelty that men could show to men. Another day, soldiers marched through the streets perhaps, rough enough, though not conquerors in a free town; and perhaps, as a very small boy to-day will find acute pleasure in a Salvation Army band, the small Saul was impressed with the trumpets, and it was explained to him that the trumpet was blown to tell the soldier when to get ready for march or battle (1 Cor. xiv. 8). Later on, he draws many illustrations from the soldier's life (2 Cor. x. 2-5 ; 2 Tim. ii. 3, 4). The custom-house perhaps did not claim the boy's attention at the beginning, any more than the tax-collector ; but they were part of the city-life, and Paul the traveller must eventually have seen as much as he wanted of the former at least (Rom. xiii. 6-7). The publican comes oftener in the talk of Jesus.

But if shops and slaves and soldiers formed a part of Tarsus life, a Hellenistic city had more variety to offer in its amusements. We have already had an allusion to the gymnasium of Tarsus. It was a matter of amusement to the Greek that Orientals were so fussy about being seen naked ; they laughed at the very white bodies of their captives, when Agesilaus had them stripped to be sold.[1]   On their side the Jews were shocked at Greek nudity.   In the reign of Antiochus Epiphanes, among the lawless enormities of Jason, who bought the High Priesthood and set about Hellenizing Jerusalem and making a little Antioch of the sacred city, the historian notes with horror the establishment of a gymnasium and the introduction of the broad-brimmed Greek *petasos*.   " He gladly planted a gymnasium under the acropolis itself, and

---

[1] Xenophon, *Agesilaus*, i. 25-28 ; *Hellenica*, III. iv. 16-19.

the strongest (or noblest) of our youths he brought under the Greek hat " [1] (2 Macc. iv. 6). To the modern in the West all this seems very innocent, but in the East race and faith are in a turban to this day. " In God's name wear red for blue," says Mahbub Ali to Kim—the Muslim colour not the Hindu. Bombay has some sixty varieties of turban, all with significance, and pictured in the Gazetteer of the city. But Jerusalem and Tarsus were far apart ; distance, environment and the lapse of two centuries changed things. Children are not particular about caste or colour if the other boy has points of contact ; and there is something about the running of a race that captures the boy's mind, even if it is naked Greeks —or, even worse, Hellenizing half-Greeks—who are running. If we cannot certainly answer the question, Was he allowed to watch the heathen at their athletics? it is easier to answer the question, Did he watch them ?

Paul, it must be recognized, kept something of the boy's mind to the very end, the boy's easy gift of " making friends with fellows," the boy's keenness—his very tangents of thought show it. " Don't you know that the runners in the stadium all run and only one gets the prize ? *Run to win* ! " (1 Cor. ix. 24). And this reprobate Jew, who had in his boyhood watched the Greek heathen at their sports, forgetful of old Jewish proprieties and Greek indecencies, goes on to make it clear, not only that he had been interested in racing, but in boxing. He does not " run uncertainly," he says, and we can believe it ; he will know which end of the course he has to reach and keep his eye on it, and " run to win." When he boxes he will not, waste his blows on the air ; the other man shall know that he can punch (so men found who ventured on

[1] See A. T. Olmstead, in *American Journal of Theology*, vol. xxiv. No. 1 ; Edwyn Bevan, *Jerusalem under the High Priests*, p. 79.

controversy with him) ; [1] and he will keep fit like a
good athlete. The whole passage is illuminative.
Paul is not " drawing illustrations from local interests "
any more than Jesus thinks out allusions to " natural
objects " ; the racing and the boxing interested
him. Of course they did ; and one might guess
that there were Tarsians, who, if they read his letters,
could have borne personal testimony to his not
hitting the air when he fought as a boy, as well as to
his keenness in running. From the energy of the man,
his extraordinary powers of physical endurance, the
vitality of his mind, it is not too much to conclude
that if he took no part as a youth in the gymnasium,
the stadium and the wrestling ground, it was not
because he would not have liked it ; the reasons must
be looked for in nationalism and religious tradition,
and the life of renunciation began before his 'teens.
One is not a Hebrew of Hebrews for nothing. But even
in antiquity children played, and fought, and ran
races. Epictetus tells what they played ; they were
" sometimes athletes, sometimes monomachi, sometimes gladiators." [2]

The theatre was another feature of Greek life to be
found wherever the Greek went, an obvious factor in
all Hellenization, pagan through and through. Running was human, boxing, too, and soldiering ; but the
stage was idolatrous, the play was a heathen ceremony
in essence, its arguments were drawn from legends of
false gods, and the performance was liable to be
grossly indecent—" a ligge or a tale of baudry." Yet
the Jews, as we learn from an inscription, had a special
place assigned to them in the theatre at Miletus. If
the son of strict Jews might not go to the theatre,
he knew all about it. " We are made a spectacle
(*theatron*) to the world, to angels and to men," he says

---

[1] Cf. Peter at Antioch, Gal. ii.
[2] Epictetus, *Diatribai*, III. xv. 5. And they quarrelled over their
games, too, from Patroclus onward, *Iliad* xxiii. 86-88.

(1 Cor. iv. 9) ; he plays Hecuba himself, with all the universe looking on ; the sight

> Would have made milche the Burning eyes of Heaven
> And passion in the Gods.[1]

Life in a Greek or Oriental town was carried on a good deal out of doors. " The city teaches the man," as Simonides said—πόλις ἄνδρα διδάσκει. Paul began to learn what we call his universalism in the streets of Tarsus as a boy, too human to feel that the other boys were not human too, whatever he was taught within doors, even if actually for a while he persuaded himself to believe it. We must not forget that life in a Hellenistic city might influence him by moods of antipathy. The family was obviously a strict one, as Pharisee in outlook and practice as the foreign soil allowed ; the discipline and the name implied division and separation, and Greeks were not always genial to Jews. We must not forget the training of the home. But here, too, in spite of itself, the household helped to broaden the boy's outlook. It was inevitable.

The two great languages of the nearer East were Greek and Syriac, to which the Aramaic of Palestine is closely akin. Tarsus stands where the two met, a frontier town. Westward, thought and speech were Greek ; eastward, and very far and significantly eastward, thought and speech were Syriac. Westward lay philosophy and literature. Syriac seems never to have had much literature till it became a Christian speech. How far eastward it reached is not always realized, but of late years Syriac books and script have been found in Turkestan. I have myself been present at a Christian

---

[1] I am told that this is fanciful; but Philo a generation earlier in Alexandria was interested in Greek amusements, e.g., in the theatre (and the psychological effects of music there, which he noticed himself), in bull fights (and the conduct of the bulls). See Drummond, *Philo Judaeus*, vol. i. p. 17.

service in Calcutta, when a liturgy was conducted in Syriac by men calling themselves Syrians, whose ancestors had been Christians in India longer perhaps than the Anglo-Saxon stock, Christian or pagan, had been in England at all. In China, at Si-ngan-fu, stands a Syrian Christian monument, conspicuous among all the inscriptions of the Church. Greek and Aramaic in some form were inevitable in Paul's upbringing. Luke tells us, further, that Paul made a speech at Jerusalem in Hebrew without preparation (Acts xxi. 40). Conceivably the speech may have been in Aramaic; Yiddish is often called Hebrew to-day. It is likely that Paul learnt Hebrew and read the Old Testament in Hebrew, but it is clear that he knew the book best in the Septuagint version. His religious and ethical vocabulary, his quotations, alike show that it was not the Hebrew but the Greek Bible that was in his heart.[1] A hint of a play on words, as impossible in Greek as in English, suggests that he at least sometimes thought in Aramaic; "long hair" and "disgrace" are not an assonance in Greek, but in Aramaic they are.[2] It is hardly thinkable that, in all his intercourse with Roman officials and magistrates, he knew no Latin.[3] There was not the Greek's contempt for that barbarian tongue to stop him, and even Greeks, though shaky now and then like Plutarch in Latin grammar, knew more of the language than they pretended.

An argument has been put forward by a learned German scholar that Paul " did not come from the literary upper class, but from the artisan non-literary classes, and that he remained with them " ; that he was

---

[1] Cf. Adolf Deissmann, *St Paul*, pp. 101-103; Wendland, *Die hell.-röm. Kultur*, p. 354, on his habit of interweaving fragments of the LXX. with his own words; H. A. A. Kennedy, *St Paul and Last Things*, p. 56.

[2] 1 Cor. xi. 14; *sa'ra* and *ṣa'ra*, or *tsa'ra*.

[3] Sir W. Ramsay holds that Paul may have preached in Latin at Lystra.

a tent-maker " whose trade was the economic foundation of his existence," who worked night and day
(1 Thess. ii. 9 ; 2 Thess. iii. 8), who wrote in " large
letters " (Gal. vi. 11), clumsily and awkwardly, with
" a workman's hand deformed by toil," and preferred
an amanuensis.[1] Poverty it is plain that Paul knew,
at all events in Corinth and in Thessalonica.[2] But
Wendland is probably right in denying Deissmann's
thesis outright, and asserting categorically that Paul
was not of the lower class, either in social status or
education, and that to count his language vulgar
and non-literary is an unjustifiable application of
Attic standards—though he allows that Paul's is not
yet a triumphant style.[3] He certainly was suspected
by Felix of being able to lay his hands on money
(Acts xxiv. 26) ; and in Rome he had his own hired
house (Acts xxviii. 30).

We learn from the Acts that, at an age which we
are left to conjecture, Paul removed, or was taken,
to Jerusalem. There, according to Paul's speech as
given by Luke, Paul was brought up at the feet of
Gamaliel (Acts xxii. 3). Whatever be the part of Luke
or of other historians in reporting the speeches of
their heroes, there need be no hesitation in accepting
the statement that Paul was the pupil of Gamaliel.
Though we are not told at what age he left Tarsus
and came to Jerusalem, the question is not without
importance. The only available evidence is internal.
That Greek was his native speech is proved, says
Wendland,[4] by his familiarity with the Septuagint.
Casual references and broken quotations will tell what
text or edition of a book a man has read ; and these,
with passages, where Paul bases arguments on the
Greek which would not rest on the Hebrew, prove that

[1] Deissmann, *St Paul*, p. 50.   [2] Compare Acts xx. 34.
[3] Wendland, *Die hell.-röm. Kultur*, p. 353. His use of the LXX
is not that of a labourer, it may be added.
[4] Wendland, *Die hell.-röm Kultur*, p. 354.

he used the Greek Bible. Deissmann ably deduces from his being a man of the Septuagint a later date than childhood for his leaving Tarsus ; [1] he must have spent a good part of his youth, or at least his boyhood, there. His "sovereign command of Hellenistic colloquial " [2] points in the same direction, and that general familiarity, which we have remarked, with the ordinary life of a Hellenistic town. It is held by another scholar that all his Hebraisms are due to the Septuagint, with the addition of a few Hebrew words, while now and then, if he happens to translate from the Hebrew, a hint of its structure can be seen in his Greek.

Greek then is his mother-tongue, and Greek his milieu—in neither case the Greek of the great classical period ; he belongs to the Graeco-Roman world, but his background is Semitic, and his religion Hebrew. He thus stands at the centre of things, equipped for the very task he was to undertake, the interpretation of Christ to the heart of the world. But before we consider his capture by Christ, we have to look more closely at the influences that played upon him and to see, if possible, how far they shaped him. If our course for the time is devious, if it yields little in positive statement about the man himself, it will enable us to see a little more of that Graeco-Roman world, which, if it did not influence him as directly this way or that way as some have held, was yet his home and his battleground. The time should not be quite wasted.

§ II

The interests of ordinary life in a Hellenistic town we have seen to be among the early associations of Paul. But Hellenistic life and Greek thought are two different things ; the Hellene remained a different

[1] Deissmann, *St Paul*, pp. 92, 93.   [2] Deissmann, *loc. cit.*

creature from his neighbours who shared his ideas and his outlook, different even if they had any element of Greek blood in their veins. The theatre and the gymnasium passed more easily into men's habits than Greek discipline into their minds. Men in that age of travel and talk picked up in popular lectures and conversation more ideas than they ever thought out, much as people do in newspapers and novels and on trains to-day. They learnt the language and even something of the style of Greece ; but the Greek spirit was not so easily caught. No example perhaps can be so telling as that of Plutarch himself ; he was Greek by blood and Greek by birth ; he was steeped in the history, the literature, and the philosophy of the older Greece ; but, however much it might have surprised him to be told so, no one could be much further from the mind and outlook of Plato.

When we turn to Paul, the obvious starting-point is given by two quotations. Luke tells us (Acts xvii. 28) that Paul in his address in Athens quoted half a hexameter, τοῦ γὰρ καὶ γένος ἐσμέν, " for we are also his offspring "—which, curiously enough, comes both in the Astronomical poem of the Cilician Aratus (translated into Latin by Cicero), and in the hymn of the Stoic Cleanthes. Till we have decided how far Luke, like other contemporary historians, felt and took a freedom in re-modelling the speeches of his characters, or (as Sir William Ramsay insists) reproduced the addresses of Peter and Paul with strict faithfulness, we cannot build much on this single fragment. A safer instance of quotation is the whole line which Paul himself cites in writing to the Corinthians (1 Cor. xv. 33).

φθείρουσιν ἤθη χρήσθ' ὁμιλίαι κακαί.

The rendering of our English version—" Evil communications corrupt good manners "—hardly suggests its source in a comedy of Menander. It does not

B

follow that Paul knew the original comedy.[1] If Paul
is responsible for the epistle to Titus in its present
form, he quoted a line of Epimenides upon the Cretans,
a line that, like several in Shakespeare's plays and a
famous quatrain in Sir Walter Scott, owes more to the
man who quoted it than to its author.

But, when we compare the pleasure in quotation
from the great literature that his Greek contemporaries
show, and the close familiarity that half-allusions betray,
it must be felt that Paul is of another school. His
quotations, his borrowed phrases and half-phrases,
echoes and assonances, point in very much the same
way as theirs to an older literature ; but with him it
is the Septuagint. Take a page of the Christian
Clement of Alexandria, who wrote about A.D. 200—
or, better, any twenty consecutive pages—and compare
the same length of passage from Paul, and the contrast
will confirm the view that Paul was not an enthusiast
for Greek literature ; he did not love it as Clement did,
and other men ; he did not know it and live in it ;
his allegiance and his tradition were elsewhere.

Paul practically says as much himself, when he tells
the Corinthians that he did not come to them " with
excellency of speech or of wisdom," that he brought
no " enticing words of man's wisdom " (1 Cor. ii. 1, 4).
When he says he was " rude (*idiôtes*) in speech "
(2 Cor. xi. 6), his meaning is quite plain. Elsewhere
he speaks of the *idiôtes* (1 Cor. xiv. 16, 23, 24) in
exactly the sense which Greeks gave to the word—the
" unlearned," the " layman," the " outsider," the

---

[1] In this connexion I tried an experiment upon a post-graduate
class in an American University ; how many knew the line—

A thing of beauty is a joy for ever ?

Everybody knew it. How many knew the author ? There was a
strong preponderance for Keats ; but those who had read *Endymion*
were a very small minority.

The recent discovery and publication of some of Menander's
plays will probably not add to the number of those who regret that
Paul did not know the poet at first hand.

"ordinary person." It is, above all, the man who has not had the education, which was summed up in the name Rhetoric, but which included literature—a scheme of culture which was first thought out and practised by Isocrates at Athens, and from which, by a direct lineal succession, Oxford culture is descended. It is true that it was a commonplace for speakers to disclaim rhetorical skill. Socrates, in a clever passage of Plato's dialogue *Ion* (532 D), says to the rhapsode Ion—"You rhapsodes and actors, and the poets whose verses you sing, are clever fellows, you know; but I can only tell you the plain truth, as an ordinary person (*idiôtes*) would." But Paul was not playing with Socratic irony; it was obvious enough that his interests did not lie along the lines of ordinary Greek culture; he did not study their great poets, he did not practise their modes of speech. If students of Greek rhetoric recognize in his writings forms and turns of speech, some thirty figures in all,[1] to which the experts gave technical names, it is more than likely that Paul could not have told the names. If a comparison with *Tristram Shandy* is tolerable in this connexion, the Fellows of Jesus College remarked with surprise upon the skill with which Walter Shandy used logical processes which he could not have labelled in scholastic language. Paul was not trained in Rhetoric, either in the narrower sense of the art of speaking or in the larger sense of Greek literary and philosophical culture.

Here we touch a most interesting question, for a great many coincidences have been remarked between Paul and the Stoics,[2] some in language and some in ideas. Thus Norden notices a "Stoic doxology" in

---

[1] A. T. Robertson, *Grammar of Greek New Testament*, p. 129.

[2] They are discussed by Clemen, *Primitive Christianity and Its Non-Jewish Elements*, p. 366; Lightfoot, an appendix to *Philippians*; W. Morgan, *Religion and Theology of Paul*, p. 28, etc.; Wendland and others.

the Romans, when Paul writes, "Of him and through him and to him are all things" (Rom. xi. 36). "Self-sufficient" (*autarkês*, Phil. iv. 11) is a word with Stoic antecedents, a word embodying a great deal of essential Stoic belief, but that is not to say that Paul uses it in any strict Stoic sense. Indeed, when he goes on to say that he "can do all things in him that strengtheneth me," it is plain how little of the original doctrine survives in the Stoic word. It had clearly been popularized. The contrast between soul and body (2 Cor. v. 1) is pronounced to be "the clearest instance of his debt to Greek philosophy,"[1] but here again Paul's outlook is not that of the Stoics. If with them he traces sin to the guilty flesh,[2] he has not their faith in the soul's ability to control the flesh and the passions of the body[3]—very far from it, as we see elsewhere (Rom. vii. 23). The Stoic emphasized "spirit" and contrasted physical and spiritual, as Paul does; but Paul's account of "spirit" is not Stoic doctrine; behind his view is a personal God who bestows it, in their judgment it is a universal force in all nature.[4] The "holy spirit" of Seneca[5] is quite another thing from the "holy spirit" of Paul. Paul's emphasis on the irrelevance of sex or slavery in the things of Christ (Gal. iii. 28; Col. iii. 11) is not unlike the Stoic insistence on the same thing in thought; perhaps the idea is borrowed or suggested, because, while it is not irrelevant to the real results of Christ's incarnation, it is not clear that Paul draws all the necessary consequences from it. Paul may speak of "reasonable, or logical, service" (Rom. xii. 1), but he is not ready to carry logic to the lengths of the Stoic. To find in his use of the allegoric method the influence of Stoicism is to ignore its wide employment by people who were not Stoics, even if they

---

[1] Clemen, *l.c.*   [2] Persius, 2, 62.   [3] W. Morgan, *l.c.*, pp. 16-19.
[4] W. Morgan, *l.c.*, pp. 28-29.
[5] Seneca, Epistle, 41, 1, 2; *sacer intra nos spiritus sedet.*

did borrow it originally. The classification of sins,
the comparison of man's body to a temple (1 Cor.
vi. 19; iii. 17), or to a vessel or a tent, the likening of
society to a body—one cannot feel that it was absolutely necessary for Paul to attend Stoic lectures to
manage such matters.

But as instances of possible suggestion, at any rate,
as parallels, accumulate, it grows clear that, living in
a world of popular lecturers, who travelled from place
to place and gave demonstrations or displays of their
accomplishments in philosophy, criticism, and style,
Paul shared the inevitable atmosphere of his time, and
caught something of the language and with it something of the ideas. Stoic terms and Stoic ideas were
not to be escaped by a man of intelligence living
among men, and used to handling ideas, even if he
did not himself frequent Stoic schools. It would
have been difficult for him to find teachers who were
not influenced by Greek ideas, even if he had wished
to find them. He went in fact to Gamaliel, of whom
it is recorded that above other Jewish teachers he was
free from prejudice against Greek thought.[1] The
case is completed when we find some of the central
ideas of Stoicism in what we may call the necessary
and unconscious intellectual equipment of Paul.

Thus to take an illuminative passage—" When the
Gentiles, which have not the law, do by nature the
things contained in the law, these, having not the law,
are a law unto themselves : which show the work of
law written in their hearts, their conscience also
bearing them witness, and their thoughts the mean
while accusing or else excusing one another " (Rom.
ii. 14, 15). There are in this passage blended elements—" The law " is pure Judaism ; yet a Stoic,
unacquainted with Judaism, might not have noticed
anything very foreign in the term ; nor would he

---

[1] H. A. A. Kennedy, *Paul and Last Things*, p. 59 ; the tradition
that Gamaliel was himself versed in Greek literature.

have recognized an undoubted echo of the language
of Jeremiah (xxxi. 31 f.) in " the law written in their
hearts " ; it would have seemed to him a not-out-of-
the-way variant upon the two great Stoic conceptions,
on which the sentence really turns—Nature and
Conscience. Conscience was a Stoic word, of their
own coining apparently—a word really needed by any
who studied man's mind, a tool of thought so obvious
that it seems odd that it was not invented earlier.
Nature was the very foundation of all Stoic philosophy ; " to live according to Nature " was their
most famous watchword. Paul here is using a conception which we do not find in the Old Testament.
" Let Nature be your teacher "—if we may give a
slightly different connotation to Wordsworth's line—
is it a Stoic or is it Paul speaking ? It is exactly with
the Stoic apprehension of a common basis under all
experience, of a common law written from the beginning in every man's mind, in his whole composition,
that Paul speaks. Sometimes he is not so successful
in catching the Stoic tone ; the question about Nature
teaching a man not to have long hair (1 Cor. xi. 14)
they would certainly have answered differently and
contradicted him. But he was probably hardly aware
how close he was coming at any time to the language
of the school, and he was almost certainly indifferent.

But to sum up his relations with Stoicism. The
School coined the language ; the roving lecturers
and the audiences that quoted them gave it currency ;
it came to Paul. He slid, as we also do, into using the
speech of our day, where it coincides with what we
observe to be true.[1] The Stoics and their followers
pointed to a great correspondence between what we
may call, in antithesis, Nature and human nature ;

[1] Cf. K. Lake, *Landmarks of Early Christianity*, p. 89, who says
that attempts made to trace the direct influence of Stoic metaphysics
in Paul only show that " their vocabulary was more widely used than
their problems were understood—a phenomenon not peculiar to
the first century."

they are made for one another ; there are laws of
Nature, and these are also the laws of human nature.
Conscience is that operation of the human mind, that
function, aspect or part of it, by which we become
aware of these laws. Nature and Conscience work
together, just as Paul says. If it was a nominally
heathen Greek who pointed it out, a good Jew can
verify it in the real world which the true God made,
and can find (as our passage shows) a hint in Jeremiah
that the true God intended the link between Man
and all Nature—the union, the community, of all
God's works—to be discovered. If Paul, as we should
suppose, absorbed these ideas from current phrase and
the common stock of axiomatic ideas, we deduce not
a Stoic school or a Stoic teacher, but a cosmopolitan
world in which ideas are no longer private or racial
property—a world conscious through the terms it
shares of a common experience and an interest in
every man's experience of God. And from other
sources we know that this was the milieu in which a
cosmopolitan Jew of Paul's day must move, whatever
his powers of resistance or assimilation.[1]

Paul, then, is not a man regularly trained in Greek
culture ; he is, as he avows, not a product of the
schools ; nor is he a philosopher, if philosophers pure
and simple at all survived and philosophy were not
merged in ethics and psychology. His traditions are
those of orthodox Judaism ; he conceived himself to
be an orthodox Jew. But an open mind in such a
world receives impressions from many sources, and he
could not use Greek speech unreflectively. It was
bound to tell upon him and it did. He met the
Greek spirit in Tarsus, city of athletes, rhetoricians
and Stoics, and the very fact that his Scriptures were
in Greek secured the influence of that spirit ; he was
to be a man of all the world. But meanwhile he was
a young Jew and orthodox.

[1] See further on this, Chap. VI.

CHAPTER II

JERUSALEM

PAUL was a young Jew and orthodox, but he was bred in a Greek world, and was more open than he would have guessed to influences outside the pale. For such trouble waits.

The circumstances of his going to Jerusalem he does not mention, and our data are scanty but not altogether insufficient. He tells us himself, in his letters, that he was " as touching the law a Pharisee " (Phil. iii. 5) ; " I forged ahead in Judaism beyond many of my own age and race, and I was more exceedingly zealous for the traditions of my fathers " (Gal. i. 14). We may recall in passing the comments of Jesus on the " traditions " and on the enthusiasm with which they were upheld. Luke further tells us how Paul divided the hostile council in Jerusalem by announcing that he was " a Pharisee, the son of a Pharisee " (Acts xxiii. 6), and how he readily explained his upbringing to King Agrippa and suggested that there must be plenty of evidence about it, if any one cared to produce it. " My manner of life from my youth, from its beginning among my own race in Jerusalem, all the Jews know. They knew me earlier, too [the Greek is not free from some vagueness], if they were only willing to testify that, according to the most exact sect of our religion, I lived a Pharisee " (Acts xxvi. 4, 5). Paul, again, in his open-air speech at Jerusalem told the people that he was brought up at the feet of Gamaliel (Acts xxii. 3). The next step comes in Luke's direct narrative ; Paul was a party to the movement of persecution. From this small hand-

24

ful of facts we have to reconstruct his years at Jerusalem, or leave it alone—unless from the grown man
and his mind we can recapture the youth, not always
a quite impossible feat, especially where the man is
remarkable for keeping through life characteristics
which every one agrees to be youthful.

Let us anticipate, and look at the grown Paul—
Paul in middle life, " Paul the aged "—impetuous and
energetic to the last ; and impetuous energy is surely
to be read in the proceedings of the persecutor. He
is large-built, fresh of mind and strongly individual,
unmistakable for any one else. If the persecutor
does not manifest the width of intellectual range and
sympathy, which the apostle shows ever to be increas-
ing in the most surprising way, we can believe that
impulses and associations of the Tarsian boyhood were
being suppressed by the logical fury of youth, and that
the chaos and frenzy of his mind were intensified by
this struggle against instinct. Two strains battle in
him, reason and intuition ; we know him as a dialec-
tician and the possessor of intuitive gifts in the same
epistle, now one and now the other—sometimes in
the same chapter. There is a great deal of both in
chapters ii. to iv. of the Epistle to the Romans ; yet,
in spite of all the great thoughts and phrases of the
fifth chapter, most people will oftener read the eighth,
where his intuition is gloriously free from his schol-
asticism. He is bound to think a thing out, to hammer
it out with reason and fact, and his sense of fact is the
thing that saves him and confuses his critics. The
tangents [1] that haunt his writings in later years show
the sudden swiftness with which he pounces on a
new idea or truth. His blaze of anger at Antioch,
when he found his colleagues were not (what he calls)
" running straight " (ὀρθοποδοῦσι, Gal. ii. 14) ; his
indignant protest : " Before God I lie not " (Gal. i. 20)
—no common or frequent phrase with him—these

[1] Cf. pp. 189, 190.

bear witness to a nature passionate in devotion to truth.
We may note also how, without his quoting himself,
as didactic persons do, he uses in an early letter and
in a later the same searching Greek verb [1]—not the
language of the easy-going—" prove all things "
(1 Thess. v. 21) and " prove the better things "
(Phil. i. 10, δοκιμάζειν). From his first appearance
as a Christian he argues—arguing, proving, and con-
founding people at Damascus (Acts ix. 22) ; just as,
years later, we find him doing at Thessalonica, Beroea,
Corinth, Ephesus, and getting regularly into trouble
with it, as human storm-centres do. Logic, love of
truth, argument, courage and intuition, with extreme
swiftness of mind and a quick temper—a man of
passion and of reason, every college knows the type,
born, like the ancient Athenians, " neither to keep
quiet themselves, nor to leave other people quiet." [2]
    Those who do not know college life may read of it
in Wordsworth's *Prelude* and many other places.
Perhaps we shall not be far astray, if we picture Paul,
launched upon a new course of study, a new way of
life, to have been not so very unlike the young
Wordsworth at St John's, both in mind and in mood
—and the first mood was in neither case the last.

> My spirit was up, my thoughts were full of hope ; . . .
> Questions, directions, warnings and advice
> Flowed in upon me from all sides ; fresh day
> Of pride and pleasure ! . . .
> I was the Dreamer, they the Dream ; I roamed
> Delighted through the motley spectacle ;
> Gowns grave, or gaudy, doctors, students, streets,
> Courts, cloisters, flocks of churches, gateways, towers.[3]

Paul was indeed not " a stripling of the hills, a northern
villager," and we do not know at what age precisely

---

[1] It is significant how characteristic words recur with him.   Cf.
pp. 195, 212 ; and also cf. Gal. ii. 20; Eph. v. 2, 25.
[2] Thucydides, i. 70, 9.   [3] Wordsworth, *Prelude*, iii. 18-35

he removed to Jerusalem. Paul is the most auto-biographical of writers, and the least. Every sentence is Paul, rather than Pauline, but chronology and quotation are work too slow for such a spirit.[1]

So far we have thought of Paul going to sit at the feet of Gamaliel very much as of a man going up for the first time to the University. But Jerusalem was a great deal more. It was the ancient capital of the Jewish people, written all over with history. We have but to recall a few names from the Old Testament to see again the city to which Paul went. The Jebusites, David, Solomon, Isaiah and Sennacherib, Nebuchadnezzar, Jeremiah, Nehemiah, what a story they make! And Antiochus Epiphanes, Pompey and Herod (for we had better leave out Alexander the Great) open up fresh avenues of memory, great records of national suffering and deliverance, and of suffering again. The Book of Deuteronomy had given the place another value altogether than the historical; here was the one place where sacrifice might be offered to Jehovah, a place, where, if theory were true, earth came closer to heaven than anywhere else. It was a pilgrim centre, as it is still. In Deuteronomy and the Psalms we can read of what it was hoped the pilgrim centre would be—

> I to the hills will lift mine eyes—
> Thy Saints take pleasure in her stones,
> Her very dust to them is dear.

In the Gospels and the Acts, and in the letters of St Jerome,[2] we can read what it became. " If,"

[1] Cf. the tangles of chronology in which Paul and Luke between them, with Galatians and Acts, involve the reader; and, e.g., the difficulty of guessing how much of Gal. ii. Paul means to tell us he really said at Antioch. Some four places will be found in the early part of that Epistle where sentences break off and take new starts. It may be Paul's explosive writing that is the cause, or the despair of a sorely tried amanuensis.

[2] I may be allowed to add Stephen Graham's fascinating book, *With the Russian Pilgrims to Jerusalem.*

wrote St Jerome about A.D. 394, " the sites of the Cross and the Resurrection were not in a crowded city, where are a curia, a garrison, harlots, actors, jesters and everything there is in any other city ; or if its only crowds were monks, then indeed it would be a desirable abode for all monks." [1] Josephus [2] affirms that under Cestius Gallus (A.D. 63-66) a census was taken of the pilgrims who came to the Jewish city and that the number was 2,700,200—a figure which " the Jew Apella may believe," as Horace profanely says. It is too like the army of Xerxes ; but, like the numbers alleged of that army, it is an indication of the swarms of Jews who came to Jerusalem, and a story in the early part of the Acts (ii. 9-11) indicates that they were almost as miscellaneous as the hosts that Xerxes led to Greece. Other sources suggest the disorders and factions of the town, which we can readily believe. Pilate on one occasion mingled the blood of Galilaeans with their sacrifices (Luke xiii. 1). To Jesus the place, with its temple full of hucksters trading in birds and cattle and making money out of the pilgrims in its sacred courts, and with the floating population of ruffians that a sanctuary drew, was " a den of thieves " (Mark xi. 17).

From the squalor of the present, people in such places, who are not engaged in exploiting the tourist and the pilgrim, take refuge in the past, in archaeology. But Paul was the last man capable of becoming an antiquary, however acute and keen his sense of the value of history, however intense his attachment to his people and its spiritual story. If Mr C. G. Montefiore finds Paul's religion before his conversion insufficiently joyous and darkened by too sombre a strain of pessimism, the contrast between the idealized Holy City and the actual pilgrim centre may have

---

[1] Jerome, *Epp.*, lviii. 4. I may refer to the chapter on "Women Pilgrims " in *Life and Letters in the Fourth Century*.
[2] Josephus, *Bell. Jud.*, vi. 9, 3 ; G. A. Smith, *Jerusalem*, ii. 397.

contributed to the darkening of life. At the same time, we may suppose that a Cilician-born Jew, with interests keen enough in the living and larger world he knew (in spite of the intense nationalism, which at this time he was clearly trying to heighten), would in moments of nature find fresh avenues back to the larger world in the great tides of humanity that swept in from everywhere, Jews, proselytes and outsiders. Perhaps, too, a man who was a Roman citizen by birth and (at least in later life) by instinct, may have found the anti-Roman feeling of the home-bred Jews something parochial. In all this attempt to recapture his years in Jerusalem, we are, as already said, dependent on guess-work ; but where we have a man of marked characteristics, guess-work need hardly be as random as its name sometimes suggests. At any rate we find the future Apostle of the Gentiles living in a focus of the world's life, provincial town as it was. He could hardly have been reminded more forcibly in Rome itself, or Alexandria, of the many sorts and conditions of men ; and this was one of his problems.

His studies in Judaism did not need to be intensive to reveal to him how the religion was divided into schools and sects. The thing was patent. The long history of Jewish thought was marked and shaped by the struggles of thinkers, as everybody knew. The prophets were famous for their defiance of popular misconceptions of God and of the ritual He wished. The careers of Nehemiah and Ezra had been full of controversy. Judaism was still divided. All Jews accepted the Pentateuch, all the Temple ; and the canon of the Old Testament was winning its way to acceptance. All these things held Jews together ; but in interpretation and observance they disagreed. Paul was the son of a Pharisee, strict by tradition, ardent by temperament, clear from beginning to end that Sadduceeism was in essence a negation of God, as indeed it was ; and, except by antipathy, there is little reason to suppose that the views of the Sadducees influenced him. The elements that shaped him in Judaism were the noble ones. That he was brought up on the Old Testament and some books of the Apocrypha (notably The Wisdom of Solomon) we have already seen. Even after his conversion, he went to the Temple to pray, and received there, we learn, a significant addition to the many calls that took him to the Gentile world (Acts xxii. 17-21). More strange is it that at the end of his journeys, on his last visit to Jerusalem, he could fall in with the compromise in practice (as it must before long have seemed to Christians) proposed to him by the friends at headquarters. Two other contributory factors have to be considered in more detail—the influence of Apocalyptic ideas, and the reaction of Greek thought as it affected the Jews of the Dispersion. To these we must return in a little.

He was a Pharisee, but not all Pharisees were of one mind. There was a common outlook, a common conviction of the supremacy of God and of His law, a common purpose to observe that law to the last jot and tittle, and to safeguard the observance by keeping within the hedges set up by tradition. A determined attempt is made nowadays by Jews and others to vindicate the Pharisees from the character which the Gospels give them; but it will take a great deal of proof to show that Jesus did not find himself in conflict with them, and that the grounds of his disagreement were not substantially those given in our narratives. There were obviously Pharisees who entirely deceived themselves—"blind Pharisees," as Jesus calls them—who combined, as is very easy to do, excessive scrupulosity about trifles with insufficient attention to the weightier matters of the law, judgment, mercy and faith (Matt. xxiii. 23). That there were others who were keener in self-criticism is shown by the

fact that Paul came of the school, and admits it readily
in later life, admits it without a hint that his Pharisaism had been hypocrisy, or that it was anything but
an experiment in religion which utterly failed—a right
enough thing to try, but a wrong thing to go on with,
when Christ was available. Among Pharisees there
were different schools of interpretation ; the followers
of Hillel and Shammai, it was said, not Elijah himself
could reconcile. Paul, as a Greek-speaking Jew of the
Dispersion, went, as already said, to Gamaliel.[1] To
pursue inquiry into the Jewish sects is not our purpose,
but to understand Paul.

The elements that go to his training are, in the
case of every man of any real force, controlled by
reflexion upon experience, his own experience and
that of others so far as it is available for him ; for his
observation is part of his experience, though not the
dominant part. The training is experience ; but
what schools and colleges and teachers contribute is
far from being the whole experience ; and the man
reflecting upon what he has seen and what he has
been is larger than all his experience together. Hence
while the elements in his environment and upbringing
that shape him count, the man himself counts much
more. What does *he* make of father and mother,
school and college and professor ? Does he re-affirm
what he has been taught ? The presumption is that
he does so on the basis of its observed correspondence
with fact. The question, then, of his native stamp
and endowment is at least as important as that of his
teachers or of the atmosphere in which he grows—
more important.

Paul kept to the end a good deal of his Judaism,—

---

[1] Mr Montefiore, *Judaism and Paul*, p. 90, prefers, for reasons
which I do not guess, to doubt the statement in Acts that Paul was a
pupil of Gamaliel ; I do not know whether Luke or Paul is to be
supposed to have lied or blundered over it. Professor Kirsopp Lake
accepts the statement ; *Earlier Epistles of St Paul*, p. 427.

some of it because he believed in it after long and
concentrated thought ; some of it, as with the Greek
ideas which he picked up in the Hellenistic atmosphere,
with a certain serene unconsciousness that it too
needed criticism. Outstanding examples, obvious at
a glance, are such famous pieces of exegesis as that
about *seed* and *seeds* in the Epistle to the Galatians—
" He saith not, And to seeds, as of many ; but as of
one, And to thy seed, which is Christ " (Gal. iii. 16) ;
or the spiritualization of Israel's experiences in the
exodus—" They were all baptized unto Moses in the
cloud and in the sea ; and did all eat the same spiritual
meat ; and did all drink the same spiritual drink ;
for they drank of that spiritual Rock that followed
them, and that Rock was Christ " (1 Cor. x. 2-4).
Such ingenuities of interpretation pleased the Jews,
and, unfortunately, later on pleased the Christians,
who learnt the method from Philo. It is true, however, that if Philo had not been there to teach them,
the Stoics were doing, and the Neo-Platonists rather
later were to do, the same thing with Homer. Still
Paul did not learn it from Stoics or Neo-Platonists ; he
got it from his Jewish teachers.

It is to be remarked at once that, while, probably,
doubts as to the validity of the method hardly crossed
his mind, it is only occasionally that he uses it, and
rarely to establish any point of first importance.
When he comes to what is fundamental, he turns
(probably) unconsciously but by instinct to his own
experience.

More than these small ingenuities came from his
school. He is never stirred by the question that has
agitated modern Christendom, as it did Marcion in
the second century—the question of the authority
and inspiration of the Old Testament. He may not,
in any passage to be ascribed with certainty to his pen,[1]

---

[1] 2 Tim. iii. 16 is a famous verse in a much-disputed epistle, some
parts of which, I feel, must be genuine Paul. It is possible that

suggest any account of inspiration, but the authority of the Old Testament was a Jewish axiom,
and it is among Paul's axioms, unchallenged, almost
un-thought-about. There the Old Testament stood ;
the prophets had been conscious that the Lord spoke
to them, and they had said so ; and history had again
and again confirmed them. As for the Law, one
question and its answer will suffice. " What advantage then hath the Jew, or what profit is there of
circumcision ? Much every way ; chiefly because
that unto them were committed the oracles of God "
(Rom. iii. 1). The Jew had indeed from of old the
oracles of God and the law of God ; and Paul had
no question in his mind as to the truth, the validity
and the permanence of the Law ; he was a thorough
Jew here, and accepted without criticism. Without
criticism, but not without interpretation. If God
eventually spoke to him in a way quite beyond mistake,
and if then there appeared divergency between God's
word as given to Paul and God's word as recorded in
the canon, the conflict was not fatal ; it merely meant
fresh thought, and new examination of the old records.
If the schools of the Jews have their differences of
interpretation, where two explanations are lawful, to
propound a third can hardly be sin—especially if the
third rendering is confirmed by revelation. Allegory
and the non-critical handling of passages and phrases
out of their context were the accepted and traditional
lines of commentary. Paul could as legitimately use
them as any other student—perhaps more so, if by
such procedure he could avoid a narrow interpretation of God's mind and rulings, if he could reconcile
apparent contradictions and justify the ways of God
to men. The unsoundness of the scholarship saved

Paul would have endorsed the rendering of it in the Authorized
Version, but it is not the only possible rendering. A disputable
translation of a doubtful passage is a slender foundation for a
dogma.

c

him from slavery to a book and a code, and left him free for fresh experience of God.

For this is the supreme contribution of Judaism to Paul and to the world. Polytheism and pantheism were the twin curses of contemporary religion, the one often immoral and always trifling, the other vague and disheartening as it always will be. The Jew at all events had no doubts at all about the reality of God, His eternity, His universal rule and His absolute power. This made for sanity and for real thought ; the paradox of a reflective Greek that the Jews might be called " a nation of philosophers " hit the mark. Philosophers had always been units ; even their schools showed tendencies to disruption ; the Jewish people stood together in a faith, at once the outcome of intense experience and long thought and the promise of clearer and ampler thought. The Jew might say it was the gift of revelation ; well, let him say so for popular audiences ; the philosophic value of his belief was just as great. It meant the unity of the universe and of experience, and eventually a thought-out world, logically based on principle. But that was not the language of the Jews. No. " God spake all these words, saying " (Exod. xx. 1). The Greek might always prefer to put things in the abstract, and certainly there were Jews who found his term *Logos* extraordinarily useful ; but the centre of Judaism was not a philosophy, nor the unity of the universe, but God, personal, final, and supreme, Maker of heaven and earth and of man, Lawgiver and Judge. God was also the Father of Israel, in some degree of Israelites also, and, in a manner of speaking, of other men ; at all events He was Maker and Judge of all men. Morality, the bounds of right and wrong, were fixed by His decree ; and once that was apprehended, there was no more to be said. To speak once more in the other tongue, when you have reached the ultimate, there can be no more to be said. In the

Torah, the Law,[1] God had revealed His will, and
change was impossible. The only loophole was interpretation,[2] and in view of everything involved interpretation was a serious task ; the issues were awful,
to mistake or to change what was written might lead
to disaster beyond thought. Severity toward those
who interpret otherwise than you do becomes on this
basis intelligible.

Paul's Pharisaism then is the logical outcome of
his conviction of the One God. If God's law is all-
important, nothing can matter more than to be sure
that one is really keeping it ; the straitest sect will
be the wisest one, the only wise one. Mr Montefiore
tries to prove that, though Paul " could fancy himself
perfectly orthodox " and a good Pharisee, his religion
differed in " those very points which constitute the
essence and bloom of a religion," viz. outlook and
emotion. He maintains that there was a broad
difference between Paul and the " Rabbinic Jew,"
whom he reconstructs from the Rabbinic literature
of a rather later day.[3] The orthodox Jew, whom he
describes, believed in the same One God, but reckoned
that the Jew stood in a peculiar relation to Him.
" The average and decent-living Israelite would inherit
the world to come, would be ' saved ' to use other
and more familiar phraseology," but not exactly on
his own merits ; " God's love for Israel, His love of

[1] R. Travers Herford, *The Pharisees*, p. 54, says " there were
reasons, no doubt, why the LXX always rendered *Torah* by νόμος
as there were reasons why Paul, who ought to have known better,
perpetuated the same mischievous error." Such purism is hard to
understand ; whatever *Torah* and νόμος first meant, two hundred
years of equation is not irrelevant in the history of words ; and much
of Mr Herford's book goes far to acquit Paul.

[2] On interpretation, see R. T. Herford, *The Pharisees*, pp. 67,
69 ; 166 note.

[3] Mr Montefiore in a later book, *The Old Testament and After*
(1923), pp. 466 ff., deals with my treatment of his picture of the
God of the Rabbinic Jew. He corrects my inferences in my *Progress
in Religion*, but most gracefully suggests that he had written unclearly.

the repentant sinner, His inveterate tendency to forgiveness, together with the merits of the patriarchs [cf. Luke iii. 8] would amply make up for their own individual deficiencies." "Salvation was the privilege of every Israelite, who, believing in God and in His Law, tried to do his best and was sorry for his failures and lapses." "Yes, God . . . is very angry," but "let a man repent but a very little and God will forgive very much." He holds that Paul's was an altogether inferior and inadequate type of Judaism, "poorer, colder, less satisfying and more pessimistic," gloomy about the fate of the Gentile world, gloomy about the possibility of overcoming evil inclination, gloomy with the sense of human frailty—in all, a "cheap and poor Hellenistic Judaism." [1]

Mr Montefiore asks eight questions about Paul, which, put in a somewhat condensed form, are these: [2] If Paul had known and accepted the Rabbinic view of the world, would he have been so pessimistic? If he had known and accepted the Rabbinic views of the Law, of piety toward God, of religious psychology, of salvation, could he have evolved the doctrines of the Law, piety, psychology, and mysticism to be found in his epistles? How could he have ignored the Rabbinic teaching of repentance? (Mr Montefiore does not think that to the Rabbinic Jew sin was less hateful than it was to Paul.[3]) If Paul had believed in the markedly human view of the Messiah held by the Rabbinic Jew, would he or could he have evolved his Christology? If he had held with the Rabbinic School their "ready and not unwilling consignment of the non-believer and non-Jew to perdition" (compatible he holds with "the most exquisite and delicate charity" [4]), where would his special mission have been?

---

[1] C. G. Montefiore, *Judaism and Paul*, pp. 93, 35, 36, 42, 94, 53.   [2] *Ib.* p. 59.
[3] *Ib.* p. 77. Cf. *The Old Testament and After*, p. 467.
[4] *Ib.* p. 56; modified in *The Old Testament and After*, p. 468.

The main questions here concern Sin and Conscience —the Gentile world—and the Messiah.

We may, I think, take the picture of the Rabbinic Jew as Mr Montefiore draws him, particularly since he does it in a spirit of admiration and indeed (unless I am mistaken) of advocacy. Mr Montefiore counts the religious outlook which he describes satisfactory and happy, so that we need hardly suppose that he is undervaluing the Rabbinic Jew. He admits that his evidence comes from the fourth and fifth centuries, and other scholars suggest the use of extreme caution in applying evidence of that date to the period of Paul.[1] But suppose we provisionally concede his historical conclusion, and find Paul in a milieu such as he suggests, it is at once clear that the contrast between Paul and the type of mind, which Mr Montefiore sketches, is very great—as great as he insists, or greater. But it does not, I think, necessarily follow that Paul, if more sombre, more pessimistic and so forth, is really on a lower plane of thought and insight. The so-called "healthy-minded" are sometimes shallow. Cassandra, historically, has often been right and the optimists wrong.

To the Rabbinic Jew, Mr Montefiore thinks, sin was not less hateful than to Paul. It is quite clear, on Mr Montefiore's showing, that the Rabbinic Jew was far less troubled about sin, assumed far more easily that his repentance was adequate, and believed with no great effort of mind that his God took the same rather superficial view of sin that he did himself.[2] It would not be unfair to quote Heine's famous remark: " God will forgive me ; *c'est son métier* " —a sentiment much less smug and by its wit eluding

[1] H. A. A. Kennedy, *Paul and Last Things*, p. 217. Kirsopp Lake, *Earlier Epistles*, p. 426.
[2] See Mr Montefiore's rejoinder, *The Old Testament and After*, p. 467 ; fundamentally I believe I am right in my inferences from the earlier statements, which the later qualify but do not cancel.

the question as to how deeply the poet had thought out the problem. Heine may be right, and the Rabbinic Jew may be right; we have to face that possibility, distant as it seems. But if they are right, then those who have thought most deeply upon religion in Greece, in Christendom, in Hinduism and Buddhism, have been lamentably astray. To set up such a view of sin, as Mr Montefiore attributes, perhaps correctly, to the Rabbinic Jew, as truer, saner and more profound than another judgment, which has the support of Plato, is to risk the charge of a certain superficiality. Paul and Plato, however their language may differ, have very much the same conception of sin. They reached it, no doubt, by rather different paths,—Plato through insistence on the intellectual and moral necessity of a righteous universe, Paul through acute realization of the holiness of God. If Paul and Plato are wrong, and the Rabbinic Jew right, that Jew has transcended his spiritual ancestors. For prophet and psalmist are with Paul in their conviction of sin and their knowledge of the misery of it, and they reached this outlook as he did. " I saw the Lord sitting upon a throne, high and lifted up," says Isaiah (vi. 1); and the immediate result of the sight was a humiliating sense of his own pollution and that of his people, a sense of his need of cleansing. Throughout life Paul's problem, and Paul's conviction, is the Righteousness of God. It is his axiom in every argument, his problem when he thinks of the Gentile world and of human depravity, his despair when he looks into his own life.

It is not necessary to read far or deeply into such a document as the Epistle to the Romans to see how impressed he is—and appears always to have been—with the seriousness of sin. Fools, the old Hebrew had said, make a mock of sin (Prov. xiv. 9); Paul stands with the world's great thinkers, aghast at the power of sin and its consequences. There are those who do

not read autobiography in the seventh chapter of
Romans—as if Paul used the first person singular here
in the style practised by rhetoricians of the second
order—as if such writing could be anything but
autobiography! "The Law is spiritual; but I am
carnal, *sold* under sin "—the words are for many too
familiar to yield all their significance without pressure
(πεπραμένος ὑπὸ τὴν ἁμαρτίαν). He is the slave
of sin, or has been, without power to do even the good
he would have wished to do, a victim of its paralysis.
"What I hate, that do I." "I know that in me
(that is, in my flesh) dwelleth no good thing; for to
will is present with me; but to perform that which is
good I find not . . . I find a law that, when I would
do good, evil is present with me. . . . I see another
law in my members, warring against the law of my
mind, and bringing me into captivity to the law of
sin which is in my members. O wretched man that
I am! Who shall deliver me from the body of this
death?" The passage is not isolated, or the ac-
cidental record of a mood; it records an experience
which Paul, and not he alone, has found central; it
is too personal and too real to be anything but of the
essential fabric of all his thought. The old Hebrew
sense of God, intensified by generations of prayer and
insight and self-criticism—and this time re-appearing
in a man of supreme genius—no wonder conscience is
one of the keynotes of his life.

At every point in the story of Paul's thought, the
question of Sin and Conscience recurs. No treatment
of his life and mind can be valid, in which the presence
and consciousness of his experience in the service of
conscience, and of his experience of the power of sin,
are not recognized as primary factors in his Theology
and primary motives in his conduct. Whether we
agree with his view of Sin, is not the issue; nor whether
we place him below or above the Rabbinic Jew or the
modern person who claims to be "healthy-minded."

For Paul the long struggle to be righteous before God, and his sense of failure in that struggle, are part of every judgment he makes upon God, or upon human life, present or future. He is a man who has failed, who has sinned, and who has been forgiven, and who can never outgrow the wonder of his forgiveness. To this we shall have to return again and again ; for the present we have to note that in these early days in Jerusalem he is accumulating the experience that made his life and is beginning to try to make clear to his own mind what it means.

When we reach questions of the Gentile world and of the Messiah, we touch issues which were practically closed for the Rabbinic Jew of the fourth century, which were perhaps not of supreme interest to his precursor, the Jew of the same type of mind (waiving the discussion of opinions) in the first centuries B.C. and A.D. The later Rabbinic Jew, in Mr Montefiore's explicit words, made a "ready and not unwilling consignment" of the Gentiles to perdition[1]; his Messiah, whenever he might come, and his coming was relegated to a distant and indefinite future, would be human and no more ; and he had ceased to try to relieve doubts, perhaps by now suppressed or banished, as an early Judaism had done, by the composition of Apocalyptic books. Paul lived in a period when the Gentile was acutely interesting. The Apocalyptic movement had grown out of the pressure of the Gentile, so that we may not improperly consider them together.

The Apocalyptic literature that survives is extraordinarily tiresome to readers who have been trained upon Greek art and thought. The writers of it are dull and tasteless as a rule, with little gift of expression and next to none at all of clearness. They are, however, receiving a good deal of attention to-day, perhaps, as often happens after a period of neglect,

[1] Montefiore, *Judaism and Paul*, p. 56.

rather more than they deserve—in some quarters, a great deal more. Except that the book of Daniel is in the canon, one would say broadly that the whole movement shows influences unfamiliar to the Old Testament. The writers are pre-occupied with history in a way strange to the prophets, though the prophets were far from indifferent to history; and they have a dimmer and fainter vision of God. To the prophet God was flamingly real; to the writers of the Apocalypses, while they believed in Him and while their object was to justify His ways to men, God is rather remote and His character so far beyond criticism as to be scarcely susceptible of being even ethical; His sovereignty outweighs questions of right and wrong. Shall not the Judge of all the earth do right (Gen. xviii. 25)? He can obviously do what He likes; and what His people would like, He will do. For the prophet, it was imperative that Israel should take the point of view of Jehovah; and he was ready with amazing courage to denounce Israel's failure to do so. The Apocalyptist conceived of God as more like an ordinary Jew, not altogether unlike the Jew of Juvenal apt

Non monstrare vias eadem nisi sacra colenti,
Quaesitum ad fontem solos deducere verpos (xiv. 103),

and possessed of all that Jew's " contempt for Roman laws." Here is what one of them says, and his words justify Mr Montefiore's " ready and not unwilling consignment " :—

" Then thou, O Israel, wilt be happy, and thou wilt mount upon the neck of the eagle and [the days of thy mourning] will be ended.

" And God will exalt thee, and He will cause thee to approach to the heaven of the stars, and He will establish thy habitation among men.

" And thou wilt look from on high, and wilt see

thine enemies in Ge[henna], and thou wilt recognize them and rejoice, and wilt give thanks and confess thy Creator." [1]

Minds less vindictive did not pronounce so bluntly on Gentile destiny, but avowed that they could not solve the problem of what God should do with the Gentiles.[2] There was no blessed resurrection for them, at least, if the Jews of the first century B.C. and the first century A.D. were right.[3]

If it is conjecture that Paul had upon his mind before his conversion the problem of the Gentile world, it is perhaps legitimate conjecture; it is at least putting two and two together. We know that he grew up in a Gentile environment; we know that he did not miss its interests, even if in education he was directed to Jewish rather than to Greek ideals; we know that, at any rate in retrospect, he associated his conversion with the call to preach Christ to the Gentiles.[4]

With Peter (for instance), on the other hand, the evangelization of the world was not at all an immediate corollary from the knowledge of Christ. Mr Montefiore concedes that any occasional qualm which Jews might have about the darkness of the heathen world would probably be oftener in Hellenistic communities.[5] It is clear, too, that there were Jewish thinkers who had already transcended the tribal view of God to which Rabbinic Judaism returned in spirit; they wrote of a general resurrection,[6] of a general last judgment, of immortality. The problem was a complicated one. If a man accepted the narrower view

---

[1] *The Assumption of Moses*, x. 8-10 (Charles), a document perhaps written in the lifetime of Paul.

[2] See the discussion in 4 Ezra viii; pp. 239, 240 below.

[3] R. H. Charles, *Enoch*, pp. 297, 300.

[4] Acts xxii. 15; xxvi. 17; Galat. i. 16.

[5] Montefiore, *Judaism and St Paul*, p. 110.

[6] 4 Ezra vii, 26-44. Cf. Fairweather, *Background of the Gospels*, pp. 276-291.

of a Davidic King, an Anointed, who should rescue Israel from their oppressors, then the question of Gentile destiny in God's scheme of things was not very important ; it might be forgotten. Even if the Messiah were a being pre-existent, at God's right hand, a Supernatural Son of Man, the matter might still be shelved somehow, if one concentrated on Israel and conceived God and His Anointed to take a nationalist view. But when taught by the prophets— by Amos and Jeremiah, in particular,—a seriously-minded Jew began to think, as John the Baptist apparently thought, that God could *make* children of Abraham out of the pebbles if He really wanted them, that righteousness is of more consequence than anything else in humanity, that good conscience and good conduct are more significant than good blood, blindly transmitted by " the will of the flesh " (John i. 13) ; then God could not be supposed to consign a good Gentile to Gehenna, or to promote a doubtful or indifferent Jew to heaven, even if that Jew were descended from the friend of God and were the seed of the patriarchs. In that case, what *was* the privilege of Israel ? If the problem of the good Gentile is solved by one theory as to the next world, the solution involves yet another problem—the problem of the bad Jew, who could no longer logically claim the privilege of Israel. This was a matter of reflexion sooner or later with Paul ; can we peremptorily say it was later and not sooner ? How should he not realize and realize early the serious position of a Jew who failed to be righteous ? And a further question rises ; what is the function of a Messiah, if righteousness and general immortality are to be presumed in the scheme of God ? What place is there for a restored Israel in a heaven where virtue and eternal life are the decisive factors ? The Davidic King must yield place to another conception of the Messiah, if a Messiah is needed at all. There were Jews who, long before the great Rabbinic period, reached the point of leaving the Messiah out altogether, or at least giving him so small a function that he might as well not be in the scheme of things. It might be truer to say that they never reached the point where it seemed needful to introduce a Messiah at all.[1]

Beside Rabbinic Jews, or their legitimate ancestors, there were then Jews interested in Apocalyptic, and Jews of a school whose greatest man is Philo. It is impossible to say how widely any particular Apocalyptic book was circulated,[2] or what attention would be paid to it by any given Jew, so to speak. A great deal would depend, as with every reader of any book, on his literary taste and interests, on his religious preconceptions and experience. The Apocalyptic writings are from a literary point of view worthless, unless we except the first half of Daniel, the author of which certainly had a gift of narrative far beyond his school. How far a strict Jew would attend to such books, whether of his own sect's mind or not, cannot be said dogmatically. But the general body of ideas, with which the writers of the surviving books worked, was in the air, and perhaps to-day we invert their real relation, and attribute more influence to the writers than they really exercised, and credit them too definitely with leading where perhaps they followed. But the wide differences between these dreamy writers, handling " things to come " between asleep and wake, chaotic in mind as in art,[3] would allow considerable freedom to the reader. He could never quite succesfully piece together one apocalypse with another, nor always the various parts of a single one ;

[1] More fully discussed on pp. 201 ff.
[2] W. Morgan, *Religion and Theology of St Paul*, p. 10 : " Apocalyptic was never the faith of more than a circle . . . But . . . it was the deepest and most earnest spirits that were attracted to it."
[3] Cf. J. H. Leckie, *World to Come*, p. 27 : " It is an excellent rule to suspect all accounts of Jewish doctrine in proportion as they suggest symmetry, order and logical coherence."

and he was driven, consciously or unconsciously, to select and to reject. Every apocalyptist is categorical and dogmatic enough, but there was not enough agreement to impose a definite faith on the Jewish people. The Hellenistic school was a further safeguard; the philosophic temper is a difficult one for the prophetic to mate with; it is another illustration of that "ancient quarrel" which, Plato says, has always existed between poetry and philosophy.[1]

So the ardent young Jew from Tarsus, zealous for God, zealous for the traditions of the fathers, is launched into what was very like University life in a pilgrim centre, in a national capital with a foreign garrison. How long he was there we do not know, nor with whom—apart from Gamaliel, and presumably other young Pharisees of his own age and sympathies (Gal. i. 14). That he was associated from an early point with the synagogue of the Cilicians is probable. The detail of that Jerusalem life is beyond us; something of the outline we can reconstruct. The opportunities for thought in such a place must have been endless, though it is not everybody that takes them in a University. Israel, the Gentiles, the Messiah, Resurrection, Immortality, Sin and Judgment, this world with its evil, the next with its promise of Right,—how was one to combine all that was said on topics of such variety and importance? Who was to decide when the doctors disagreed, as we know they did?

Once again, we have to remember that we are dealing with an exceptional man, the maker of an epoch, intensely serious, perplexingly swift of thought, and apt to reach the fundamental more thoroughly and more quickly than we suppose. He has been studied by millions; of the followers of Jesus none has been anything like so formative; every Christian who has read him with any attention has formed some

[1] Plato, *Republic*, x. 607 B.

impression of him, some judgment upon him. But to judge such men takes gifts of sympathy and experience more or less commensurate with their own ; and these are not common. In the story of the Christian church two men stand out, qualified beyond others by genius and experience, to understand Paul— Augustine and Luther. Much material, unknown to either of them, is available for the modern scholar ; but one is disposed to question whether after all it is so important as we sometimes suppose—whether it really matters at all, compared with the insight, which in Augustine and Luther was given by God and developed in life. Genius rather than scholarship is the touchstone by which to test genius.

CHAPTER III

DAMASCUS

ONE phase of religious thought in Paul's Jerusalem we have not yet touched—the Christian movement. If it is hard to be at all precise about the currents in Judaism, it is at least as hard to be certain about the early church in Jerusalem. Something turns on the date at which Luke wrote the Acts, and still more on the sources which he used, and the degree of knowledge which he really had of Palestine. When he wrote the Gospel, he explained his purpose and plan in his preface, and scholars of late years have successfully studied his method in careful comparisons between Mark's Gospel and Luke's borrowings from it, and they have also made out another source which both Matthew and he used in addition to Mark. In the latter part of Acts it is plain that Luke depended on Paul himself and Paul's friends. That he was with Paul on some parts of the journeys seems most probable. Whatever sources he used for his account of the Jerusalem church, it is hard to think that they were at all of the same historical value as those which he used for the Gospel, or as his own notes of Paul's talk and of their journeys together. It is fairly plain that, while a man of wider range and far more literary capacity than Mark, and clearly dissatisfied with Mark's style and language and general usage of Greek,[1] Luke was very faithful, as ancient historians were perhaps too apt to be, to the source before him. The source (if not sources) for the early days of the church in

[1] See the very interesting study of Henry J. Cadbury, *The Style and Literary Method of Luke*.

Jerusalem must rouse a good many suspicions, unless
we are to say that Luke is responsible for the parallelism
of the miracles with Jewish history and legend, which
I think can hardly be urged. Luke is accused at a
later point of making all sorts of eirenical adjustments,
which it does not concern us to discuss in detail ; he
may have found Paul's statements and those which
he got elsewhere hard to reconcile. Narrative at all
events was a gift denied to Paul. It may be possible
to disentangle everything ; people have tried it in
various ways ; but happily it is not our task.

When we come to ask about the church in Jerusalem
before Paul joined it or even began to persecute it,
we have the full disadvantage of depending on a not
too critical historian writing of a land and situation,
which he did not intimately know, in dependence on
a very curious authority. It is quite clear that the
community was full of fervour and courage, quite
changed from what it had been before the Crucifixion.
Then it had been uncertain of the mind and the
future of Jesus, and very slow to take in what he said ;
it had scattered when the attack was made upon him.
Now it had a testimony to give—that Jesus was raised
from the dead ; it was perfectly sure of this, and
stood all sorts of persecution. But it was still confused
on many points ; it was full of the Holy Ghost ; it
gathered adherents freely, but not all of them, we are
told, of reliable quality (Acts v. 1-11). Its ways
were odd ; it elected an Apostle by a final drawing
of lots, and it practised communism — the latter
leading very soon to trouble, while the former practice
was not, so far as we know, repeated. Altogether
there is, in spite of all the enthusiasm, the courage
and benevolence, a want of nearly every other quality
that we associate with the mind of Jesus.

Luke gives us a number of speeches delivered by
Peter. To Sir William Ramsay all students of the
New Testament are indebted for a great deal of new

light on Luke's fidelity to the facts of the Roman Empire and its geography—a signal contribution. But when he asks us to believe that Luke is verbally faithful to Peter, so faithful as to keep a Greek word which Peter used in a speech but afterwards discarded for a better in his Epistle,[1] those who study ancient historians can only open their eyes in amazement. When he also turns " the angel of the Lord " who " came upon " Peter [2]—the normal term for a theophany in pagan narrative and for an angel's coming in the New Testament—into Manaen, Herod's foster brother,[3] he makes Luke's procedure the harder to explain. Scholars generally will not want to press the verbal faithfulness of those speeches ; it will be a good deal if they are free to allow some correspondence of content. Certainly the speeches are quite different in texture from the recorded talk of Jesus in the Synoptic gospels, which is all short—it is fragmentary, and one sees that it is authentic, saved by its own life and humour and pungency ; the story of the Prodigal Son is the longest connected piece. Peter's speeches are very different and a cautious historian will handle them uneasily. Dr Hastings Rashdall holds that, when we reach the speech of Stephen, we have far more certainly " a genuine and most interesting monument of the earliest Christian thought." [4] With Stephen and Gamaliel we come into the area where Paul can be counted among Luke's authorities, and Paul apparently had reason to remember the gist of that speech, perhaps some of its words.

Some light may be shed on that early church from what is actually known of its later history, which is little ; from the Epistle of James, and from the character of Jewish Christianity so far as it kept aloof from the general body of Christ's followers. There

---

[1] Compare, in the Greek, Acts iv. 11, and 1 Peter ii. 7.
[2] Acts xii. 7.   [3] Acts xiii. 1.   [4] *Idea of Atonement*, p. 77.

D

results a rather slow and uncertain Christology;
Christ is not all that he becomes to Paul, to the
writer to the Hebrews, to the fourth evangelist, to
the author of the Apocalypse. That early church
was the trustee of the sayings of Jesus, and preserved
them, for which alone we owe it a boundless debt;
it comprised the witnesses (before Paul) of the resurrection and it bore its testimony; it had something
to say of the ascension—a matter easier for men who
believed in a geocentric astronomy and a solid sky,
with Horace, perhaps, and the Apocalyptist.[1] It was
not however very clear as to the person and work of
Christ. Even the speeches of Peter, while touching
on the resurrection, the ascension and the second
coming (Acts iii. 20), do not go beyond calling Jesus
"the holy and the just," "prince (ἀρχηγόν) of life"
(Acts iii. 14, 15), "prince (ἀρχηγόν) and saviour"
(σωτῆρα)[2] (v. 31), and associating with him "forgiveness" (v. 31)—the last a very important point, if
not thrown back by natural reflex from the language
of a later day. Finally, the early church remained
very much unaware of where it was going.

For, to put the issue bluntly and at once, it seems
hardly to have been conscious that it was in any
peculiar sense a "church." The word may involve
not a little anachronism, and it certainly suggests too
many associations, too many controversies, to be used
of this body of early Christians in Jerusalem without
further reflexion. We must try to picture a group
of people, as we have seen, without any very clear
Christology, but conscious of a new loyalty and of
a new experience, which they wished to share with
their neighbours—so happy it was. We read of Peter

[1] Horace, *Odes*, III. iii. 7, *si fractus illabatur orbis*; and Rev.
xx. 11.

[2] The presence of the word, σωτήρ, itself suggests a later date
for the present form of the speech. It belongs chiefly to the later
strata of the New Testament.

preaching apparently on the street from a door or a
window (Acts ii.) but also in Solomon's Porch of the
Temple (Acts iii. 11), which was in fact for a time
the recognized meeting-place of the group (Acts v. 12).
There were gatherings of avowed adherents of Jesus
by themselves, but the routine or ritual—we must
not be too precise—of their religious life had still to
some extent a centre in the Temple; "day by day
they continued with one spirit (or mind) in the
Temple" (Acts ii. 46). At the very end of the Acts
we find the same thing; Paul, on the advice of the
brethren in Jerusalem, went through some conspicuously Jewish rites in the Temple (Acts xxi. 26, 27)—
a procedure not very consonant with the latest of his
writings, which show a further development. How
strange all this was may not occur to every reader of
the New Testament at once. But when one recalls
the episode of the cleansing of the Temple by Jesus,
and reflects upon what he found there—a market full
of birds and cattle, the whole apparatus of money-
changing and buying and selling, a "den of thieves"
reeking of cow-dung and blood, and crowded with the
agents of a mercantilized religion—it grows strange
that men and women, taught by Jesus a new way in
religion, could still endure to worship in such a place
along with those who killed him; but they did. We
read, moreover, that "a great crowd of the priests
became obedient to the faith" (Acts vi. 7); and, if
we ask whether they continued to minister along the
old lines in the old place, it is hard to think that they
abruptly ceased to do so. But how long did they
continue, and how came the cessation of their sacri-
ficial service?

The reference to the synagogue of the Cilicians
reminds us of a double strand in Judaism. The
Temple obviously did not minister to all the spiritual
needs that the synagogue had taught Jews to recognize. The practice, maintained by Paul for years,

of resorting to the local synagogue, wherever he went, and beginning his mission by preaching there, suggests that Stephen's activity was similarly in a synagogue, and that it was in the synagogue of the Cilicians he preached "full of charm and power." There was bound to be cleavage. Temple and synagogue were inevitably to be impossible centres for Christian preaching. There could not permanently be much sympathy between men who said that Jesus is Lord and men who said " Jesus is anathema " (1 Cor. xii. 3). Division, taking the form of persecution, was inevitable and it cleared the issue. The strange thing is that Temple and synagogue could have been used so long.

Professor B. W. Bacon of Yale distinguishes two persecutions, the first by the priestly party on political grounds, which soon ceased ; the latter a more important one raised by the clash of Stephen with the Hellenizing Jews, and the Cilicians among them. And here Paul comes into the story, as the church has never forgotten ;—" the witnesses laid down their clothes at a young man's feet, whose name was Saul." [1] With what synagogue but that of the Cilicians could that "citizen of Tarsus" be connected? He must have been involved in the controversy with Stephen from the very first ; he was not built to be neutral or even moderate. So he goes on and makes " havock of the church, entering into every house, and haling men and women committed them to prison," [2] and thereby disseminates the contagion he is trying to stamp out.

From the story of Stephen and his speech, from the standard objections of the Jews to early Christianity, from Paul's own letters, we may feel our way to some account of the ground he took in opposition to the new religion. Luke *may* have thrown back into the early period the fuller recognition which the differences between the Jewish and Christian communities

[1] Acts vii. 58.   [2] Acts viii. 3.

at last reached. We have to remember that Paul's was a life of " revelation," however we define the term ; and he did not necessarily see from the beginning all he discovered with time, nor need we suppose patent to the insight of the Jews of the first half-century what a later generation could see without any insight at all. The two religions, as the new one developed, were bound to move further and further apart ; from the first it was inevitable. Jesus was not crucified for nothing by the common action of priests and Pharisees. If his disciples did not guess the reason, his enemies were clear enough. With those enemies Paul was consorting, and what they saw and spoke of, it is hard to suppose him slow to understand. We may summarize the main points under four or five heads.

Whatever Israel might properly hope for, or expect, in a Messiah, if a Messiah there was to be at all, it was clear to Paul and his friends that Jesus could not possibly be the Messiah. If Christian historians produced pedigrees connecting him with David, they also preserved enough of his talk to show that he set very little by the connexion. " How say the scribes that Christ is the son of David ? " he asked.[1] Perhaps the Messiah was not to be strictly a son of David, but no one as yet had suggested that he was to be a peasant, a carpenter, a homeless vagrant ; that, so far from restoring the Kingdom to Israel, he was to be crucified by the foreigner. A Messiah crucified was to the Jews a stumbling-block,[2] a contradiction in terms ; and so it remained. The Law had said quite plainly that " he that is hanged is accursed of God," and had given special injunctions for the immediate burial of such a person before sundown ; his body was not to remain all night on the tree " that thy

[1] Mark xii. 35.
[2] 1 Cor. i. 23 ; cf. Justin, *Dialogue with Trypho*, 32 ; also *The Conflict of Religions in the Early Roman Empire*, chap. vi.

land be not defiled." [1] We know that this was a
passage which Paul thought over, and in later days it
gave him a comfort that was not to be expected. The
Christian propaganda of the crucified Jesus as the
Messiah had thus in it everything to revolt a patriotic
Jew, who loved his race and its hopes, who was conscious of the mockery of the foreigner, who believed
the Law to be the very word of God, given by angels,
and in a manner of speaking almost an incarnation of
God. The cross was for centuries the point of
attack, and while, as we see, it became the very centre
and inspiration of Paul's religion, he remained sensitive
to the shame of it. [2] He knew exactly what men felt
and said about it, because he had felt and said the
same.

As for the Resurrection of Jesus, there again Paul
had opportunity to learn how it affected men. The
Greeks at Athens simply laughed when he spoke of it,
and the discussion was at an end at once. [3] Luke tells
us that, from the first, the priests and Sadducees were
vexed that the Christians " preached through Jesus
the resurrection of the dead " [4]—it was all counter to
Sadducee belief, as we know. That Paul counted
the story a sheer fabrication, seems confirmed by the
emphasis which, later on, he always lays on the risen
Jesus, and on his vision of him alive. Those who
alleged that Jesus was raised from the dead were
" false witnesses against God," [5] so that their talk was
not only silly but sinful.

Another point was the Law. Luke is very fitful in
his treatment of chronology ; apart from his statements that Paul was eighteen months at Corinth
(Acts xviii. 11), two years at Ephesus (xix. 10) and
two years a prisoner at Caesarea (xxiv. 27), he gives no
dates of any consequence in the Acts. The reference

[1] Deut. xxi. 23 ; Gal. iii. 13.
[2] Gal. v. 11 ; 1 Cor. i. 18-ii. 3.
'Acts iv. 2, 18, 33 ; v. 28, 40.
[3] Acts xvii. 32.
[5] 1 Cor. xv. 15.

to the coming of Gallio, while Paul was at Corinth, gives us our solitary fixed date. Gallio's proconsulate fell in A.D. 52. We are left to guess how long was the period between the Crucifixion of Jesus and the conversion of Paul; it has been estimated at something vaguely between one year and six. In that interval it became perfectly clear to people who cared for clearness that the Gospel was not going to strengthen the position of the Law. When Jesus said : " Think not that I am come to destroy the law, or the prophets," and predicted that no jot or tittle should go unfulfilled, either Matthew (v. 17-20) or his modern interpreters may be accused of lack of imagination, if the one, or the other, really suppose that Jesus meant his followers to maintain the Law of Moses, as the Pharisees tried to keep it. It was very early evident that, in the new relations with God which Jesus had made possible for men (long as it was before the church made up its mind to a definite theory to cover the facts), one thing at least was certain—the days of righteousness by the Law were past, the Law was becoming obsolete. According to Luke, it was not till Peter had committed himself with Cornelius that the question was discussed with any urgency among Christians at Jerusalem, and the rest of the Acts is never long free from echoes of the controversy ; so conservative can Christians be and so unobservant. Their enemies saw the end a great deal more clearly and more quickly.

Accordingly one part of the charge against Stephen concerned the Law. The scandal put about was to the effect that " we have heard him speak blasphemous words against Moses and against God " (Acts vi. 11). When he is brought to trial, it is put more explicitly. " This man ceaseth not to speak blasphemous words against this holy place and the law ; for we have heard him say, that this Jesus of Nazareth shall destroy this place and shall change the customs which Moses delivered us " (vi. 13). To change customs was

tantamount to destruction of nationality.[1] Stephen's
defence turns chiefly on another controversial point,
really of more significance, viz., the suffering, rejection
and death of Jesus; but at the end he touches on
Temple and Law, not obscurely for those who understand, while to his court it meant that he pled guilty.
" Howbeit the Most High dwelleth not in temples
made with hands; as saith the prophet, Heaven is
my throne, and earth is my footstool : what house
will ye build me ? saith the Lord : or what is the place
of my rest ? Hath not my hand made all these
things ? "[2] This, coming after a survey of Israel's
history, and with the conclusion : " Which of the
prophets have not your fathers persecuted ? " and
the counter-charge that the court trying him " have
received the law by the disposition of angels (as it
was ordained by angels) and have not kept it," confirmed the worst alleged against the Christian community. They *had* principles of universalism, which
must tell against Israelite privilege ; they were *not*
loyal to Temple and Law. To translate all this into
blasphemy against Moses and God was no more than
controversy can always manage. And, latent in his
defence, was a suggestion of an explanation for the
sufferings of Christ, which appears not to have been
lost on Paul, hostile as he was for the time.

In any case we have a strong indictment for an
ardent young Jewish patriot to bring against the new
sect—the change of Israelite custom, involving the
disappearance of Israel's nationality ; contempt for
the Law and a clear menace to the Law's continuance

[1] The mark of a tyrant was to change national customs (Herodotus,
iii. 80). The stories of Cambyses' treatment of Egyptian religious
customs (Herodotus, ii. 16, 38) and of Macedonian resentment of
Alexander's Persian robes (Arrian, *Anabasis*, vii. 6, 2 ; 8, 2)
illustrate this.

[2] Acts vii. 48-50 ; quoting Isaiah lxvi. 1, 2, a passage used by the
Apologists against the Jews, Justin, *Trypho*, 22 ; *First Apology*, 37;
Barnabas, 16, 2 ; Cyprian, *Testimonia*, ii. 4, c.

and validity; a hideous parody of the Messianic hope; and, implicitly, the final abandonment of Israel to Roman rule. There were also matters personal to Paul; if their view of God was right, all his endeavours after righteousness according to the Law were misdirected and needless; he had blundered, and wasted his energy; what was gain to him was after all really loss;—a conclusion that no man could welcome. And we must not forget the man's passion for truth and his resentment of lies; he could not but resent the falsehood of the Resurrection story in any case; how much more when it involved God? No wonder that Paul was " consenting " to Stephen's death—or, to render the Greek (συνευδοκῶν) in language of our own day, that he thoroughly approved of it.

I cannot help feeling that Gamaliel's action had a share in developing the persecutor in Paul. Luke tells us how, at an early appearance of the Apostles on trial, " there stood up one in the council, a Pharisee, named Gamaliel, a doctor of the law, had in reputation among all the people," and advised the Jewish authorities to wait and see; to let the men alone; " for if this counsel or work be of men, it will come to nought : but if it be of God, ye cannot overthrow it ; lest haply ye be found even to fight against God." [1] Hesitation is the badge of the scholar tribe. Erasmus was a difficulty to men of his day; he would not definitely side with Luther nor wholeheartedly condemn him. We may readily believe that this information from within about Gamaliel came to Luke from Paul, and that the moderation of his teacher impressed him, both before and after his conversion. If afterwards he felt the wisdom of the older man, at the time it would have been less than human nature for the young and ardent Paul not to resent the " trimming " of the cautious Gamaliel;

[1] Acts v. 34-39.

and Paul always had plenty of human nature, and was quick to respond to its promptings. It would not be unnatural if this spectacle of vacillation in one whom he regarded fired him with indignation,[1] and if indignation drove him (as it sometimes did later on) into action more fierce than we might properly have supposed native to a disposition so obviously built for friendship. But after all there would be little to surprise us in that.

But there is another phase of the matter yet to be considered. In two narratives of the vision at the gate of Damascus, we read that the words : " It is hard for thee to kick against the goad " were among those that came to Paul. It has been suggested that the phrase was from Pindar ; but the indignant ox, harnessed to the plough, tossing the yoke which it cannot throw off,[2] and kicking out at the ploughman whom it cannot reach, was not a sight for which it was necessary to go to the poems of Pindar. Paul may very well have seen it that very morning on his journey ; and the poor beast, kicking in vain at a man separated from it by the length of the plough, and only hurting itself afresh with each kick at the inevitable yoke, may have stayed in his mind as a picture of humanity, till it was brought home to him : " Thou art the man."

It is most likely that, in spite of his indignation with Gamaliel, Paul felt some qualms suggested by his friend's uncertainty—qualms none the easier for his trying to overcome them (as men do) by committing

---

[1] In Romans xvi. 7, Paul alludes to " my kinsmen Andronicus and Junia, my fellow-prisoners, who are of note among the apostles, who also were in Christ before me." Can we add their conversion to the grounds of indignation and of ferment within him ? The coupling of their names (the feminine Latin and implying Roman citizenship) suggests man and wife ; who were they, and who was " Herodion my kinsman " of verse 11 ?

[2] Cf. Juvenal, xiii. 20 : *Ducimus autem Hos quoque felices, qui ferre incommoda vitæ Nec jactare jugum vita didicere magistra.*

himself more deeply. It has already been suggested
that he had also to fight against the consequences of
long familiarity with the Hellenistic world ; here too
he was divided against himself, and (as befalls men in
such a state) he was the more violent on one side
because he wished to be on both sides. A youth
passed in Gentile surroundings, a manhood devoted
to work among Gentiles, hang together; and
somewhere under the surface it is hardly overbold
to surmise that a lifetime's instinct was making a
fierce struggle against the theory of a season—his
humanism against his tribalism ; and the latter betrays the uneasiness of its temporary triumph by its
violence.

Then again, in the speech made from the steps to
the crowd in Jerusalem, we are reminded by Paul
himself of his part in the martyrdom of Stephen
(Acts xxii. 20), planned by men of his own synagogue,
in all likelihood with his approval from the first.
Whatever part rewriting — condensing, abridging,
" altering things to keep them the same "—had in
Luke's work, we may be pretty sure that he was better
informed of Paul's mind, and even of his usual ways
of speech, than he was in Peter's case. Ordinary
probability supports us here. What impression must
that death of Stephen have made on a young man,
bigoted, but affectionate and open-hearted, and uneasy
in mind ? We know from himself how his nature was
torn in two by the struggle against sin ; and here was
a man, being slowly butchered, and entirely at peace
with God. Paul felt the contrast ; he was himself
not at peace with God. The miserably slow process of
the death left Paul the longer time to study the dying
man, his face, his bearing, and the scene. A century
and a half later, Tertullian tells us of the effect of the
martyr's death in his day,—the tranquillity of the
martyr amid the hideous shouting and hatred of the
mob, the uneasiness of the spectator, and the force

of the contrast.[1] " No one would have wished to be
killed," he says, " unless he knew he had the truth." [2]
It seems, indeed, as if Tertullian were telling his own
story there ; [3] and there is a good deal in common
between Tertullian and Paul—the swiftness of mind,
the passion for truth, the headlong temperament.
Paul may very well have reckoned Stephen's death a
landmark.

Finally, on this point, to whom does Luke owe the
story of the vision dying Stephen saw ? Who of the
bystanders would tell it to Luke ? Paul seems as
likely to have heard Stephen's last words for himself
as to have learnt them from Luke. The dying man,
face to face with death, eternity and judgment to
come—the things that made Paul, as well as Felix,
tremble,—said he saw in an opened heaven the glory
of God and Jesus standing on the right hand of God ;
and in converse (as it appeared) with Jesus, expecting
to be with him in a moment and forgiving the men
who were killing him, Stephen died, happy. Life
often teaches men to be suspicious, or at least cautious ;
and Paul must have turned all this over in his mind
a great many times. He cannot always have found it
quite easy to convince himself that the men who
threw the stones, the mob who would have stolen the
clothes, were right in God's sight ; or that Stephen
was acting a part and was lying with his last breath.
Stephen had been no trimmer in life ; and he appeared
to be candid in death. His face was not the face of
a liar—it was more like an angel (Acts vi. 15). If so,
then *what* did he see ? Was it possible that Jesus
still lived, as the Christians said ? Paul had not our
modern psychology, which, modern as it is for the
present, has perhaps not solved all the problems. He
was confronted with a dilemma ; either Stephen lied

---

[1] Tertullian, *Apology*, 50 ; *ad Scapulam*, 5.
[2] Tertullian, *Scorpiace*, 8.
[3] See *Conflict of Religions in Early Roman Empire*, p. 320.

to the last, or else—or else there might be something in the Christian story of the risen Jesus; and, if he dismissed the second alternative, the former was not very easy either. We can imagine him perplexed in the extreme—growingly angry with himself and as a result more violent, as if to force himself away from distasteful hypotheses or doubts, and more savage with his work of persecution. *Ego fiebam miserior et tu propinquior*, wrote Augustine of a similar interval in his own experience—" I grew more miserable, and thou nearer; thy right hand was even then to catch me out of the mire and to wash me, and I knew it not;" and he too speaks of the fear of death and judgment, which never left him through all his changes of opinion.[1]

Paul took refuge in action, as men do; but even action has its interludes, one cannot be active every moment—least of all a man of his swiftness of mind, and suddenness of thought. Action in his case, when it meant widespread arrests and a journey to Damascus, involved associates. We can guess what these associates were—how little congenial to the troubled man in charge of them, and how ill they showed in contrast with their victims. Every arrest repeated the reminder of the dying Stephen and the men who killed him. So the Damascus gate is reached.

Here, if it seem that we have been using conjecture already, more conjecture awaits us, and happily a new area of clearness and certainty beyond it. There has been, as there was bound to be, a great deal of discussion as to what happened at the gate of Damascus. Professor Percy Gardner, for instance, says that there is no excuse for taking the Lucan account for sober history; that Luke has a love for the marvellous, and the bright light, the vision and the words may be due to him; and that the three narratives differ in

_____
[1] Augustine, *Confessions*, vi. 16, 26.

essential points.[1] Professor B. W. Bacon holds that
the discrepancies, which Luke might perfectly well
have removed, if he had cared to take the trouble,
prove " the uncritical popular character " of the
story.[2] It can, however, hardly be maintained, by
any real student of Luke, that Luke invented the
whole episode, the light, the words, and the vision;
whatever he does with them in his narrative, it seems
incredible that he is not drawing upon Paul's own
account of something that happened.

But the discrepancies are surely not central, or
essential. How much did the companions hear or
see ? is not a question of prime importance. If
Paul, or Luke, fluctuated on this point, it should be
remembered that affidavits sworn to by the companions
would probably have varied a good deal, or, if they
had all agreed, would have been no better evidence.
In any case, what the companions may have supposed
to have happened, matters to nobody. If it is said
that Luke ought to have made all his narratives tally
to the last detail, history is not written by lawyers
nor logicians, nor perhaps any other literature that
lives. As to what we are told that Paul saw, heard
and said, the agreement is substantial, though in
addressing Agrippa Paul rather " telescopes " his
narrative, as he did the story of the Antioch disagreement when he wrote to the Galatians. A table
may clear things at this point, giving the narratives of
chapters ix., xxii. and xxvi. in parallel columns :

ix.	xxii.	xxvi.
verse	verse	verse
3 Suddenly there shined round about him a light from heaven.	6 Suddenly there shone a great light from heaven round about me.	13 I saw a light from heaven above the brightness of the sun shining round about me and them that jour-neyed with me.

[1] P. Gardner, *Religious Experience of St Paul*, p. 29.
[2] B. W. Bacon, *Paul*, p. 45.

ix.	xxii.	xxvi.
verse	verse	verse
	9 They that were with me saw indeed the light, and were afraid.	
4 He fell to the earth.	7 I fell unto the ground.	14 We were all fallen to the earth.
4 He heard a voice saying unto him.	7 I heard a voice saying unto me.	14 I heard a voice speaking unto me
		14 in the Hebrew tongue,
7 (they hearing a voice)	9 (they heard not the voice)	
4 Saul, Saul, why persecutest thou me ?	7 Saul, Saul, why persecutest thou me ?	14 Saul, Saul, why persecutest thou me ?
		14 It is hard for thee to kick against the pricks.
5 And he said,	8 And I answered,	15 And I said,
5 Who art thou, Lord ?	8 Who art thou, Lord ?	15 Who art thou, Lord ?
5 And the Lord said,	8 And he said unto me,	15 And he said,
5 I am Jesus whom thou persecutest ;	8 I am Jesus of Nazareth, whom thou persecutest.	15 I am Jesus whom thou persecutest.
5 It is hard for thee to kick against the pricks.		
6 And he, trembling and astonished said,	10 And I said,	
6 Lord, what wilt thou have me to do?	10 What shall I do, Lord ?	
6 And the Lord said unto him,	10 And the Lord said unto me,	
6 Arise, and go into the city,	10 Arise, and go into Damascus ;	16 But rise, and stand upon thy feet.
6 And it shall be told thee what thou must do.	10 And there it shall be told thee of all things which are appointed for thee to do.	
		16 [The call to go to the Gentiles is given.]

To-day psychologists will group this episode with similar or apparently similar ones in the experience of other men ; and it is not unreasonable. I believe that in such cases the words are generally few and are indelible from the memory. That Paul saw or seemed to see a great light, shining all round himself and his companions, and that he fell, will strike no one as odd to-day ; and it fits in exactly that he should uniformly give the words alike, and that they are direct and few. Any one who has had any experience of the receipt of words, whatever his theory about their origination, will know how clear and definite they are, and will be able to give them long after, and frequently to add the exact spot at which they " were given " or " came." Paul also " saw "—and not infrequently, as his own writings and Luke both tell us. The first remark to be made may be given in Weinel's words : [1] " The particular form, which Paul's conversion assumed, was surely caused quite as much by the strange psychology which was then universally accepted, as by the picture of Christ taken over from Judaism." A modern man, not unfamiliar with the psychology of to-day, might see the same figure and hear like words, and yet not suppose that what he saw was objective nor that what he heard was audible to another, and still might realize that it was a critical moment, which would be decisive for him.

It is put in this way to-day. So many things are working within him, as we have seen, and in conflict ; and with a flash—it is odd how spontaneous English phrase hits off a co-incidence—comes a light, and at any rate one problem is solved. Suppose (it is said) that the sufferings of Jesus, his rejection and death, are, as Stephen said, exactly along the line of the true prophets, and, so far from discrediting the Messiah, prove his true succession and authenticate him ? And

[1] H. Weinel, *St Paul, the Man and his Work*, p. 148 (tr.). Cf. below p. 185.

again, if Israel claimed or expected some acceptance with God, or some consideration from God, in virtue of the merits of the patriarchs (as we saw), can the sufferings of Jesus serve the same end, and, instead of being the final proof of God's damnation of him, mean a new footing for men in approaching God? Now both these ideas require development and definition—tasks on which Paul and others have spent their lives; but their sudden realization may go far to explain what happened at the Damascus gate.

I think it is reasonably maintained that visions, in or out of the mystical state, and words received (and other experiences, whatever they may be, that fall into this class) have their form and content from what is already working consciously or subconsciously within the man's mind who has the experience. It comes, then, briefly to this: are we to say that the line of thought, culminating suddenly in a new clarity, produces the vision, or that the vision leads to the clarification of the thought? Probably many psychologists to-day, professed and amateur, would prefer to say the former; Paul said the latter. There is this to be said for the modern view, that different minds reach conviction in different ways—slowly or quickly putting things together, and gaining a new view as the result, but figuring the process to themselves in different terms, putting it in different language, and sometimes associating the change with some experience or sensation which may be novel. Plato's "old quarrel between poetry and philosophy" is not unconnected with these differences. Reason and intuition and instinct are terms used to express the routes by which conviction is reached; though it is not clear that they do not imply all exactly the same route travelled over at different rates of speed. When John Bunyan was seized with a new view of things, he might see it, he often did see it, in a mental picture; things fell naturally into picture form for him, as they

E

do for the artist. But Bunyan was also conscious of hearing a voice—at least, as he thought it out, he had the sensation (as we put it) of hearing it : " It would sound so loud within me, yea, and, as it were, call so strongly after me, that once, above all the rest, I turned my head over my shoulder, thinking verily that some man had, behind me, called me." [1] The *daimonion*, the vague " rather supernatural thing," of which Socrates spoke [2]—the warning he used to get somehow—is another illustration of my point. It is arguable that Paul " visualized " his profoundest experiences—*saw* when he felt most deeply—saw or heard (or both) when a premonition (which also is a vague word) reached him, or when a course (as in travel [3]) became clear to him, or, as at the Damascus gate, when a new idea or adjustment of ideas swept without warning into his mind.

At the same time our warrant for excluding the possibility of a risen Jesus of his own choice showing himself to Paul, as the disciples said he did to them, cannot be unimpeachable. However difficult it be to prove it, we have no moral right, or intellectual right, to rule out that alternative. It was so that Paul always interpreted this experience, though others of the kind he referred to the angel of the Lord. Angels and spirits are indeed constantly reported as seen by persons of a lower culture than that to which we aspire ; but again we have no right perhaps to dogmatize on what may be possible to persons who have gone further than we have.

But after all whether the word or vision be (to use hackneyed terms of to-day, not quite scientific but useful) objective or subjective in its origin, that is not the most important point. Does the idea conveyed,

---

[1] *Grace Abounding*, §§ 94, 95.   [2] Plato, *Apol.*, 31 D.
[3] Cf. Acts xvi. 6, 7, 9. The last of these was a vision in the night, perhaps a dream : on which compare a Jewish view given in Ecclesiasticus xxxvii. 14 : " A man's soul is sometime wont to bring him tidings, more than seven watchmen that sit on high on a watchtower."

or, if we prefer it, the thought grasped, the issue realized, correspond to the real ? Does it take us further into the interpretation of all our experience, or does it side-track us and land us in some impossible contradiction ? Paul checked his revelation by the rest of his reflective and emotional life, rationalized it, and found in fact that it was no odd or stray addition to his outfit, but a key that unlocked for him the meaning of his own experience, the meaning of Israel's history —patriarchs, prophets, and psalmists, and the purposes of God for the whole of mankind. " It pleased God, who separated me from my mother's womb and called me by his grace, to reveal his Son in me " ; so says Paul to the Galatians (i. 15, 16). If, with some historians, we say that this is all that can be said as to his conversion, and decide to suspend judgment on Luke's data, Paul's statement here is enough. He *knew* at once that a great change of life was before him ; and, if Luke had not told us, we could have guessed that he would ask, " Lord, what wilt thou have me to do ? " He continues, to the Galatians : " Immediately I conferred not with flesh and blood," and he explains that when, later on, fourteen years after, he talked things over with those " who seemed to be pillars," those " who seemed to be somewhat " had nothing additional to give him, ἀλλὰ τοὐναντίον —" but contrariwise." [1]

To this revelation of the living Jesus Paul constantly returned. The conviction, reached then for ever, that Jesus lives, became the most effectual and operative force in his own life. " He habitually conceives of Christ as clothed in the δόξα or Divine radiance in which he first beheld him at Damascus," [2] and the experience was confirmed by a lifetime. It could not, one feels rightly or wrongly, have been so momentous, if it had not been led up to in some such way as we have supposed. A decisive experience must properly

[1] Gal. ii. 9, 6, 7.   [2] H. R. Mackintosh, *Person of Christ*, p. 54.

decide something; and, if there was nothing that needed to be decided and was decided, the intensity of Paul's feeling has very little meaning. The great epoch-making conversions, however sudden some of them may seem, have generally not been unheralded. To the men whom Paul brought to Damascus, to the authorities who sent them, and (as we learn) to the Christians, Paul's conversion was a bolt from a blue sky; but he knew the prelude of storm as they did not.

It will be well to survey the points that were decided. First of all, Jesus lived; the Resurrection story, Paul now saw, was true. God had shown him His Son;[1] no experience could be more wonderful, more definitive. The whole of Paul's subsequent thought is based on the truth of the Resurrection, on Christ working in the power of an infinite life, a " working whereby he is able to subdue all things unto himself "[2] —" declared to be the Son of God with power, according to the spirit of holiness, by the resurrection from the dead."[3] Jesus from that moment is for Paul a divine being, and the identity is patent of the historical Jesus and the Risen Christ.[4] It will not be out of the way to recall here the vision of the dying Stephen—it is the same that Paul sees, and the co-incidence (if the word may be used without its suggestion of accident) is significant. The psychologist may hold that the one has suggested the other; every vision, every mystical experience, it may be held, has its starting-point in something without. But, however we may explain it or phrase it, the connexion is surely not a chance one.

In the next place, the Cross is explained, and it wins the central place, which it kept in Paul's thinking. Christianity for Paul " consists, first and last, of experiences generated in the believer by the Cross."[5]

[1] Gal. i. 16.   [2] Phil. iii. 21.   [3] Rom. i. 4.
[4] R. H. Strachan, *Individuality of St Paul*, pp. 77, 90.
[5] J. Denney.

It is no longer a stumbling-block, as Paul says it remained to the Jews, who missed its meaning; he holds its meaning, and it becomes for him the criterion by which everything in heaven and earth and history is judged. The " suffering " of Christ, a scandal to the Gentile philosopher as well as to the Jew, becomes the very thing that makes him Christ, the proof of his Messiahship, the revelation of his nature, and his real and eternal glory. It is the pledge of a love on God's part that no one could have dreamed, nor, without the Cross, believed.

In the third place, the whole difficult problem of Righteousness, of Sin and Forgiveness, is solved. The Cross is reconciliation, and " we have peace with God." [1] To this tortured man, haunted with the sense of failure, anxious about God's judgment, and convicted already, there was new life in the revelation that God loved him to the point of giving His Son for him—" God commendeth his love toward us in that, while we were yet sinners, Christ died for us." [2] Hereafter, terror is not among the emotions roused by the thought of God in the mind of Paul; it is the love of God that absorbs him and surprises him, and (as a critic has said) disorganizes his grammar—a love too great to get into words and sentences, a love that produces aphasia—as the epistle of Peter puts it, " joy unspeakable and glorified." This new conviction has the power to break the bonds of old habits, old prejudices, and old preconceptions, and to lead Paul on to new life—new with a newness that never grows stale and with the freshness of perpetual revelation. Wonder, according to Aristotle, is the source of philosophy; and Paul's undying wonder makes his theology.

The problem of Israel is solved too. God is not rejecting Israel; but the choice of Israel proves to be a better thing than Israel supposed, it is not an end

[1] Rom. v. 1.   [2] Rom. v. 8.

in itself, but a means to a higher and more wonderful
end. It was not that Israel is chosen and there's an
end of it ; not at all, to Israel is foreshown, and with
Israel is shared, God's larger purpose for mankind.
The oracles of God are given to Israel for the world,
and not for Israel alone. In the matter of the Law
Paul seems to have moved some distance. At first he
appears to have held a Jewish view that it was given
by angels.[1] His later epistles suggest that he was
occupied with other themes, when once in Romans he
had worked out his ideas upon the Law—greater
themes, the place and work of Christ in all time and
all existence. But in any case the Law was never
going to be God's last word ; or why should He have
sent His Son ? Paul never loses his attachment to
his people ; he hopes against hope that their acceptance
of Christ will come in time, and prove " life from the
dead " [2]—the consummation of the world and the
resurrection itself.

Lastly, the difficulty about the Gentiles is dissolved
into thin air. All his early friendships and interests
were right after all ; Gamaliel's interest in Greek
literature was right ; the theory, that had given Paul
so much pain, was all a mistake ; God loved the
Gentile as He did the Jew, and Paul could find room
for his own heart to expand in God's world of men.

So much was clear at once, but the full value of
it Paul was not to discover except with time. Many
things had to be re-thought ; and even the points
mentioned are probably clearer and sharper-edged in
our summary, with the rest of Paul's life and his
epistles before us, than they were at the moment to
him. How he developed is plain to any one who will
read his epistles in chronological order, how profoundly
and how swiftly—and, not improbably, with an in-

[1] Gal. iii. 19. In Col. ii. 8, it is possible that Paul includes the
Law, but also possible that he refers to heathen ideas only.
[2] Rom. xi. 15.

creasing rate of acceleration. It has been conjectured that the interval in Arabia, which he mentions to the Galatians,[1] was largely given to reflexion, but that must remain a guess. By the time he wrote to the Galatians, his account of the great change in his life is drawn with edges sharp and clear enough. That is no uncommon phenomenon. Augustine's *Confessions* describe a conversion completer and more abrupt than could be surmised from his writings of the period, and the question has been raised as to which give the truer picture [2]—not a very profound question. To the man looking back it is plain how great the change was, and that it was final and decisive; to the man at the time its full meaning was not so evident, and (as we should expect of men like Augustine and Paul) he will not say more than he has realized, he will say probably a good deal less than he might—naturally and wisely. " I were but little happy, if I could say how much," [3] and a man of any depth will often impress onlookers as taking great happiness or great changes, which may come suddenly, with a surprising coolness. Jesus himself hints something of the kind in his parable of the seed and the soils; the seed in the good ground shows less for a while than the seed in the shallow earth, but no one in the long run can doubt that it was really sown. The great change comes in Augustine, and he is quieter about it than some readers of the *Confessions* would have expected; but he knew, and Paul knew, that it was a decisive moment; how much in life was changed neither could at once know.

[1] Gal. i. 17, 18. It may mean a total absence of about three years from Jerusalem. Luke and Paul are both careless or absent-minded about dates.

[2] I would refer my reader with pleasure to William Montgomery's most interesting and attractive volume, *St Augustine, Aspects of his Life and Thought*, which gives a very human picture of the most charming of saints with unusual skill and sympathy, and with sound historical discernment.

[3] *Much Ado About Nothing*, ii. 1, 318.

Chapter IV

"NOT HAVING MINE OWN
RIGHTEOUSNESS"

ONE of the great difficulties in the interpretation of religious experience is the unnoticed divergence of terminologies. Where the differences of race and thought are broad, some but not all students will be on the alert from the start, aware that there is no easy translation of terms round which the minds of men have long been at work. There are traditions, suggestions, nuances, which make it impossible to be certain without close examination that we have caught the real meaning or exhausted the whole wealth of meanings. It is particularly difficult for a monotheist to understand polytheism, eminently so for a monotheist who comes at the end of a long age of dominant monotheism. God in English and *theos* in Greek have to be used as equivalents; but are they? Between them lie all that Hebrew and Christian have taught the world of God; and even in Plato the equivalence has to be scanned in every passage. It is hard, too, when men for eighteen centuries have been using Paul's words, now importing into them unconsciously their own ideas derived from a later and perhaps another scheme of things, now consciously attempting to re-interpret, with or without a religious purpose of their own—it is very hard to be sure that the familiar word means precisely what we have been told or what we think we have discovered. Paul was a Jew, and most of his interpreters have inherited a culture and an outlook at least as much Greek, at least as much Latin, as it was ever Jewish.

It is easy to say that St Cyprian, a Roman lawyer of the third century, converted to Christ but not wholly transformed, still a Roman lawyer, very little influenced by Greek thought, ignorant of Hebrew, a man of parchment and pasteboard, is an ideally bad interpreter of Paul. Is it so easy to own that a modern scholar, a man of books and lexicons, who never knew at first hand the pagan world, never spoke with a heathen except in an educated dialect of some Western speech—a man whose tradition is Greek antiquity mediated by the inheritance of the Renaissance, the evolutional theories of modern science and some smattering of recent psychological speculation—may be as far astray as Cyprian? When one reflects how partially one knows one's own environment, how little one understands of things so obvious as the Town Council's duties (to say nothing of its politics) or the educational system of one's own country as it bears on the education of actual children, how little one guesses of the economic or religious ideas of the family across the road or of the servant waiting at table, it is obvious that ancient men might be as ignorant of such things, and as inattentive to them. The Mohammedan and the Hindu may know how to annoy each other and utterly fail to understand each other's minds and why such and such things annoy. Fundamental misconception is not the peculiar gift of the uneducated either, as English history teaches us. A great deal of the interpretation of Paul suffers from being archaeology applied without enough historical care.

It is almost useless to try to understand a man on the basis of coincidences of his language with the language of others. Both may use the same term, and, so far from its implying unity of outlook, it may really mark their dissidence ; all depends on connotation, and association, and still more on the central idea to which the term, and what it is meant to

convey, are related. When, then, we are told to look for
Paul's religious affinities in the contemporary mystery
religions (if contemporary they were), or even in contemporary Judaism, whatever the relations which we
may find, Paul's central ideas were not taken from
the mystery religions and are not to be found in them,
and the supreme and decisive factor in his life contemporary Judaism rejected. A great man's debt to
his countrymen and his teachers may be underestimated
by himself, it often will be; but it may be grossly
overestimated by posterity. Plato, for instance—is
he the product of Periclean democracy and Orphic
religion ? We can see how both affected him, but
we have to take pains to see how independent he is
of both, how very much more a man of all time than
a man of that time.

Some similarity of experience is required in an
interpreter. A student, modern to the core, who
could not conceivably take initiation into any mysteries
seriously, who is not supremely concerned with sin
nor interested in Jesus Christ or immortality, may
have contributions of value to make to the study of
Paul, but he will need more than genius to be an
interpreter of him. Luther remains a great interpreter of Paul; for, whatever ought to be deducted
because of sixteenth-century controversies and all the
history, traditions, and politics that colour them,
whatever must be modified by later-gained precision
in scholarship, Luther has the same largeness and
variety of mind as Paul, the same experience of failure
in the struggle for righteousness, the same realization
of a new life given by Christ ; and these after all are
the central and decisive things in Paul. John Wesley,
a man of less range than Luther, touched the experience of Paul and so far is a warrantable interpreter.
Of many of Paul's recent interpreters, admirable men,
widely read in archaeology and comparative religion,
something is to be said not unlike Bunyan's criticism

of the " ancient Christian " at Bedford from whom he had such " cold comfort " : " Talking a little more with him, I found him, though a good man, a stranger to much combat with the Devil." [1] There is, as Wendland says,[2] a unity in Paul's fundamental thoughts, an inner connexion. Before Damascus he hated Jesus ; after Damascus he loved him ; but, before and after, he knew what sin was—from experience ; and he knew, from what it meant to himself, that God could not compromise with it ; before and after, righteousness was his ideal, a matter of daily thought.

Those who like contrasts are apt to draw one between " the lucid free rational spirit "[3] of the Greek and the Jewish conscience anxious and even morbid about sin. The contrast has its value, even if we recognize the rather casual recognition given to sin by the Rabbinic Jew, according to Mr Claude Montefiore,[4] and the serious account taken of it by Plato. The Jew was committed by the tradition of his people to the keeping of the Law ; " for Judaism religion was the hallowing of this life by the fulfilment of its manifold duties." [5] There was the Law itself in the background, never forgotten, with its picture of a jealous God insistent on righteousness to the utmost ; there were the writers of wisdom-literature, moralists of a somewhat safe inspiration ; above all there were the great prophets of Israel ; and at last in their succession there was John the Baptist, though we cannot say that

[1] *Grace Abounding*, § 141.
[2] Wendland, *Die hell.-röm. Kultur*, p. 352.
[3] R. W. Livingstone, *The Greek Genius*, p. 181 ; who emphasizes that Plato is not of the type commonly drawn of the Greek.
[4] In his earlier book, see p. 35 ; but in the later work he qualifies what he had written.
[5] *Jewish Encyclopaedia*, *s.v.* Saul of Tarsus. Cf. also R. Travers Herford, *The Pharisees*, p. 58, " to live *for* the Torah, *by* the Torah, and *with* the Torah was the ideal which Ezra cherished for the national life."

he influenced Paul; all these pointed the Jew one way and made a real contrast with Greek religion. There was incalculable gain in having a God whose moral standards were more and more recognizably ahead of the best men, rather than gods whose legends proclaimed them markedly below even average human beings.

But the ordinary Jew, sketched by Mr Montefiore, devoted to his religion but easy-going about it, is not the type that we have to study. Paul was a Pharisee, as he avowed, and he took his religion seriously. It was essentially not unlike other religions where the acquisition of merit is the goal; and in spite of modern attempts to make the Pharisees look better and brighter, the verdict of Jesus upon them stands, unless we are to say that, in religion unlike other spheres, the verdict of genius is less important than that of the common-place.[1] Even a religion of merit is an advance upon a religion of magic, but it is open to peculiar dangers. Fear is, after all, a primary motive both in religions of magic and of merit, and it is not the best motive; it is fitful; it is easily dulled; and, even when most steady, it does not lead to real development of the mind and conscience; it over-developes certain sides of the character at the cost of the whole nature. The whole endeavour of a man intent upon merit was apt to become self-centred. Luther, who knew from experience, remarks on the " opinion of righteousness " and its effects.[2] There was a danger of legalism— that regard for the letter and contempt of the spirit which form together the great temptation of all lawyers. " Associate religion with law, and the latter will gain ground with the swiftness of an infectious

---

[1] R. T. Herford, *The Pharisees*, pp. 204-211, severely rates Jesus for his ignorance of the Pharisee position, the unintelligence and want of sympathy that he showed, and the sharp temper betrayed in his language, though he admits some great qualities in Jesus.

[2] Luther, *Galatians* (Engl. tr. 1584), fol. 152 b.

disease." [1] " I fast twice in the week ; I give tithes of all that I possess " ; [2] and other references to the tithing of mint and anise and cummin will recur to the reader's mind, and much else that men have quoted from Jewish legalism. These are the dangers of small minds, and a legalistic outlook on religion seldom allows the mind to grow. Men of this build lose all sense of perspective ; their attention is turned like schoolboys to the marks they have won, and they become impressed with their own achievement. Fixing their eyes on God's Law they lose sight of God. [3]

But Paul had a mind of more energy ; " his psychology," as Mr Montefiore says, " is not ours. His doctrine of sin is not ours." He is too deep and too real to be taken in by himself, as Jesus shows us that the Pharisees were apt to be. If he says that he had been by Pharisee standards " blameless," [4] it is when he has thrown them over for other standards and has ceased for ever to " go about to establish his own righteousness." [5] He has the habits of a psychologist, he is one by instinct and nature ; he reads his own soul and the souls of other men. His treatment of food-taboos in his letter to the Corinthians deserves to be recalled oftener than it is. It is the judgment of a man supposed first to have been an adherent of Pharisaism and later on to have been influenced by the adherents of mystery religions ; but he sees through the whole nonsense of prohibited foods, of religious vegetarianism and the perils of meat infected by idols. The passage should help us to measure the man, a mind not at all of the type that thinks in

[1] Weinel, *Paul* (Engl. tr.), p. 69. [2] Luke xviii. 12.
[3] R. T. Herford, *The Pharisees*, p. 231, " Judaism in general, and Pharisaism in particular, was a religion which put the doing of God's will in the first place, and faith in the second place ; faith, moreover, not in a Person but in God Himself."
[4] Phil. iii. 6. [5] Rom. x. 3.

terms of magic, a nature that will never tolerate
pettifogging conceptions of anything. He cannot be
supposed to have imagined righteousness a matter
of mint and anise and cummin. No, he struck for
higher things ; he " followed after the law of righteousness," pitched his ideals high, high as the standards of
God—and he failed to attain them. So much we
saw, in considering his conversion.

"Be not deceived," he wrote later on to the
Galatians,[1] "God is not mocked ; " and he used a
rather colloquial term—a man does not " screw up
his nostrils " at God with impunity. A Jew, Paul
had not grown up for nothing in a community that
spoke and wrote and thought perpetually upon a
Last Judgment. If in one of his earliest extant
Christian letters he speaks of the Lord Jesus being
revealed from heaven with his mighty angels, and in
flaming fire taking vengeance on them that know not
God,[2] the vocabulary and the phrase, if we eliminate
the words " the Lord Jesus," are clearly of Jewish
origin ; he identifies Jesus here with one familiar
aspect of the Jewish Messiah. A similar adaptation
by Jesus of a Jewish picture of the last day confirms
this,[3] and establishes historically the sort of thing that
haunted the mind of Paul in his Jewish days. A man,
he says in a later and greater letter, may by hardness
and impenitence lay up wrath for himself in the day
of wrath, when God's righteous judgment is revealed.
God, as the old psalmist saw, renders to every man
according to his deeds ; and for those " who do not
obey the truth " (a very noticeable phrase, very
suggestive of Paul's outlook) there will be indignation,
wrath, tribulation, and anguish, whether the man be
Jew or Gentile ; and it will come to the Jew first in
fact. Perhaps Paul had once thought, " to the Jew
afterwards," but in any case he had never supposed
the Jew would get off scot-free—" there is no respect

[1] Gal. vi. 7.   [2] 2 Thess. i. 7, 8. See p. 233.   [3] Matt. xxv.

of persons with God." [1] Here is one more feature of the influence of monotheism in contrast with Greek polytheism and Greek monism ; the human individual has to do with a personal God, who attends to his case as if there were no other such case to occupy Him in the universe. Men commonly do not think in this way in modern times, nor with the strictness that Plato used in distinguishing between good and evil ; and we pay the penalty of careless thinking and society suffers with us. To recover the mind of Paul, this conception of God's judgment, of God's personal dealing with the individual sinner, of the reality of the punishment, must be grasped and understood—and imagined, too. The modern thinker supposes himself less apt to confuse picture and substance ; he need not suppose himself more sensitive than Paul to the reality here.

For, that Paul does not merely look to the future, the seventh chapter of Romans amply proves with its dreadful description of the losing battle with the flesh. Paul stands near those ancient thinkers, who, from Plato onward, found matter the source of evil and antagonistic to soul—matter phenomenal, transient, and mortal, working against the eternal and real element, the body the prison of the soul. Paul's term is " the flesh," and a reference to the Greek concordance under σάρξ will quickly reveal the line his thoughts of. it took. No flesh shall be justified— the weakness of your flesh—when you were in the flesh—in me, that is, in my flesh, dwelleth no good— with the flesh I serve the law of sin—they that are in the flesh think the things of the flesh, they cannot please God—the fleshly mind is enmity against God ; such is a handful of his phrases, taken from the Epistle to the Romans. Elsewhere, if we may take the Epistle to the Ephesians as representing his mind (as I believe, whoever may have been his secretary, and however

[1] Rom. ii. 5-11.

freely the secretary treated this letter and the letter to the Colossians), Paul goes further and says : " We wrestle not against flesh and blood "—not, we may be sure, a reversal of his view in the Epistle to the Romans—" but against principalities, against powers, against the rulers of this world's darkness, against spiritual wickedness in high places," in fact, the whole daemon world. In the struggle the will is divided and betrays him, as Augustine in his turn found ; he can will but not do ; the flesh has control of the will or some part of it, and paralyses it. The " thought " of the flesh, the " desires " of the flesh, infest the will ; and as a Christian Paul prays for " the keeping of the thoughts," no idle prayer.[1] It should be noted at this point, as Professor Percy Gardner observes, that Paul does not accuse himself of the vices of the Greeks, of actual unchastity in any of its many forms. But what went on in his mind was enough to make him feel himself alienated from God, and to make him own that this alienation was deserved.

When we consider the effects of sin as Paul knew them, it is interesting that we are able to compare with his writings a work, written probably in Hebrew and in his own day, an orthodox work which is fairly representative, we are told, of the Judaism against which Paul re-acted—the *Apocalypse of Baruch*.[2] Others had held that sin began with the angels that fell ; this author, like Paul, lays it at Adam's door, and finds its consequences in physical death, psychological and physical decline and spiritual evil, for men and for angels. " Owing to his transgression untimely death came into being, and grief was named, and anguish was prepared, and pain was created, and trouble perfected, and disease began to be established, and Sheol to demand that it should be renewed in blood, and the passion of parents produced, and the

[1] Phil. iv. 7. See p. 189.
[2] R. H. Charles, *Apocrypha and Pseudonyma*, ii. 470.

greatness of humanity was humiliated, and goodness languished. What, therefore, can be blacker or darker than these things ? . . . For he was a danger to his own soul ; even to the angels was he a danger. For, moreover, at that time when he was created, they enjoyed liberty. And some of them descended, and mingled with women. And then those who did were tormented in chains." [1] There is more than a hint of rhetoric in this, but not without genuine thought. Yet " though Adam first sinned and brought untimely death upon all, yet of those who were born from him each one of them has prepared for his own soul torment to come, and again each one of them has chosen for himself glories to come. . . . Adam is therefore not the cause, save only of his own soul, but each one of us has been the Adam of his own soul." [2] As to the Law, " man would not rightly have understood My judgment, if he had not accepted the Law, and if his fear had not been rooted in understanding." [3] The writer is emphatic upon the value of good works : " Hezekiah trusted in his works and had hope in his righteousness, and spake with the Mighty One . . . and the Mighty One heard him " (lxiii. 3, 5) ; " those who have been saved by their works, and to whom the law has been now a hope, and understanding an expectation, and wisdom a confidence, to them wonders will appear in their time. For they will behold the world which is now invisible to them, and they will behold time which is now hidden from them. And time shall no longer age them. For in the heights of that world shall they dwell, and they shall be made like unto the angels, and be made equal to the stars, and they shall be changed into every form they desire, from beauty into loveliness, and from light into the splendour of glory " (li. 7-10) ; " the righteous justly hope for the end, and without fear depart from this habitation

---

[1] *Apoc. Baruch,* lvi. 6-12.   [2] *Apoc. Baruch,* liv. 15, 19.
[3] *Apoc. Baruch,* xv. 5.

F

because they have with Thee a store of works preserved in treasuries " (xiv. 12) ; if others did evil, it was due to Zion, that on account of the works of those who wrought good works she should be forgiven (xiv. 7).

Paul has some of these ideas ; " by one man sin entered into the world and death by sin, and so death passed upon all men, for that all have sinned . . . by one man's offence death reigned by one " ; [1] " the wages of sin is death " ; [2] " the earnest expectation of the creation waits for the manifestation of the sons of God. For the creation was made subject to vanity . . . the bondage of corruption. . . . The whole creation groans and travails in pain until now." [3] He believes that, with sin, death and pain and anguish, grief and trouble, came and remain. He seems much less sure that each one of us is the Adam of his own soul ; and, if anything like half of what modern speculators and observers have said of heredity is true, he is probably right in not holding that every child comes into the world equally a sheet of white paper with the option of remaining white. That had not been his experience ; " sin came to life and I— died " ; [4] it is not rhetoric, it is a record of tragic and bitter experience, Laconic, sufficient. " O wretched man that I am ! Who shall deliver me out of this body of death ? " A German scholar [5] guesses that the word " I died " is a memory of Paul's first deep consciousness of sin and failure when a child, a memory of a youth darkened by the shadow of sin falling on a gifted nature, and growing intenser with years till it is distress and anxiety. We have seen already how it affected him when we studied his conversion.

---

[1] Rom. v. 12 f.   [2] Rom. vi. 23.

[3] Rom. viii. 19-22 ; it may be urged that Paul means travail-pains, as he says συνωδίνει birth-pains and not death-pains in v. 22 ; but pain runs through the rest of the passage.

[4] Rom. vii. 9.   [5] Deissmann, Paul, p. 94.

Paul is not content with the one pungent phrase. The question of sin was not one to be turned off in a sentence. He recurs to it again and again. He contrasts with " the new man " " the old man and his nature crumbling or wearing away along the lines of the desires that deceive," [1] the wasting of the moral nature by the passions, till a man is " *dead* in trespasses and sins," [2] a view very like that of the Stoics. In the Epistle to the Romans he writes out of his own autobiography, not only in the famous seventh chapter already quoted, but also in the first chapter. The refrain runs through it " God gave them up "—first to uncleanness, next to vile affections, finally to a " reprobate mind," a mind that refused to perform the functions of a mind without betraying its incapacity. For he speaks elsewhere of conscience cauterized (1 Tim. iv. 2), and stained (Titus i. 15),[3] the mind darkened (Eph. iv. 18), and stained (Titus i. 15), the heart deadened (Eph. iv. 18). He uses the analogy of senses lost, and he pictures the man himself left to be the victim of guides that lead astray, of scouts that do not report ; he suggests a nature robbed of its natural self-protection, a mind that (in the language of the old Greeks) is like a coin not genuine, or a citizen who cannot make good his claim to citizenship,[4]—a human soul at last without hope and without God in the cosmos,[5] the huge vast cosmos, empty it would seem of all that can make a man endure it and face it, if we may speak a little in Stoic style. A man is saved by hope, Paul holds ; [6] and if a man has no hope, no God, and no mind left to work his way with, what of him ? And the author of the *Apocalypse of Baruch* spoke of storing up good deeds ; and other Jews thought it would serve if they fulfilled the Law

---

[1] Eph. iv. 22.   [2] Eph. ii. 1.
[3] That is if the Epistles to Timothy and Titus are Paul's own, or Pauline.
[4] ἀδόκιμος.   [5] Eph. ii. 12.   [6] Rom. viii. 24.

as far as they were able, the best way they could ; and with a nature like this !

A battle then against the flesh, against Sin (which in his language becomes personified), against principalities and powers of darkness—fears within and fightings without (if we may forestall a phrase of his Christian life [1])—and the man's nature steadily growing less and less able to sustain the conflict, as conscience lost faculty after faculty, and the will was more and more divided—it is little wonder that Paul describes such a man as without hope. If we are saved by hope, to what does despair lead ?

So much for the human side ; and God ? As we have seen, a man's sense of sin corresponds with his sense of God, and is indeed made by it. There were Jews, as Mr Montefiore tells us with a hint of satisfaction, who took sin, as one might say, sensibly ; but mankind rarely remembers with gratitude the contributions made to the world of ideas by what is locally known as commonsense. The uncommon man is more apt to be the real contributor, and Israel had produced a succession of them. Paul was a student of the prophets, who had spoken of God and of sin ; and his experience confirmed theirs—up to a point. They were right as to the enormity of sin, as to the transcendent majesty and purity of God ; there could be no compromise between God and man's sin ; but the prophets had not shown how the gulf was to be bridged. Jeremiah and Hosea had come nearest it ; Hosea had spoken of God's love in an epoch-making way ; Jeremiah, worn out with the folly and wickedness of Judah, and his own admitted and obvious futility, had forecast a time to come when God would make a new covenant with the house of Israel. This new covenant, he foresaw, would be on the basis of a changed human nature, in which the observance of God's law would be a fundamental instinct, the

[1] 2 Cor. vii. 5.

natural outcome of all within. No one could say that this change in Jewish character had arrived. The writers of Eschatology write on the tacit assumption that it had not yet come; they have little hope that it could come in the existing order of things. They urge that there must be judgment and selection; that God's triumph is in the future, perhaps in the far future—if indeed any one could call it triumph, when the great mass of the human race, and perhaps a large proportion of Israel—God's highest work, God's personal choice—should be written off as final failure.[1] No, the chaos and breakdown of human nature, and of Jewish nature, was the more evident, the more earnestly a young Pharisee struggled to make anything of his own soul; the material gave way.

Yet God and man, he felt, must somehow manage some adjustment, but not at all costs. To abate anything of the awful purity and majesty of God would be asking God to be less God; it was not to be thought of; and, besides, if one did think of it, it would not be done; God would not and could not be less than He is; He is righteous, and there is an end of it. Tacitly the Jew accepted what the Greek thinker had reached—Righteousness is not susceptible of compromise by God or man; God cannot thinkably waive jot or tittle of absolute Righteousness.

Paul, at first, like the Apocalyptists, was entangled in legalistic conceptions of God. If God is righteous, if righteousness is to prevail in God's universe, it must be clear to everybody—sooner or later it will be definitely and finally clear—that God must pronounce a last word upon Sin; and that word would be spoken by retributive Justice. Modern scholars, Jewish and others, do not find in the Old Testament or other

[1] Cf. 4 Esdras viii. 14, " If then with a light word thou shalt destroy him who with such infinite labour has been fashioned by thy command, to what purpose was he made ? " See also chap. x, pp. 239, 240.

Jewish literature the principle that God's right to forgive is limited by His retributive justice, that God cannot forgive without some satisfaction or propitiation, adequate to the offence.[1] They may be right in their contention that there is no Jewish antecedent ; there is however in Plato a parallel very close—God is not to be won over, says Plato, by prayers or sacrifices to palliate wrong.[2] Hindu thinkers, I do not know at what period, have reached substantially the same view, expressed in their central doctrine of Karma. But neither Plato, nor Paul, is to be supposed limited to the opaque views of his predecessors. So long as a man thinks in a legalistic way at all, he must think things through on the basis on which he starts, if he is to be clear at all. God may, as it is urged, have temporarily deferred sentence, He may have shown forbearance in passing over sin done aforetime ;[3] but deferred sentence is not necessarily cancelled sentence or abolished law. The picture, which Mr Montefiore drew of the God of the Rabbinistic Jew, shows weakened lines, and implies principle lost ; it is a loose-hung God, the very type that Plato hated and despised. The painful conception which Paul held of God is preferable to the notion that God administers His laws slackly, will accept easy equivalents, and will allow an off-and-on working of law in His universe.

What the Judgment achieves in the scheme of thought reached by Paul is really revelation and vindication of the fundamental nature of God. In any well-ordered system or universe the punishment will correspond with the crime, or it is irrational ; and by its correspondence it shows and proves the real nature of the sin as conceived by the legislator.

[1] See William Morgan, *Religion and Theology of St Paul*, pp. 87-90 ; though the treatment in my text owes more to the conversation of Principal David S. Cairns, of Aberdeen.

[2] See generally Plato, *Republic*, ii. 364, 365 ; *Laws*, x. 885.

[3] Rom. iii. 25.

Whether the system be a human one and the legislator human, or the system be the universe and the legislator God, the same principle holds. The punishment exhibits the nature of the sin, and it reveals the mind of the legislator ; it shows how he stands to the question of right and wrong. In the case of a Draco or the Roman Twelve Tables, the penalties will betray local and racial notions. But in a higher law, in the highest of all, the study of the penalties for sin will reveal God's character. His uncompromising condemnation of sin in His universe, and the punishment assigned to it, serve also to exhibit the real outlines and characters of right and wrong—a fundamental contribution to the idea of Cosmos, without which a universe cannot be ;—and they further serve to exhibit the character and attitude of God, to vindicate Him from any complicity with sin or with compromise.[1]

Paul, to secure the character of God, must either supply a righteousness of his own answering to the requirements of the Law—for in all this, there is inevitably some confusion of the idea of law and the Law or *Torah* given by angels through Moses ; Paul equates them—or else Paul must admit (and he does admit with a fervour that people who think chiefly of their own skins will never understand) that he himself has failed and is amenable, and must be, to the punishment assigned by God to a failure such as he has achieved. To compromise or to palliate is to derogate from the conception of God ; and that Paul is too honest and too God-centred to do, even if his honesty makes him despair.

But Paul changed his mind in view of a great discovery. He could not give up, and did not, the fundamental conviction of God's supreme righteousness—" let God be true and every man a liar." [2] But he discovered in the Cross of Christ a moral and

[1] Cf. Rom. iii. 5.   [2] Rom. iii. 4.

spiritual more-than-equivalent for the Judgment. The Cross did something, and did it so thoroughly, that it made men's existing conceptions of God's judgment seem antiquated. It took at once that central place in history, in human outlook, in the universe, which had been held by the Great White Throne. It solved the problem of God's righteousness and man's sin. The problem was to square moral instincts with grace. Greek and Jewish notions of God's forgiveness failed, as Plato and others saw, because they involved the simple giving-away of the very ideas of law, order and righteousness, and because moreover this giving-away of what is fundamental appeared arbitrary, unbalanced, and a great deal too easy ; it undid the universe, and yet cost nobody anything. One thing that the conception of Judgment carried with it was the idea of the moral and spiritual cost of sin ; no man (let us say) expecting to be damned, with the completeness and finality that the word carries whatever picture we frame of the state produced, could conceivably think lightly of sin. Nor, Paul held, could a man think lightly of sin, when he saw and realized the Cross of Christ. The Cross enabled a man to share God's view of the seriousness of sin, but without despair ; it allowed him to hope, to trust, to live, without cheapening God or righteousness. Repentance, μετάνοια, was not the rather easy Jewish process of the Day of Atonement, but a genuine sharing of God's outlook at all costs to oneself, a disinterested emotion as opposed to one sprung of self-seeking, an affirmation of God's ways. The Cross was for Paul a revelation of God's ways and of God's nature, so surprising in its inconceivable generosity that it melted his heart, and that, throughout his whole life, he could never think or speak of it without the element of wonder and surprise. " God was in Christ reconciling the world to Himself ; " in the Cross He showed Himself, His heart, and His love ; and doing so He captured the self, the heart and the love of men, who thereupon came over to His view of sin and of everything else. The Cross revealed at once the brightness and warmth of God's love and the horribleness of sin ; and if a man accepted the love of God as a result, he could not forget how exceedingly sinful sin had been shown to be. A service done for him by God in Christ, at the price of so much suffering and humiliation—made a spectacle for men and daemons and angels—a forgiveness that cost God so much, could never leave a man capable of thinking lightly of sin. Christ was indeed putting away sin by the sacrifice of Himself ; and for all time sin, the record of the broken law, remained " nailed to His Cross," as Paul says.[1] The Cross shows them both nailed up, Christ and sin, a " placarding "[2] at once of the two supreme factors in a moral universe, God's love and sin's hatefulness. No wonder that for Paul there was no getting away from the Cross, no transcending of it (as in some partially derivative faiths) for a higher view of God ; there was no higher view of God for him, because there was no truer or more essential revelation of God. God became unthinkable for Paul except as revealed in Christ ; and so, if we are thoroughly and profoundly honest, He remains.

No one would expect in so brief a compass a full statement of Paul's conception of God in Christ. Indeed, as suggested before, if every chapter, if every line, is not full of what Paul is trying to express and trying to discover, the biography, or the characterization of the man, or whatever it be, is futile, and even false. " To me," he said, " to live is Christ ; " and, of course, it was ; and as one is never done with life, Paul was never done with Christ—he would probably say he had hardly begun. Even a very little reading of his epistles in the order of their composition will show how amazingly he grew in his insight into Christ,

[1] Col. ii. 14.　　　　[2] Gal. iii. 1.

how progressively he found more and more in him. It was said in our introduction that a man of this type is irreducible to system, and it is true. His vocabulary is not in the least that of a lawyer or even of a philosopher of the systematic type. He flings out words and thoughts almost in desperation. Perhaps the best commentary upon them and upon his methods is given by Clement of Alexandria, when he speaks of Christian language as to God : " If we ever name Him calling Him, though not properly, one, or the good, or mind, or absolute being, or Father, or God, or Demiurge, we do not so speak as putting forward His name ; but for want of His name, we use beautiful names, that the mind may not wander at large, but may rest on these. None of these names, taken singly, informs us of God ; but, collectively and taken all together, they point to His almighty power." [1] It was so that Jesus used parables, none of them telling the whole story, none of them susceptible of being pressed in minute detail, but all taken together giving a wonderful picture of God. So Paul's metaphors, analogies, legalistic arguments, spiritual flashes—who can correlate them, who would wish to ? Not Paul himself, a thinker too vivid, too human, too great, to be systematic. A system of Pauline thought will always be wrong somewhere ; what the student of Paul has to do is to realize by experience, somehow, what that love of Christ, revealed in the Cross, and far above all law (for it transforms law into instinct), meant to Paul. Otherwise do not let him give the name of Paul to what he draws.

" If any man be in Christ, it is a new creation," says Paul : and the latter phrase seems to have been one that appealed to him, as it comes twice in letters several years apart. It is his equivalent for what the fourth evangelist later on calls being " born again," and, I think, a good deal more. It is not only that the man

[1] See Clement of Alexandria, *Stromateis*, v. 81, 5-82, 3.

is given hope to face the world with, in the place of despair ; the whole world seems changed, a different place, and so it is, for there is a new God over it and in it, a loving friend and not a supernatural lawyer. Deissmann has reckoned that Paul uses the phrase " in Christ " a hundred and sixty-four times, perhaps with the rendering " in God " of the Septuagint Psalter before him.[1] A new universe and himself in Christ—and that old and painful righteousness, " according to the law blameless," which he had striven so hard to acquire, is absolutely irrelevant ; he is in a new order of ideas. The acquired righteousness— and most of us know the consciousness of doing well— he counts not a gain but a loss, he prefers *not* to be conscious of it, *not* to be aware of any accumulation stored in the treasury of God, but to have only such title to righteousness as Christ may give him, a righteousness of faith. In plainer words, what that old righteousness was supposed to secure, viz., happy relations with God, God is now known to volunteer on His part to those who will believe that He does so, and will accept what He offers. The righteousness which thus rests on faith, on counting God as good as His promise, is not from one point of view righteous-ness at all ; but it serves as well, it is the acceptance for nothing of what had previously had to be bought. On the other hand it works out at a far more effective righteousness, for it is not self-seeking nor self-sus-tained ; self is absent from it, and it is instinctive, the natural and spontaneous reaction of affection to affection ; the good that is done is done without conscious purpose but to please a friend ; it would be done in truth as readily out of gratitude, if that friend by any chance were never to know.

One or two points must be safeguarded. The language of Paul is, as we saw, various. Like other men of vivid mind, he gives a thought many expressions.

[1] Deissmann, *St Paul* (Engl. tr.), pp. 121, 132, etc. Cf. p. 212.

But he never suggests that God has to be reconciled or appeased—on the contrary, it is men who have to be reconciled to Him, like the wife (in the Corinthian letter [1]), who gives up her quarrel with her husband. God is not asking for suffering. He volunteers to do the suffering Himself, God in Christ " commending " His love to us, sinners as we are. A great deal of trouble has been made for people who belong to a scientific or psychological age rather than to an age of legalism, by the phrase " imputed righteousness " ; but it is hardly of the first importance. All schemes of salvation, in which this idea plays a prominent part, have a legalistic basis and imply an outlook, and not that most closely congenial to the love of God ; and " the love of God which is in Christ Jesus, our Lord," is the central thing with Paul. If he touches the legal, as he does, it is fairer to take his words as an argument on the old assumption (which he has discarded) rather than on the new, which becomes the principle of his life. His relations with God and Christ are quite obviously beyond expression in legal terms. The form, which a new experience takes, still more that in which it is expressed, depends a good deal on literary antecedents, on existing religious vocabulary, on philosophical postulates and dogmata, and indeed on those who are to listen or to read. The great contribution of Paul here is his gift of a new language, in which Christians have continued ever since to express their deepest emotions. The whole vocabulary of Grace is Paul's ; and, as one of his English followers put it, " 'tis a charming sound."

Paul will not be understood, if we try to work out his new life in terms of the old idea which he abandoned. But a new realization of him, and indeed of Christ, will be gained with every fresh attempt to collect and to understand the multitudinous variants, in which he tries to express the new life. He is not playing

[1] I Cor. vii. II.

with formulae here; he is as little scholastic as a young lover; and experience lies behind every endeavour he makes to say how much he owes. Far nearer his feeling, far nearer the fact, than any juristic analogy, is his confession that " God has shined in our hearts, to give the light of the knowledge of the glory of God in the face of Jesus Christ." [1] He has passed for ever from the region of schemes and satisfactions and settlements into that of sunshine and peace—a peace that passes understanding, as he says.[2] Sunshine and peace are the conditions of spiritual growth. Storm and stress may challenge men and so develop them, but only if the challenge to find a deeper peace is stoutly accepted, and if the peace is found. Paul had accepted the challenge offered to his dogmatism by the Christian movement. He had faced the facts, above all the fact of the crucified Jesus; he had penetrated to the meaning; he has won through to certainty and found God.

[1] 2 Cor. iv. 6.   [2] Phil. iv. 7.

CHAPTER V

THE LIFE OF OBEDIENCE

As characteristic a sentence of Paul as any we have in his own writings or in Luke, is one in his speech to the King and the Roman governor. "Whereupon, O King Agrippa, I was not disobedient to the heavenly vision." [1] "When it pleased God . . . to reveal his Son in me that I might preach the good news of him among the Gentiles, immediately I conferred not with flesh and blood ; " [2] so he writes to the Galatians. A century and a half later, Tertullian describes conver-version no less decisive : "Who is not stirred by the contemplation of it [i.e., the death of the martyrs] to find out what there is in the thing within ? " [3] "Every man who witnesses this great endurance, is struck with some misgiving and is set on fire to look into it, to find what is its cause ; and when he has learnt the truth, he instantly follows it himself as well." [4] *Et ipse statim sequitur.* In both cases a martyrdom is a part-cause. To look with open face into the glory of the Lord (i.e., Jesus), as on to a mirror on which the sun is shining, is to be lit up oneself, to be transformed. [5]

Why, we are asked, does Damascus mean to him a new vocation ? Why does the vision of Jehovah enthroned, high and lifted up, while His glory filled the temple, mean first a new sense of sin to Isaiah, and then a call to go on behalf of God, where God shall send him ? Why is Jeremiah, if reluctantly, still irresistibly a prophet ? Why has Amos to leave

---

[1] Acts xxvi. 19.   [2] Gal. i. 15, 16.   [3] Tertullian, *Apol.*, 50.
[4] Tertullian, *ad Scapulam*, 5.   [5] 2 Cor. iii. 18.

94

his flock in the South ? Why must Buddha share his illumination ? The instances might be multiplied to great length. Why can a man see Truth and not be able to leave it alone ? " A man who can hold his tongue can hold anything," wrote the wittiest churchman of our day ; but in philosophy, and poetry, and religion, to see is to speak. There is no alternative. " If I do this thing against my will, a stewardship is committed to me ; "[1] but Paul did not do it against his will, and by now he could act with an undivided will. He instantly realizes what is involved. All that has been pent up in him, all the instincts crushed by his resolve to be a thoroughgoing Pharisee, everything—love of men, Gentile memories, the craving for the largest-hearted God possible — is released at once and joyful. John Bunyan says that he himself under somewhat similar circumstances felt as if he could talk about the love of God to the crows by the roadside, and legend (or perhaps history) says that Francis of Assisi did. Paul and Bunyan had other game.

A man is responsible to men for what he knows, and responsible to God for telling them in full. Much folly is talked to-day about the emphasis laid on personal salvation, on individual conversion. So far as we can learn from our records, it has been God's most effective way of saving communities ; and the saved man knows it and gets to work ; and Paul did. Without hedging or accommodating, outspoken and definite from the first, he let it be known where he stood—" first unto them of Damascus, and at Jerusalem " and then in Tarsus,[2] and so on into widening circles, in " regions beyond," [3] " not where

[1] 1 Cor. ix. 17.
[2] Cf. Acts ix. 30 ; xi. 25. These two references suggest (alas ! as too often in Luke, without dates) a ministry of some duration in the native place which must have been interesting.
[3] 2 Cor. x. 16.

Christ was named."[1] And, like real converts, like men who make the supreme discoveries, he is prepared to proclaim his message at all costs to himself.

For Paul Jesus is "Lord"; it is the name for Jesus that is peculiarly and pre-eminently Paul's own. If we are told that this was the name given by Greek adepts to Serapis, Paul at all events knew more of Jewish religion than he ever did of Egyptian [2]—so much is certain; and he had met the term in the Septuagint, a book with which we know him to have been familiar.[3] "To this end," he says,[4] "Christ both died, and rose, and revived, that he might be Lord both of the dead and of the living." Christ's lordship is proportionate to his own place and person; and as Paul knows more of Jesus Christ every year, the lordship of Christ is enhanced and emphasized. If Paul escaped from the servitude of the law of Moses, with a relief that never died away, he passed under the law of Christ. He says it with a sudden jerk, partly to explain himself to others, partly in happy reminder to himself.[5] A man, writes Professor F. G. Peabody, " is set free as he passes from one kind of law to the other. Liberty is allegiance to the higher law "; there are " laws that broaden and enlarge life." [6] He has a centre now—not one that he is secretly in revolt against, but one to which all life is true'd; and it means a steadying of interests, a correction of ideals, an expansion of outlooks—the experience which Wordsworth describes in the *Ode to Duty* :

> I supplicate for thy control,
> But in the quietness of thought;

---

[1] Rom. xv. 20.

[2] Once more note the slightness of Paul's connexion with anything Egyptian, Apollos included.

[3] Compare Rom. xiv. 11; Phil. ii. 10, with Isaiah xlv. 23, Septuagint.

[4] Rom. xiv. 9.   [5] 1 Cor. ix. 21.

[6] *Afternoons in the College Chapel*, p. 72.

Me this unchartered freedom tires ;
I feel the weight of chance desires :
My hopes no more must change their name,
I long for a repose that ever is the same.

Paul, too, as we have seen in a passage previously quoted, feels the need of having his " thoughts kept " ; [1] but with him the centre is not the conception of duty, but the living person who (as he repeats) " loved me and gave himself for me." [2] If there is truth (as there is) in the old saying, *fabri fabricando fimus*, a truth expressed in English by apprenticeship, what was it for Paul for years to be " a fellow-worker with Christ," [3] hammering the same anvil, handling the same things, and learning how ? To live with an artist and to watch his touch, to catch his angle of vision, to learn at last to anticipate how his mind will work, is a supreme opportunity for any man who has an eye for greatness and truth. In no fanciful way, but literally, we may say that Paul lived so with Christ ; at least, it was his ideal, and the combination of such an ideal with personal love and gratitude is an incomparable training. There is illumination in the contrast between Marcus Aurelius, with his inheritance of Stoic dogmata, his sense of duty in a loyalty to an impersonal ideal, his solitude and his deepening belief in the ultimate futility of his endeavours, and Paul, happy in daily intercourse with a personal Master and convinced to overflowing that there can be no doubt of that Master's triumph.

The converse of Master in that ancient world was Slave, and the term is constantly applied to himself by Paul. An attempt has been made to use the Pauline phrase " slave of Christ " as evidence for some intimate knowledge of the mystery religions on Paul's part.[4] Apuleius represents Isis as saying to the converted

---

[1] Phil. iv. 7. [2] Gal. ii. 20. [3] 2 Cor. vi. 1.
[4] Reitzenstein, *Die Hellenistischen Mysterienreligionen*, pp. 78, 81, etc.

G

Lucius, " You will remember clearly and keep laid up in your inmost mind that the remaining course of your life to the very end of your last breath is mortgaged to me." [1] He says further that against " those, whose lives the majesty of our goddess has claimed for her service (*servitium*), unhappy chance has no opportunity." [2] The initiate of Isis is frequently called in Greek " slave of the goddess " (or, vaguely, " slave of god "). But Apuleius lived a century after Paul, so perhaps Paul did not borrow from him ; and while Paul might have borrowed perhaps from those whose views Apuleius reproduced, it is not certain that he knew them, while it is certain that he knew another great branch of the human race and another and greater literature, where such expressions were not unfamiliar. Names like Obadiah, Abdiel, Obed-edom, Abdullah, Abdur Rahman, are reminders enough that the idea of a man being the slave of a god has been all along common to the Semitic race. Even if Paul was ignorant of the elements of Hebrew etymology—and there is nothing the least abstruse in the formation of such names—he could read the Psalter in Greek, and in the 116th Psalm, were the words : " O Lord, I am thy slave, I am thy slave, and the son of thy handmaid." The very words became Pauline ; for " Lord " the Septuagint gives κύριος, and " slave " is represented by the ordinary Greek δοῦλος. It is hardly necessary to send a modern Christian to the Upanishads—though he might have a better chance of finding them than Paul the documents of the mystery cults—for what he can read in his Authorized Version. Mr Farnell at all events is satisfied that " the slave of God " came into Christian use from Semitic sources. [3]

Mr Farnell also gives us a suggestion as to another famous expression of Paul's—" I bear in my body the

[1] Apuleius, *Metam.*, xi. 6. [2] *Metam.*, xi. 15.
[3] Farnell, *Greece and Babylon*, p. 193.

stigmata of the Lord Jesus." [1]   A passage is cited from Herodotus to show that a slave in Egypt may secure virtual emancipation by going to a certain temple of Herakles and having branded upon him " certain sacred marks " [2] (στίγματα ἱρὰ), though we are told that no Egyptian parallel has been found for such a general right of asylum. Mr Farnell says that the practice of marking the body by branding, cutting or tattooing, with some sign that consecrated the man as a slave of a deity, may have been of great antiquity, though the evidence only goes back to the sixth century B.C., but that it is essentially not Hellenic.[3] Paul, once more, had nothing to do with Egypt ; most probably he had not read a line of Herodotus. But the branded slave of men was no uncommon sight, and Paul is probably merely extending his general conception of the slave—not an unnatural thing to do, as he looked at his body and saw the scars, records of stripes and stones,[4] and of that " dying of the Lord Jesus " which he carried about in his person ; [5] his body had had a good deal of " buffeting." [6]

Paul uses the illustration taken from slavery very freely, and it is worth while to note that so did Jesus. " Necessity is laid upon me " (1 Cor. ix. 16) ; " I enslaved myself to all men that I might gain the more " (1 Cor. ix. 19)—such passages are plain enough. He speaks of his apostolate as a stewaidship, and the Greek οἰκονόμος like the Latin *villicus* was a slave. Even thoughts are brought into obedience (2 Cor. x. 5). The heading of several epistles tells the same tale ; and the idea is further extended when he speaks of " ourselves your slaves because of Jesus " (2 Cor. iv. 5). This

---

[1] Gal. vi. 17.
[2] Herodotus, ii. 113 ; and note of How and Wells.
[3] Farnell, *Greece and Babylon*, p. 194.
[4] Cf. 2 Cor. xi. 24-27.   [5] 2 Cor. iv. 10.
[6] 1 Cor. ix. 27 ; ὑπωπιάζω in this passage is another reminder of Greek boxing, a vivid one, much vivider than the English.

definite and clear relation to Christ, his own complete subjection, is often an immense relief to him. Men criticized him and his gospel; it was foolishness, the resurrection was silly, the cross a great obstacle. Well, if they did criticize him? "Who art thou that judgest (dost criticize) another man's servant?" he asks; "To his own master he stands or falls"; and then, in his sudden way, with the familiar tangent he adds, "Yes, and he shall be upheld, too." [1] So, in the passage of Galatians, the *stigmata* are indeed a badge of freedom; "henceforth let no man trouble me; I bear in my body the *stigmata* of the Lord (i.e., proprietor) Jesus." Man's judgment—even Corinthian opinion—is a negligible factor; [2] even his opinion of himself, as he points out, is unimportant; indeed, he does not trouble to estimate himself and his services; he is a steward, and " he that estimates me is the Lord." So there it rests. In his use of the term " saint," or dedicated person, we find implied very much the same ideas [3]—Christ's ownership and use of him, Christ's responsibility for the message he delivers, Christ's protection, his identification with his Master and the great joy of being used by Him.

With something of the same thought, Paul tells the Galatians, " I have been entrusted with the Gospel of the Gentile world " (ii. 7); and " it is asked of stewards that they should be faithful." [4] Paul, with a message committed to him, is determined that it shall be delivered exactly. On this point he speaks with emphasis to the Corinthians in more than one letter. " Christ sent me to preach the gospel: not with wisdom of words . . . Christ crucified, unto the Jews a stumbling-block, and unto the Gentiles foolishness. . . . When I came to you, I came not with excellency of speech or of wisdom, declaring unto you the testimony of God. For I determined not to know anything

---

[1] Rom. xiv. 4. See also p. 190.   [2] ἐλάχιστον, 1 Cor. iv. 3.
[3] See *Jesus in the Experience of Men*, chap. x.   [4] 1 Cor. iv. 2.

among you save Jesus Christ—and him crucified . . .
not with the enticing words of man's wisdom. . . .
The natural man receiveth not the things of the
Spirit of God." [1] In the other letter (we need not
now try to discover how many letters, or parts of them,
are embodied in our two Epistles) he speaks of his
endeavour to be sincere. Sincerity is not so easy a
task as some people think ; it is not always easy to be
sure that one is telling the truth, even if one tries,
either to others, or to oneself ; and simplicity is one
of the most difficult things to achieve. But Paul,
like many of his followers, and for the same reasons,
has tried to be candid with himself, alike in self-
criticism and in apprehension of the truth. His conversion had begun in self-criticism and the resolve to
have ultimate fact in absolute veracity.

Bunyan's undertaking to be straightforward and
plain in telling his story,[2] illustrates Paul's mind—
as an unintended parallel will. " I could also have
stepped into a Stile much higher than this, in which I
have here discoursed, and could have adorned all
things more than here I have seemed to do ; but I
dare not : God did not play in tempting of me ;
neither did I play, when I sunk as into a bottomless
Pit, when the *Pangs of Hell caught hold upon me* ;
wherefore I may not play in relating of them, but be
plain and simple, and lay down the thing as it was."

" We," says Paul,[3] " have renounced the hidden
things of dishonesty, not walking in craftiness, nor
handling the word of God deceitfully ; but by manifestation of the truth commending ourselves to every
man's conscience in the sight of God." The English
of the Authorized Version is not here very clear in
detail, nor is Paul's Greek. At least two views may be
taken of the first clause. It may be yet another
emphasis on that thought, of which the epistle is full,

---

[1] I Cor. i. 17-ii. 14.   [2] Preface to *Grace Abounding*.
[3] 2 Cor. iv. 2.

of the awful openness of the life of the Christian.
" We have been made manifest to God," he says—
thrown open, seen through by God ; we must one day
be thrown open and manifested before the Judgment
Seat of Christ ; and we aim, he suggests, at being open
and manifest to men here and now—" commending
ourselves to every man's conscience in the sight of
God," who knows our " shameful secrets," if we have
any. He draws a picture of a life where all the windows
of the soul are thrown open, where the sun searches
every corner of the room.[1] In this case—and whether
it be Paul's precise meaning in this passage or not, it
is certainly his sense—he puts forward a plan of openness of life without secrets ; if he, or any one else, is
to serve Christ, he must be open for all men to see into
him and to see through him ; and if there is anything
wrong, it seems better that men should know it at
once, as they will later on " when God judges the
secrets of men." [2]

On the other hand, Paul's Greek may bear another
meaning of " secret shame." He was evidently conscious in the Greek world of the criticism of those
who had studied Rhetoric and Philosophy. The
passage already quoted from First Corinthians shows
so much. He, so sensitive to men's feelings and minds,
could not escape the unspoken criticism ; he read it,
and felt it, at once—and, with it, he was conscious of a
feeling of shame. He would have liked—something in
him would have liked—" to step into a Stile much
higher than this " ; but he will not attempt it. He
uses on the contrary, in this part of his epistle, three
very striking words to bring out his endeavour " to be
plain and simple, and lay down the thing as it was."
" Not walking in trickery nor vamping the word of
God," he says here ; [3] and, a chapter or so earlier,[4]

---

[1] Cf. verse 6.   [2] Rom. ii. 16.
[3] 2 Cor. iv. 2, πανουργία, δολοῦντες.
[4] 2 Cor. ii. 17, καπηλεύοντες.

he says he will not " try the tricks of a retail trader on the word of God." The Greek distinguished between the merchant who travelled from city to city, and the retailer who sat in the market, as sorry a figure in person as he was in mind ; " the unsound kind of *Chrêmatistikê* (money-making) is so-called (τὸ καπηλικὸν), not because none but κάπηλοι practised it, but because it was exemplified in, and best illustrated by, their way of trading, with which every one was familiar," says Mr W. L. Newman, commenting on Aristotle.[1] No man shall say that Paul has dressed up the Gospel, touched it up or toned it down, boomed it, or concealed the sacrifices it involves ; he has not attempted fine language or artful presentation (though some said something of this sort [2]) ; he does not even try to put the thing in what might be supposed to be the right way. No ; in the centre of the story were a stumbling-block and an absurdity ; and Paul is content to leave them there, with great plainness of speech and an open-air sincerity.[3] Obedience and loyalty on the one hand, and experience on the other, lie behind his procedure. The Cross of Christ has to be faced and thought out ; and, as Paul knew, the challenge of the Cross, the offence of the Cross, were potent agents in bringing men face to face with the supreme issue.

In the sentence addressed to King Agrippa Paul brought vision and obedience close together, and we have already seen, in the analogy of the craftsman and the apprentice, how naturally the two things belong to each other. Obedience means vision. The records of Luke, confirmed by passages of Paul's own writing, tell of visions which Paul had from time to time, to which we have already referred [4]—visions,

---

[1] Aristotle, *Politics*, i. 9, 2, 1257 B.   [2] 2 Cor. xii. 16.
[3] 2 Cor. iii. 12 ; 2 Cor. ii. 17.
[4] Chap. III., p. 66. Cf. Acts xxii. 18 ; xvi. 7, 8, 9 ; xviii. 9 ; xxiii. 11 ; xxvii. 23 ; 2 Tim. iv. 17 ; and 2 Cor. xii. 1 ff.

dreams, hints, " concerns and stops," as Quakers used
to say. To emphasize the mode, the form, the shape,
in which these things from time to time came to
Paul, would be to miss the real issue. Dreams, visions,
and " strong suggestions," come to temperaments of
various makes, but are not necessarily particular
revelations of God's will, even if the recipients so
suppose, nor need they be always as nugatory as sometimes has been held. Examination is necessary both
of the man and of contemporary ideas. Reitzenstein [1]
suggests that Paul perhaps had no peculiar Psychology
of his own, but " speaks the Greek of his time."
Professor H. A. A. Kennedy,[2] whose acquaintance
with Paul seems to be more intimate, says that
practically every leading idea of Paul's in these matters
has its roots in Jewish soil. The contradiction may
not be very great. But the parallel of Socrates'
daimonion warns us to decide slowly. Whatever the
form or shape of the supposed communication, when
we survey Paul's career, as when he surveyed it himself,
it is hard to imagine a life more full of divine guidance
in every field of thought and activity, a life in closer
relation with God. The Lord stood by him, he says,[3]
and put strength into him ; and when we recall how
many other men and women since Paul have had the
same sense, and have lived with the same mastery over
circumstance and accident, even the quickest thinker
must pause a little before deciding it is all delusion or
co-incidence—both rather loose terms. Co-incidences
seem little apt to occur where minds do not quite
co-incide. At the end, Paul says, " I know whom I
have believed " ; [4] and even if we dispute the complete authenticity of the Epistles to Timothy, that

---

[1] *Die hell. Myst. Relig.*, p. 42, maintaining that πνεῦμα in Paul's
writings has the same meaning as in the magical papyri. " The same
meaning " is always a risky phrase, when genius is concerned.

[2] H. A. A. Kennedy, *Paul and Mystery Religions*, p. 154 ff.

[3] 2 Tim. iv. 17.　　　　　　　　　　　　[4] 2 Tim. i. 12.

sentence at least is confirmed and supported in every Epistle he wrote. Like the salutation,[1] it is in his own hand, the authentication of every letter ; " *so* I write."

At another point we have to notice the so-called psychological or psychopathic manifestations which Paul mentions—that " speaking with tongues " which he perplexes us by avowing,[2]—the vision of the third heaven " above fourteen years ago," [3] which at least suggests a not excessive frequency of such occasions. For the present our task must be to study the evidence which Paul affords of spiritual guidance in a region where he and all sane men would count it of far higher import. Even the feeblest-minded person, who experiences voice and vision, whether we call him (or her) recipient or patient, will refer them to some theory with an intellectual basis, insecure it may be, but laid by reflexion not by revelation. The vision is always classified, however mistakenly ; and the recipient or patient relies in the last resort on tests not of vision but of general experience.

Popular Psychology to-day distinguishes between the once-born and the twice-born, with (I think) a temporary preference for the former—a preference which may have its origin in mental inertia. For the twice-born there is this to be said, that to have been " baptized with *all* experiences " [4] opens a man's eyes more than to have had one experience, however happy ; it stimulates reflexion and intellectual process, and it is more apt to result in action—in that propaganda which for real people is always illuminative. The new life always means more to people who have grown up in the old and have escaped from it. The psalmist's experience is true—

[1] 2 Thess. iii. 17 ; cf. 1 Cor. xvi. 21 ; Col. iv. 18.
[2] 1 Cor. xiv. 18 ; cf. Chap. viii., p. 186.   [3] 2 Cor. xii. 2.
[4] I borrow this phrase, misquoted slightly, I believe, but a happy summary of what George Fox said or meant about himself.

He took me from a fearful pit,
And from the miry clay,
And on a rock He set my feet,
Establishing my way.

He put a new song in my mouth,
Our God to magnify :
Many shall see it, and shall fear,
And on the Lord rely.[1]

It is the new song that counts, from Homer down-
wards, even if it is as old as Homer's.

The first point here is to notice once more the new
peace of heart and mind that we have remarked already.
Whatever vagaries manuscripts and their copyists may
in certain passages suggest to timid editors, Paul
avows the possession of peace with God.[2] How much
it means, no man can tell ; and no man can know how
much, unless he has been conscious of life without
that peace. It passes understanding, as Paul said.[3]
The striking passage in the central chapter of the
Epistle to the Romans illustrates what Paul has in
mind. "The spirit also helps our weakness, for we
know not what we should pray for as we ought, but
the Spirit itself makes intercession for us with groan-
ings that cannot be uttered. And he that searches
hearts knows what is the mind of the Spirit," which
(some verses earlier) cries in us " Abba, Father."
Luther hits the real meaning here, as a man of similar
experience will ; all that the man, or the Spirit in
him, can manage is " a little sound and a feeble groan-
ing, as *Ah ! Father*," and the Father understands [4]—a
simple vocative without petition, and connexion is
established ; " He knows about it all, He knows, He
knows," and the human heart is at peace. Such peace
is, if we may use popular jargon, not static but dynamic.

---

[1] Psalm xl.   [2] Rom. v. 1. Cf. p. 221.   [3] Phil. iv. 7.
[4] Luther on Galatians, Chap. IV. (fol. 192 a, of English translation, second edition, 1580).

" Peace," wrote Benjamin Jowett, commenting on
Paul, " must go before moral growth as well as after ;
there will be no growth while uneasy with God." [1]
We have already noticed Paul's description of what
is found in Christ as a " new creation." [2] He may
mean by κτίσις the act of creating or the creation
as it exists after being made. But whether a new-
making or a new world, in it is a new man,[3] a more
explicit phrase, a man over whom sin no longer has
dominion ; he is escaped from its paralysing virus.
He is finding, in the striking phrase of the Fourth
Gospel (which was yet to be written) life, and life more
overflowingly. In his own phrase, Paul knows now
how the law of the Spirit of Life in Christ Jesus sets
him free from the law of sin and death [4]—a spirit of
power able to effect what the Law of Moses, and
the whole apparatus of regulation, maxim, caution,
and commandment, could never do.[5] Life is given by
life, and by nothing else. The parasite sin, as Professor
Peabody has put it,[6] is killed by strengthening the
organism on which it preyed ; evil is overcome not
negatively but positively, by good.[7] " As we have
received mercy, we faint not," Paul says,[8] using the
Greek word that suggests the cowardly slackening of
energy rather than the involuntary fainting, to which
the English term is now generally narrowed down.
With good hope now within him, Paul can face anything and everything—all the wonderful discoveries of
the spiritual life; for a new creation is not quickly
exhausted or quickly realized. It is routine that
deadens interest, and there his old legalism was weak ;
he had everlastingly to be doing the same precautionary

[1] Jowett, *Paul's Epp.*, vol. ii., p. 266.   [2] 2 Cor. v. 17.
[3] Eph. iv. 24, with the contrasting phrase in Rom. vi. 6.
[4] John x. 10 ; Rom. viii. 2.
[5] See P. Gardner, *Religious Experience of St Paul*, p. 34, on Paul's
sense of freedom in escaping from the minute regulations of the Law.
[6] *Evenings in the College Chapel*, p. 173-4.
[7] Rom. xii. 21.   [8] 2 Cor. iv. 1, οὐκ ἐγκακοῦμεν.

things, and he was of too large a build, too original.
He needed a positive centre, a stimulus, and a freedom ;
and in Christ he found all these, and he loved Christ
for the glorious freedom he found in Him, for the
charter of adventure that Christ gave.

At a later point we shall have to consider more
closely the relations between Christ and the Spirit as
Paul viewed them. Here we have to do with the new
life, the life in the Spirit, a life of heightened individuality resulting at once from the release from the
old burden, and the freedom to develop the new relation with God. The spiritual man, Paul says, is subject
to no man's criticism ; he is out of their range ; " no
man can read what he is ; " [1] his life in a way is hid
with Christ in God,[2] centred in the spiritual and in
touch with the eternal. One of the effects of sin, as
we saw, was to deaden mind and conscience—darken,
stain, and cauterize, were Paul's words. The guidance
and teaching of the Spirit—" the Spirit of wisdom
and revelation, in the knowledge of God " [3]—is to
enlighten the understanding, to the point of realizing
all that Christ means, to give a new faculty of intuition
into spiritual things, restoring the lost powers and
heightening them. God's Spirit alone can be credited,
he suggests, with knowing the things of God, which
are only to be spiritually discerned ; the man who
has that Spirit will read them and " compare " them.

The " depths of God," in his startling phrase, are
searched by the Spirit. Now the weakness of much
popular religion, inside and outside the Christian
Church, is the tacit assumption—never explicitly
avowed, for the sense of reverence would forbid—that
God is known, known already. The possession of
some real knowledge of God is every man's postulate
in discussion ; he assumes he knows God, and with
a minimum of examination. The modern Christian

---

[1] 1 Cor. ii. 14 ; Moffatt's translation.
[2] Col. iii. 3.   [3] Eph. i. 17, 18.

very often does not examine his concept of God and misses its very composite nature ; and his assumption results in endless confusion of mind. It is a real gain when we grasp that we do *not* know God, apart from the study of nature, which confessedly yields imperfect results, until we approach the subject through Jesus, whom we really know better than we know God. Paul had the advantage of being well aware that he had fundamentally misread God, of knowing that he had only begun to have any understanding of God at all, when he caught the meaning, the first meaning, of the Cross ; and yet he had been entirely sure of his knowledge of God, when he had quite missed God's real nature. From his conversion onward, he is less of a dogmatist and more of a learner ; and knowledge and vision come from obedience. " The depths of God " it is Paul's life-work and supreme interest to explore; he does not exhaust them. One of the reasons why Paul has been so inadequately studied of late years is that he was for long construed as a final authority, and his writings taken as a compendium of Theology, while his own idea was that he was a learner. " Who hath known the mind of the Lord, that he may instruct him ? " he asks, quoting the Septuagint, and using " the Lord " to represent God ; and he concludes, " but we have the mind of Christ." [1] The passage is a vindication of the one right way of approach to God, as Luther saw and said with emphasis.

One fruitful source of new knowledge was the active practical life which Paul led. The Spirit, as he believed, communicated to him what he was required to do, and where he was to go. There were, as Paul indicates, those who criticized him on this score, and suggested that he was apt to change his plans with disconcerting abruptness,[2] and to lay all at the door of the Spirit. We need not linger over the criticism at this point ; its real value is that it shows that Paul

---

[1] 1 Cor. ii. 16; Isaiah xl. 13.   [2] Cf. 2 Cor. i. 17.

was constantly on the outlook for signals and instructions, and that these uniformly bore upon his work. He was driven into endless preaching, teaching, and argument—constant collision on the deepest planes of thought and feeling with all sorts of men, and always for a practical object. It is not suggested in his own writings, nor in Luke's, but the evidence is set out by both for the fact, that he lived a life not unlike that of Socrates, always in colloquy with some man or other —colloquy that turned, as quickly as he could get it to turn, to what he held central, the mind of God as revealed in the Cross. Every discussion gave him a fresh opportunity of insight into the human mind and its re-actions to the idea of God ; and thus his obedience to the call to evangelize contributes to his " baptism with all experiences." A man so earnest, so apt quickly to reach with men the most serious things of all, so swift to refer all that he saw or divined in men's approaches or departures to what he knew already of Christ—" comparing spiritual things with spiritual "[1]—was bound inevitably to grow. Such a life has another side ; it involves a man who takes it seriously in the instinctive habit of instantaneous prayer ; he has to be in momentary communication with his Captain, always ready for the signal, the hint, where to press forward, what to emphasize, and so forth. He is watching God and watching man very closely in every such encounter ; and his prayer-life is made by the habit ; and something of what his prayer-life was, he lets us see in the Eighth of Romans.

At the same time Paul was not a natural saint. If he had not lived so long ago, and if his writings had not been included in the canon, he might not have been classed as a saint at all. He has the defects of his qualities, as we shall see or have seen in other chapters ; he has his battle with sin after as before his conversion. The principalities and powers showed no sign of allow-

[1] I Cor. ii. 13.

ing a victory " without dust," as the ancients put it.
Here, too, in the battle with weakness and temptation,
with solitude and irritability (too little of men and
too much of them), with discomfort, privation, and
danger, with restlessness and despair,[1] there was
revelation in finding himself " more than conqueror
through him that loved us " ;[2] and Paul does not
seem to have outgrown the wonder of it.

He weighed this fact of constant support, of the
steady supply[3] of a strength which he was conscious
he had not in himself, and he drew an inference. He
grew more and more certain of his Christian position
and realized that he was only at the beginning of his
experience. The gift of the Spirit as he knew it was
not finality ; it was only " the earnest money "
($\dot{a}\rho\rho a\beta\dot{\omega}\nu$).[4] He tells the Philippians that he is
" persuaded that he that hath begun a good work in
them will perfect it to the day of Christ Jesus ; "[5]
and he believes that God will finish in Paul himself
what He has begun, and that the Spirit is the " earnest
of our inheritance." Sometimes the figure is varied,
and the Holy Spirit is the seal with which God marks
His own.[6] At a rather later day, though still within
the period of what we may call the early church, the
metaphor of sealing was applied to baptism ;[7] the
sealing of the brow was part of the initiation into the
rites of Mithras ;[8] but to Paul baptism was not what
it became to the Church. To a Jew of his day Christian
baptism was one of several baptisms, significant indeed
—for a man is " buried with Christ in baptism,"[9]
crosses a line and leaves an old life with its associations
behind, and is dead to the world and his old friends—

---

[1] 2 Cor. i. 8, 9.   [2] Rom. viii. 37.   Cf. at large 2 Cor. iv. 7-11.
[3] Gal. iii. 5.   [4] 2 Cor. i. 22.
[5] Phil. i. 6.   [6] 2 Cor. i. 22 ; Eph. i. 13.
[7] Hatch, *Influence of Greek Ideas* (Hibbert Lectures), p. 295 ;
add reff. to 2 Clem R., 26 ; Hermas, *Simile*, ix. 16, 4.
[8] Tertullian *de praescr*, 40.   [9] Col. ii. 12.

but it is not magical in any degree. Paul, as we shall
see, never in his extant writings alludes to his own
baptism. It seems more reasonable to interpret Paul
by Paul rather than by Hermas or by Hermes,[1] and to
suppose his meaning to be that the gift of the Holy
Spirit is God's seal upon the Christian, a stamp of
ownership and a promise.[2] This interpretation seems
more consonant with the language of the great Hebrew
prophets, whom we know to have influenced him, the
great interpreters of God whom he had known from
boyhood.

It is to be noted, if it is not already clear, that the
metaphor of earnest money or of seal is insufficient. A
seal is essentially a dead thing and inert; earnest-
money is in its way useful. Neither exhausts, and
hardly either metaphor even suggests, what Paul seems
to mean. The Holy Spirit is for him above all things
life; and in the heightened life, the new spiritual
and intellectual energy, the new joy and exercise in
freedom, he sees, not unreasonably, the promise of a
yet further development of life and energy. This view
of the matter brings it more into line with all spiritual
and intellectual development, every stage of which is
a promise and a guarantee of another, and yet of
others still beyond; so that Paul's phrase gains weight
from its coincidence with a law of our nature, and
the recognition of what the gift actually is (the
heightened vitality) and of what it promises (still
fuller and deeper life) adds certainty to Paul's interpretation of his experience. Something of the same
kind is to be seen in Bunyan; *Grace Abounding* tells the
story of his religious life; so do both the parts of
The Pilgrim's Progress, but with what a different note
of assurance and gaiety! When acceptance of Christ
and obedience to him have actually worked out in a

---

[1] Not those of Rom. xvi. 14.

[2] H. A. A. Kennedy, *Paul and Mystery Religions*, p. 240, doubts
any reference to baptism in the term " sealing."

new realization of life, a new power to overcome, a new venturesomeness and general vitality, there must result a new certainty in a man's conviction.

To sum up then, and perhaps to anticipate points that must be more fully handled at a later stage, Paul finds that obedience has resulted in vision. A worker as well as a thinker, a man born for intimacy with other men and with a genius for friendship, he begins with the obvious duty of " preaching Christ " to the men he meets and then to men whom he has to go and seek ; from Damascus and Tarsus he looks on to Rome and to Spain.[1] But " preaching Christ " is not always what a man expects it to be. He is involved in the effective interpretation of Jesus Christ along the lines of experience—and of all sorts of experience. He finds revelation in work, in the world, among men. More than once, in moments of great crisis—at Corinth, at Jerusalem, on the ship—a quiet hour brings illumination of all the storm and stress in which he is moving—" Be not afraid ; be of good cheer, Paul ; for I am with thee." [2] That the revelation is not to be discounted as subjective or psychopathic or imaginative, or whittled away with any other unreflective adjective, is shown by the man's development. Once more we may remind ourselves that, like Plato, Paul is not a system, or a scheme of ideas, but a man living among men, testing thoughts,[3] and constantly developing his ideas. His growth is traceable in his epistles ; those written to the Thessalonians are hardly comparable with the letters to the Romans and to the Philippians, whatever we make of that entitled " To the Ephesians."

With years—and this is not every man's experience—

---

[1] Rom. xv. 24.

[2] By blending the passages (Acts xviii. 9 ; xxiii. 11), one realizes that the phrases are those familiar to readers of the Gospels as the constant language of Jesus, μὴ φοβοῦ, θάρσει.

[3] 1 Thess. v. 21, πάντα δοκιμάζετε.

Paul's sympathies widen, and he grows at once in attractiveness to men, and in liking for them, and understanding of them. The delicate tact of the letter to Philemon is familiar, but we sometimes forget how utterly alien to Paul in race and social standing, in intellectual and religious outlook, nearly everybody mentioned in the letter had originally been. There were other men of yet other types who felt his appeal— a Felix, a Julius. We shall have to return to his friendships,[1] but for the moment the width and multitude and variety of them sustains our point of his spiritual growth ; and the impulse that set him to win men, with growing tact, and sympathy ever more real, was his surrender to the ideals and purposes of Christ— his obedience. If he latterly uses vocabulary which suggests to students of other systems than Judaism an intimacy with them that once was not suspected, then, without supposing his original Jewish outlook to have been contaminated with pagan affinities, or his loyalty to clear thinking and to Christ to have become touched with magical hypotheses, one may attribute it to a growing patience, if not perhaps a growing sympathy, with ideas once alien, and with men once alien who thought in terms of those ideas. If Paul will be " all things to all men," [2] he will perhaps be ready to use any vocabulary that will bring home to them the real value of Christ. The use of alien vocabularies is always risky ; you may borrow the word and use it without fully realizing all its connotation ; [3] but Paul was not a man of vocabularies. Whatever he said came with the whole man and his whole experience behind it, and his words meant what he chose them to mean—as is always the way with great personalities. What people who never saw him face

---

[1] See pp. 178, ff.   [2] I Cor. ix. 22.
[3] The Master of a Cambridge College, who praised a missioner as " a perfect rotter at good works," may suffice as an illustration.

to face, never saw the quick hand flung out,[1] and never heard the talk that men could listen to for hours,[2] made of his manuscript letters was bound to be another thing. However, our present point is his enlarging range in friendship.

With this went inevitably, as we have seen, a closer reading of human nature, a fuller knowledge of other men's weaknesses and of his own, and a firmer belief in men when fortified by Christ dwelling in them. In spite of that fuller knowledge of his limitations, which years bring to all men—or, perhaps more truly, because of it—he grows more conscious of a power behind him [3] and within him. He realizes more and more from experience the value of the Gospel for all sorts and conditions of men, its universality.[4] The proof of this lies in his growing gift for finding his way through the tangles of the nascent church—tangles intellectual, moral, and social. He is abreast of every situation, and if he begins with a face to face encounter, a frontal attack on Peter at Antioch, later on men complain that he captures them by guile.[5] On the claims of Christ he compromised as little at the end as he did at the beginning ; but he was always ready to arrange a difficult situation by throwing his own claims and feelings overboard. He takes more and more trouble to understand men's perversities and obscurities, their prejudices and blunders, to con- ciliate them, and by dint of sheer friendship to bring them to understand how far their ideas were really " according to Christ." " And this I do for the Gospel's sake." [6]

How much more he progressively found in Christ will require at least another chapter ; but here we may close with the suggestion of an American thinker,

---

[1] Acts xiii. 16; xxi. 40 ; xxvi. 1 ; different movements of the hand are implied in the two words used.   [2] Acts xx. 7.
[3] 2 Tim. iv. 17.   [4] 1 Cor. i. 24 ; Rom. i. 16.
[5] 2 Cor. xii. 16.   [6] 1 Cor. ix. 23.

that "the persistent and continuous dedication of the will" is more than natural endowment; that "capacity grows out of desire much oftener than desire out of capacity." [1] In short, Paul was made by the steady habit, based on affection, of "bringing into captivity every thought to the obedience of Christ." [2]

[1] Peabody, *Afternoons in the College Chapel*, p. 167.
[2] 2 Cor. x. 5.

Chapter VI

" THE PREPARATION OF THE GOSPEL "

THE Christian Church early reached the conviction that the hour of Christ's first coming was not a matter of accident. God had His purposes clear—" before the foundation of the world," and all history was the working out of His design " that in the fulness of times He might gather together in one all things in Christ." [1] The disclosure of this purpose and its development were clearly to Paul a constant source of wonder and interest. It was part of his Jewish inheritance to believe that God had any real design in history at all. To the Stoic all things moved by irresistible necessity in a cycle, long indeed but finite ; and when the cycle was complete it was begun again, and the " sorrowful weary wheel " (to borrow an expression from a gold tablet found in an Orphic's grave) went on for ever and ever, as ages of rotation progressed only to general conflagration and meaningless renewal. The Jew must have counted such a belief a blank negation of the very idea of God. The great prophets saw otherwise than the Stoics, and the business of the apocalyptic writers was to forecast a genuine design of God's, which should end in a real triumph. Little wonder that Paul found purpose in God's work ; little wonder that to a weary world a course with an end to it, a chance of achievement, appealed, that it satisfied the human instinct for reality. The curse of the tread-mill in old prisons was that it went on for ever and effected nothing ; the Stoic's world was a treadmill as surely as its inhabitants were prisoners.

[1] Eph. i. 4, 10.

117

In an age when scholarship and science—intellect on its acquisitive side—have first challenged and then largely deadened the philosophic element in man, overpowering it with masses of not wholly digested fact and casting doubt on the validity of its function in any case, it may sound a little naive to find once more design in history. But the historical student of to-day, however scientific his conception of history, will allow a presentment of the factors which worked for the establishment of the church; indeed it would not be scientific history at all if these were omitted. So, whatever our interim theory may be—and perhaps it will be better to essay the task without too much theory—we may address ourselves to the nidus from which came the church.

It is perhaps hard for a modern thinker, even after years of war, to realize that to the ancient the separation of races was at least as natural as their meeting and co-operation. Yet India should give us a hint to expect it. In that country, on an avowed basis of religion, communities have stood apart for ages; but below the basis of religion is often one of race. A member of the little Jewish group known as Bene Israel will not marry a Jew of Cochin, " Black " or " White," nor a Bagdadi Jew, nor a Jew from Europe. There is at least one group of Moslems, of Rajput origin, real or reputed, whose members will not marry outside it—a rare case of caste invading Islam. How should a Parsi marry a Hindu, or a Brahmin, generally speaking, a low-caste woman ? Athens, in the age of Pericles, on political or economic grounds, reversed her practice, and refused citizenship to the child who had not two Athenian parents ; and that meant, I suppose, that the union of Athenian with non-Athenian was hardly marriage.

Yet there were things that bound Greek to Greek, as every Greek knew, and as surely severed them from foreigners and barbarians. " Many and great are the reasons that hinder " Athenians from making common cause with the Persians, say they to the envoys of Sparta ; " first and greatest, the images and houses of the gods set on fire or reduced to ruins," and " secondly, there is the bond of Hellenic race, by which we are of one blood, and of one speech, there are the common temples of the gods and the common sacrifices, the manners of life which are the same for all." [1] Blood, language and literature, religion with its gods and oracles and games and heroes, common culture and common customs, bound the Hellenes together, and marked them off from all the world beside. " The very interest in barbarian states and tribes, including the uncivilized, implies the growing consciousness of a common Hellenism " ; [2] and, as this consciousness developed, hatred or contempt for the barbarian grew with it. Isocrates, of course, preached war against Persia for forty years, and his policy perhaps colours his general views. " The Eumolpidai and the Heralds at the celebration of the mysteries, because of our hatred of the Persians, forbid the holy things to other barbarians as well, just as they do to murderers. So natural is our hostility to them, that of all stories we linger most pleasantly over the Trojan and the Persian Wars. . . . I think Homer's poetry got the greater glory, because he sang well the praises of those who fought the barbarian ; " and the Greeks, he continues, gave to Homer's art its place in competition and education that the young might learn the old hatred and imitate it.[3] Aristotle says that the Greeks regarded barbarians as " naturally slaves." [4] In both authors " by nature " means a great deal more than it does with us ; it is not the equivalent of " by disposition "

---

[1] *Herodotus*, viii. 144 ; cf. Dr Macan's note in his edition of *Herodotus*, iv.-vi., vol. ii. p. xxvi., giving illustrations from the historian.

[2] Macan, *loc. cit.*   [3] Isocrates, *Paneg.*, 157-159.

[4] Aristotle, *Politics*, i. 6, 6, p. 1255a ; and compare i. 5, 9.

or " temperament," but rather that in the nature of things, by natural law, Greeks are enemies of Persians, as we might say that cats are of mice, or horses of camels,[1] and that by natural endowment certain tribes are slaves, as sheep are four-legged. Nature was coming to mean more and more to Greeks ; so that, when racial anti-pathies are referred to Nature, Greeks imply that they are fundamental, beyond reason and beyond change.

At first, it is true, the Greek impressed the Roman, who was anxious for a while to be recognized as by blood related to one of the heroic races that fought at Troy. But by Cicero's day things had changed. Of course, in public speech, the orator will uphold the primacy of the people to whom he speaks, but even when his case requires him to represent the Sicilian Greeks as the most reasonable of men, he now and then lets slip phrases which betray the Roman contempt for the whole Greek tribe. Apart from his Greek freedman, Tiro, he has no Greek correspondent, and his letters show constantly how lightly he thought of them—" I am sick," he says, " of their want of character (*levitas*), their obsequiousness, their devotion, not to principle, but to the profit of the hour." [2] A hundred and fifty years later there was the same contempt, as Juvenal shows with his *Graeculus esuriens*. [3] And all this in face of Roman admiration for Greek litera-ture and delight in Greek art.

How the Jew felt for Greek and Roman alike, we have already seen. The attitude of the Gentile to the Jew is shown by Juvenal,[4] and in a significant passage of Epictetus, who asks : " Why do you play at being a Jew, when you are a Greek ? " [5] Celsus, about A.D.

---

[1] Herodotus, i. 80 ; cf. Polybius, v. 84, on the African elephant's dread of the Indian elephant's smell and of his trumpeting.

[2] Cf. J. P. Mahaffy, *Silver Age of Greece*, pp. 162-169 ; Cicero, *Epp. ad Quintum Fratrem*, 1, 2, 4.

[3] Juvenal, iii. 78, and the whole passage.

[4] Juvenal, xiv. 101-104.

[5] Epictetus, *Discourses*, ii. 7, 19 ; with some odd allusion to baptism.

178, denounces as foolish and impracticable the Christian sentiment that it is desirable for all who inhabit the empire, Greeks and barbarians, in Asia, Europe, and Libya, to agree to one law or custom [1]—this after two centuries of the imperial system. Finally, on this point, the surprise which Paul clearly expected his friends to feel, and perhaps felt himself, at the revelation of " God's secret " that there were to be no longer Jew and Gentile, Greek and barbarian, bond or free, is evidence of the deep-seated sense of race, which had survived Alexander and his successors, and the Roman conquest. Blood and custom and religious usage were expected to keep Gentile races apart ; and the exclusive knowledge of the true God was a barrier that separated the Jew from all other breeds.

Yet the forces at work in the world were surely and steadily working against the tradition and in favour of God's design, as Christians later on realized. Alexander the Great had changed the face of the world ; he had carried the Greek outside all known geography, he had introduced him to new lands, new races, and a new task.[2] All the kingdoms of the world and the glory of them were to be amenable to the Greek spirit. Hellenism began ; the whole of mankind was to be taught to think ; criticism, examination, the sense of proportion, were to rule in art and literature and religion, in every activity of the mind of man. Greek Buddhas from the Swat valley and from Turkestan, and Greek literature, letters and business documents, from the sands of Egypt, are material reminders of the union of the whole world in one culture, in one attitude of mind. The city state with its dour determination to have no relations with its neighbour—sheer mastery of that neighbour excepted—began to look very

---

[1] Origen, *contra Celsum*, viii. 72.

[2] See Edwyn Bevan, *House of Seleucus*, Vol. I., Chap. I.; and p. 28 of the same book.

parochial and trivial. Athens ceased to be an Empire and became a University, and what she had failed to do as the one, she did as the other. The ready homage offered to Athens by all civilized mankind was only challenged by Alexandria, and only in so far as Alexandria itself adopted Athenian ideals. Greeks went everywhere, by every trick of question and satire, and by every art of beauty, tempting the tribes to become citizens of one great Republic of the human mind ; and not in vain. The Greek trader might be as sordid and money-loving as his Semitic rival and neighbour in Alexandria or Antioch, in Babylon or Kandahar ; but he could not help being the missionary of something better. In proportion as men everywhere understood or even picked up the Greek attitude to life and the world, to things material and ideal, the world became one. The Bactrian felt the influence and coined gold pieces with his own head and a Greek inscription. The Jew felt it and wrote books in a new vein, *Ecclesiastes* and *Ecclesiasticus*, the *Wisdom of Solomon*, Greek dramas on the Exodus,[1] and the library that bears Philo's name. The Phoenician felt it, turned Greek and taught the Greek and the Roman Stoicism. How far the races commingled their blood, it is hard to guess ; Alexander held strongly that they ought to, and he promoted thousands of mixed marriages. But literature is not generally interested in half-castes, and we only hear of them by accident. If it had not been that Paul wished for the moment to conciliate Jewish prejudice, we might never have heard that Timothy had a Greek father—perhaps not quite as Greek as the technical term suggests to us—and a pious Jewish mother and grandmother, both, it may be noted, bearing Greek names.

Rome inherited the Empire and the task of Alexander. Perhaps the most striking thing in the testi-

---

[1] The work of an Ezekiel, extracts from which are given by Eusebius, *Praeparatio Evangelii*, ix. 28, pp. 436-447.

monies of the rest of the world to Rome's work is the emphasis on peace and on the freedom of travel. Pliny was of course a Roman, but he may give us a text. At the beginning of the twenty-seventh book of his *Natural History*, he speaks with interest of the growth of botanical knowledge ; how one herb of healing comes from Maeotis (the Sea of Azov), another from Atlas " beyond the pillars of Hercules, where Nature herself ends," others from British isles outside the world, and so forth ; and all are interchanged freely, thanks to " the boundless majesty of Roman peace "— " may that gift of the gods, I pray, be eternal! for in truth the Romans seem to have given a second daylight to mankind." " You see," says Epictetus, the Greek slave and Stoic philosopher, " that Caesar seems to give us great peace, that there are no longer wars, nor battles, nor great brigandage or piracy ; but a man may travel in every season on the roads, and may sail from the rising to the setting sun." [1] Philo the Jew praises Augustus, " who not only loosened but abolished the bonds in which the whole habitable world was previously bound and weighed down ; who destroyed both the evident and the unseen wars, which arose from the attacks of robbers ; who set the sea free from the ships of pirates and filled it with merchantmen." [2] In the last century of the Empire in the West Claudian says the same [3]—and those who have studied Greek tragedy will feel the irony of this last voice of Rome on the very eve of her dissolution :—

> Rome ! Rome alone has found the spell to charm
> The tribes that fell beneath her conquering arm,
> Has given one name to the whole human race,
> And clasped and sheltered them in fond embrace,

[1] Epictetus, *Diatribai*, III. xiii. 9.
[2] Philo, *de Legatione ad Gaium*, 21 ; cf. Skeel, *Travel in the First Century*, p. 30, a book as attractive as it is scholarly.
[3] Claudian, *Cons. Stilich.*, iii. 150. Claudian was an Egyptian Greek who wrote in the language, rhythm, and spirit of Virgil. (Dr T. Hodgkin's translation.)

Mother, not mistress, called her foe her son.
And by soft ties made distant countries one.
'Tis to her peaceful sceptre all men owe—
That through the nations, wheresoe'er we go,
Strangers, we find a fatherland ; our home
We change at will ; may watch the far-off foam
Break upon Thule's shore and call it play,
Or through dim, dreadful forests force our way,
That we may tread Orontes', Ebro's, shore—
That we are all one nation evermore.

Tertullian, about A.D. 200, and the Persian Afrahat, who wrote homilies in Syriac a generation or two later, have both the definite idea that Rome is to last as long as the world, and that Rome and the world will go together. But they of course were Christians.

How far men in general recognized the significance of the new order, when Rome became definitely mistress of a united world, or even when the civil wars ceased and an imperial master ruled from Atlantic to Euphrates, it is hard to guess. It is not easy for one generation to realize what stirs the imagination of another. Our data are fragmentary and various. Agrippa superintended the completion of an *Orbis Pictus* in Rome, which perhaps Julius Caesar first ordered.[1] It was delineated on the walls of a portico, and it is held that it was not really a map as we might have supposed, a map with the proper configuration of lands and seas, but it was designed to figure the order and distances of places on road and coast and river, the size, look, and features of the provinces and districts of the Empire, and all on a level more or less available for those who used the portico. Map or plan, or whatever it should more properly be called, it was the outcome of years of surveying work, and it must have brought home to Romans that unity of the world, which their fathers had achieved and they guarded. Virgil's great note cannot have resounded in vain.

[1] Pliny, *Natur. Hist.*, III., 2, (3), 17. See Merivale, *History of the Romans*, iv. pp. 401, 402.

Tu regere imperio populos Romane memento
(Hae tibi erunt artes) pacisque imponere mores
Parcere subjectis et debellare superbos.

Romans must have realized something of the better
aspects of their achievement. But whether they or
their subjects grasped what Caesar symbolized by
putting Gauls in the Roman Senate, it is hard to say ;
Augustus, with his eye on old Roman prejudice,
turned the Gauls out. Claudius, Paul's contemporary,
was able to bring Gauls in again—a thoroughly weak
emperor achieving what a strong one had feared to do
or had disliked.[1]

It is notorious how freely persons in search of
education or of historic sites, or with a philosophy to
expound [2] or an initiation to vend, travelled the whole
Mediterranean. When about 499 b.c. Aristagoras of
Miletus suggested to King Cleomenes of Sparta that
he might with advantage lead a Spartan army to Susa,
and carelessly let fall that it meant marching three
months' journey from the Mediterranean, he was
ordered to be out of Sparta by sundown—a revelation
of the unfamiliarity of the idea of travel.[3] Paul, as we
know, travelled like a modern commercial traveller, who
forgets how many times he has crossed the Atlantic;
he has the habit, and hardly thinks about it.

In a later day, about a.d. 380, Prudentius, the great
Latin Christian poet, again and again inculcates the
Providential ordering of all this unification of mankind—Christ willed the course of kingdoms in due
sequence, and the triumphs of Rome, in order that,
when the ages were fulfilled, he might impart
himself ; God would bind together nations discordant
in speech, various in worship, and bring all under one
sway, a union of hearts ; no union would be worthy
of Christ, did not one mind link race to race ;—Christ

[1] Cf. Suetonius, *Julius*, 80.
[2] Cf. Strabo, c. 673, on Tarsian travellers.　　　[3] Herodotus, v. 50.

is author of the walls of Rome, who set the sceptre at
Rome as head of the world and bade mankind submit
to the Roman toga and arms, that all the jangling races
might learn customs and culture, that all their tongues,
their genius and their rites might know one set of
laws ;—this was achieved by the Roman empire's
successes and triumphs, the way was prepared for
Christ's coming.[1]

In this cosmopolitan world the Christian Paul was
entirely at home. A Roman citizen, he had no quarrel
with the government, nor generally with its officials.
If magisterial action at Philippi was hasty,[2] it led him
to mention his citizenship the sooner to Claudius
Lysias.[3] At Ephesus the Asiarchs took the pains to
do him a good turn.[4] Where Greek was spoken, and
where Jews resorted, he went, but hardly to outlying
mountains where Celtic prevailed. As Deissmann has
put it, the places connected with Paul are almost
without exception to be found noted on even the
smallest map ; and he points out that a number of
them are already on railway lines and some approached
by steamships as well to-day—not that we are to
suppose that the capitalists who built the lines were
thinking of Paul, but that he and they alike have had
eyes to recognize real lines of communication, and the
real centres to which men will inevitably gravitate.
Tarsus, Jerusalem, Damascus, Konieh (Iconium),
Ephesus, Laodicea, Colossae, Hierapolis, Thessalonica,
Beroea, Athens, Corinth, and Rome dot his itineraries.
He certainly did not flee the world. Our next step
is to ask what he found in this new cosmopolitan
world, in which Alexander first and then the Romans
had broken down the barriers and brought the races
together.

---

[1] The four passages summarized are : *Adv. Symm.*, i. 287 f. ;
Adv. Symm., ii. 582 f. ; *Steph.*, ii. 413 ; *Adv. Symm.*, ii. 618. See
Life and Letters in the Fourth Century, Chap. XI.
[2] Acts xvi. 22, 37, 39.   [3] Acts xxii. 25.   [4] Acts xix. 31.

The spiritual outlooks of the age are peculiarly interesting and not a little complicated. Primitive animism here, there savage superstition, hold their own, reinforced by magic, by belief in daemons now reduced almost to a system, by astrology and by philosophy. At Lystra we are told that the common people and then the priests were prepared to believe Paul and Barnabas to be gods appearing in the likeness of men [1] —a notion which Euripides and his friends would have thought old-fashioned enough in Pindar. Plutarch's so-called *Moral Treatises* are the great exposition of the prevailing view that gods and daemons are two classes of beings ; and these writings and the books of Apuleius, written about fifty years later, are the great classical sources for daemon-lore. There we have from the non-Christian side much the same general view set forth as meets us in the Christian apologists,[2] who drew some of their material from Jewish apocalyptic.[3] But good or bad, whether souls of men ascending to the ranks of gods, or fallen angels who had rebelled against Jehovah,[4] there the daemons are. Now they mediate between gods and men, " bearers hence of prayers, thence of gifts," guardian spirits of men ; now they claim godhead on false pretences for themselves. They are everywhere— bringers of disease and lunacy, givers of oracles, authors of everything odd or strange, infesting human life and making it terrible by night and by day, for even " sleep makes no truce with superstition "— " ten thousand tyrants, haters of men," Tatian calls them. Magic, poisoning, conjuring, and astrology all flourished, the last a new and dreadful source of despair. It is not till one reads Plutarch, the Jewish apocalyptic

[1] Acts xiv. 11.   [2] E.g. Barnabas, 7.
[3] Cf. Clemen, *Primitive Christianity and non-Jewish Sources*, pp. 83-94, 109-114, 367-8 ; Kennedy, *Paul and Last Things*, pp. 325-327.
[4] Enoch, xiii. ; cf. Enoch, viii. 1 ; ix. 6 ; x. 4-6 ; liv. 1 ; lxxxviii. 1.

writers, the Christian apologists, and the fragmentary notices of the heresies, that one can realize the enormous incubus that the congested superstitions of all the world imposed upon mankind. Every race had its ghostly or spiritual terrors, and none could be neglected. The liberating power of the Gospel cannot be understood till one realizes what the daemons cost mankind.

There was not in the world intellectual energy enough to repel the attack of recrudescent superstition. We have seen in our day what absurd beliefs can be generated in dark rooms among people who lack philosophy and have no practical acquaintance with conjuring.[1] In those days, as Tacitus cruelly says, " the great geniuses had ceased." [2] Culture was indeed widely diffused ; but there was too much receptiveness and too little criticism in the intellectual atmosphere. There had been great progress in natural science in favoured quarters, under the rule of Alexander's successors. Astronomy, mathematics, geography, medicine had been greatly advanced ; but there was a want of chemistry, and psychology, in its modern developments, was of course not to be expected. Conjuring,[3] chemistry, and a little psychology explain many things to-day, for which in antiquity superstition alone could offer an explanation, and against which reason could only bring a mute contempt or the charge of lying. But, as we can believe, the witnesses to be cross-examined were very often not lying at all ; they *had* seen things for which there was no rational explanation. There not enough popular knowledge of disease ; the frequent charges of poison, which we meet in the works of Tacitus, are one indication

[1] As Bishop E. W. Barnes has said, " England during the last seventy years has become progressively less religious and more superstitious."

[2] Tacitus, *Histories*, i. 1.

[3] See Elias Henry Jones, *The Road to Endor*, the story of a Ouija board in a prisoners' camp in Turkey, as lively a narrative as could be wished, and a merciless exposure of spiritualistic methods.

of this, and the ready credence given to daemon-possession is another. Medicine was commonly empirical and traditional. The scientific problems discussed in their books of Natural Questions by Plutarch and Seneca reveal a world where cock-and-bull stories found ready credence, and critics could only guess or quote ; investigation generally there was none. The plain fact was that the political life of eight centuries in Europe and Asia had, with all the stimulus of Greek environment, contributed none the less toward the reduction of the numbers of those whose brains worked actively ; they were killed in party frays in Greece, in the wars of Alexander's successors, in the civil wars of Rome ; and the steady trend of all government to monarchical hands discouraged what was left of human genius.

Yet we must look at another side of the story. In a way that always strikes the student of the great classical Greek writers with surprise, the development of personality had continued. Men, no longer citizens and statesmen, remained individuals, and became in fact individualists in practice, social and religious. There are traces of weariness of the flesh ; Hellenistic people as well as Jews find Plato's antithesis between body and soul, between material and spiritual, congenial ; they recognize evil as a force in the world, as a spiritual factor too. They are dissatisfied with themselves, not penitent (penitence is a Christian grace) but resentful, wishful to get clear of the annoyance of the sense of failure, the sense of uncleanness and defilement. It is not the same thing as Paul's deep sense of sin and of moral failure and impotence, but people have grouped them together. There is a nervousness and an uncertainty about conduct, a craving for expiation. Theophrastus, Cicero, Horace, Plutarch, Juvenal, and Seneca all show people of the type, worried, frightened, credulous, and afraid they may be very wrong, too afraid to think anything out

I

very clearly, and others more intellectual but uneasy, and, as Seneca says, " afraid not so much of drowning as of sea-sickness." [1] We know how in revivals of outgrown religious ideas intellectual clearness is apt to be counted almost blasphemy or impiety. With this sense of insufficiency and uneasiness goes a craving for divine support. Much is said vaguely about mystery religions to-day, but again Apuleius gives us the great classical illustration. How far he was really as pious as he suggests, may be doubted. A vivid sense of humour is like the caps and rings with which heroes of legend make themselves invisible. The reader can never be quite certain with people like Apuleius how much is humour and how much is serious ; piety may be protecting itself with humour, or humour may be making fun of piety, or both operations may be going on at once. Such phaenomena are still found. But at all events the *ego* of *The Golden Ass* is wonderfully converted at last, and goes from one expensive initiation to another, and sees the gods whom others, it is obvious, craved in earnest to know.

There was weakness in the popular explanations of the universe. Men were not sure whether all was fate—the εἱμαρμένη of the ancients — or all was chance (τύχη). The stars in their courses made for determinism ; but the wild and revolting accidents of life, the toss-ups on which kingdoms and thrones depended, and the devastations that followed the caprices of would-be kings, suggested that Menander was after all right, when he, or one of his characters, said outright that sheer fluke (ταὐτόματον) was probably god. Add to this distracting alternative the activities of daemons in Gentile regions—the wars of angels and devils in more Jewish areas—and what a world it is ! The universe is either a great deal too disorderly, or

[1] Seneca, *de tranquillitate animi*, 1, 2 *in statu ut non pessimo, ita maxime querulo et moroso positus sum : nec aegroto nec valeo ;* 1, 17 *non tempestate vexor sed nausia.*

else everything in it is riveted a great deal too tight ; in either case thought and life become torment. Just as in medieval and modern India life in a world haunted with spirits, and the awful wheel of law, with its expiatory re-births, drive and have driven men to find new roads to sanity, so in the ancient world the fear of this life, the fear of re-birth into it, the fear of the unknown, compelled men to try to find some sure foothold in the divine.

A great deal has been written of late years about mystery religions—the cults of Cybele, of Isis and Serapis, and at last of Mithras, to keep to the great names, and a good many more cults as to which we can hardly be certain of their periods, their places or their general diffusion. Men were undoubtedly turning to the Orient for light, as M. Cumont has shown us. The barbarians, after all, were the older peoples, or at least their civilizations were older ; and the old had more chance of being true, and so had the strange, the obscure, the exotic—*omne ignotum pro magnifico*. Promise enough, and people will believe you ; every quack knows that side of human nature. Speak mysteriously of sin and purification, hint at hopes, and men distracted with worry will believe with a minimum of delay or examination. The Greeks did not know much of the religion of Egypt, though Egypt after all lay at their doors, and they had traded and lived there for generations. Egyptologists are very severe, some of them, with Herodotus, and for Manetho there is little but contempt ; he was thoroughly inaccurate, as far as he can be tested by modern research, and, it would seem, dreadfully dull.[1] But the Greeks got something that answered—Egyptian to the degree perhaps that eighteenth century Gothic was Gothic, or Macpherson's Ossian was Celtic ; if it was not exactly the real thing, it was very exciting, romantic

[1] Erman, *Egyptian Religion*, p. 217, calls Manetho's book " a melancholy piece of bungling."

and mysterious. How Hellenized it all was, they did
not guess, because they did not know the original
language or cult. At any rate truth lay in synthesis ;
if you believe and practice everything, you must somewhere be entirely right. If you are expiated, and your
sins are taken away temporarily, it must be to the
good, and the oftener the better ; the question of
sinful instincts need not be raised. A little philosophy
is good, as Callicles says in Plato's *Gorgias* ; too much,
he says, ruins life, and that it would certainly ruin
religion Plutarch is quite convinced. So sacraments
were the thing, to give a man " salvation "—whatever precisely that might be — to win him " re-
generation " (παλιγγενεσία), re-birth, and eventually
" deification." Men and women formed associations
for worship and sacrament. *Taurobolio renatus in
aeternum* is an inscription over a grave, of a later date
than Paul's—" Born again in the *taurobolium*, the
baptism of bull's blood, for eternity."

We do not know precisely the dates of the documents
which reveal to us the liturgies or the theories of
those who leaned to such cults. We do not know how
widely the cults were spread or the documents circulated. The polemic of the Christian fathers down
to the very end of paganism is mainly against the
Olympian gods, the well-known gods, and not against
the divinities of the mystery religions, well aware
as they very often were of the ways and language
of " Gnostic " teachers. But Wendland's moving
description is not without evidence — " an old
and rich world of culture, dying and in agony,
yearning for a new creation and re-birth, in all
the unrest of a search for God, an unrest never
to reach a goal ;—so shows itself to us the declining
paganism." [1]

---

[1] Wendland, *die hellenische-römische Kultur*, p. 186. Compare
Wilamowitz too (*Kultur der Gegenwart*, i. 8, p. 92), the soul was
"sensitive, responsive to sentimentalism and egoism, romantic, modern."

But paganism was not declining in Paul's day, and had no thought of it ; it had, like Hinduism a century ago, nothing but the consciousness of such eternity as a universe, probably to end in flame, would enjoy and impart. It was not even very conscious of its weakness. Greek polytheism had always been weak in moral content. The mysteries of Greece were for the holy, not for the profane ; but the conception of holiness was one that accepted the harlot with no suggestion of her abandoning her trade. So much is evident from the stories of the Greek orators and Eleusis, and it is evident again in the works of the elegiac poets of Rome. Neither Demeter nor Isis was very squeamish. When purification and holiness are spoken of, all depends on the conceptions of sin and holiness prevalent, and these in turn depend on the conception of God.

In the centuries of Greek life it is little to be wondered at that the technical terms of philosophy and religion were somewhat cheapened in popular use, as they are in other societies. Many people to-day can talk of evolution who never read Darwin, and more can make loose use of psychological terms. *Mysterion* comes to mean what the Romans called *sacramentum* (a vague term, unless the date and other circumstances of the particular use are considered), and it also means a secret. When Paul writes : " In everything and in all things I have been initiated (μεμύημαι) both to be full and to be hungry, to have too much and to have too little," [1] the playfulness of the language proves a colloquial use, but not necessarily personal knowledge of Greek mysteries. Φιλοσοφεῖν, to " philosophize " about a situation was used by Greeks in the same easy way, without implying personal study in Porch or Academy. Other words,[2] perhaps

[1] Phil. iv. 12.
[2] See generally Wendland, *die hell.-röm. Kultur*, pp. 156, 185 ; Clemen, *Christianity and non-Jewish Sources*, pp. 68, 233.

less likely to be popular, are found common to Paul and to the documents of the mystery-religions— documents (once again) hard to date. The contrasts between spirit and soul and flesh (πνεῦμα, ψυχή, σάρξ, σῶμα), between spiritual and heavenly on the one hand, and on the other between natural and earthly (πνευματικός, οὐράνιος, ψυχικός, ἐπίγειος), are noted, and such terms as transform and transfigure (μεταμορφοῦσθαι, μετασχηματίζεσθαι). Some of these are shared by the Stoics of Paul's day,[1] and some are as old as Plato. Where language is so widely prevalent, a particular association between two groups of people, who use the same popular psychology, will be hard to establish to the exclusion of others.[2] Some other terms, similarly shared it is said, Paul may have got from Judaism. In the case of others again, it is suggested [3] that Paul may have gained insight from his converts into what mystery religions had been for them ;— he might have, that is, if we are right in assuming first that his converts came from those ranks and classes of society (generally well-to-do Greeks and Hellenists) which supplied the adherents of those initiations, and, second, that some of them had actually been initiated ; the two assumptions are not the same. Mr Montefiore, in his desire to dis- tinguish between Paul and more conventional Jews, suggests that Paul may " have cast a wistful eye over the border, where the votaries of the Hellenistic mystery religions were claiming that they could conquer sinfulness at a bound." [4] This again assumes identity

[1] Cf. Seneca, *Ep.* vi. 1, *Non emendari me tantum sed transfigurari.*

[2] Cf. Professor C. C. J. Webb, in *Constructive Quarterly*, Sept. 1918, p. 445 : " The evidence for the historical connexion of Chris- tianity with the known mystery religions of the Roman Empire is much less strong than is sometimes assumed." See also the striking essay on "The Gnostic Redeemer," in Edwyn Bevan, *Hellenism and Christianity.*

[3] H. A. A. Kennedy, *Paul and Mystery Religions*, pp. 280-1.

[4] Montefiore, *Judaism and St Paul*, p. 116.

in date and outlook, and perhaps in the use of terms, which is yet to be proved.

The strong contrast in Paul's piety, says Wendland,[1] the dangerous antithesis of spirit and flesh, the tendency to asceticism, the inclination to hypostatize (personalize) or materialize spiritual functions and religious occurrences (Vorgänge), the conception of mysteries and revelation, the picture of the world in stages or storeys (cf. the third heaven), Paul's experience of the journey upward, his realistic representation of the higher types of spirits and of the servitude of men under their power and of the battle against them, the yearning for redemption, broadening with Paul into cosmic significance—all these have analogies in purely heathen mysticism. Wendland compares the relation of Plato to Orphism—a borrowing of terms with rejection of substance and a strong antipathy. We may admit the analogies ; we have to allow the appearance of common terms, e.g. salvation ($\sigma\omega\tau\eta\rho\acute{\iota}\alpha$), the idea of re-birth ($\pi\alpha\lambda\iota\gamma\gamma\epsilon\nu\epsilon\sigma\acute{\iota}\alpha$), but, once more, we have to be cautious about the dates of our mystery-documents, and we have to realize, first, that the connexion is not proved, and will not be till the dates are better established ; we have to compare Paul's use of Greek philosophic terms and occasional literary expressions, which he owed to the milieu and the atmosphere in which he lived, rather than to personal adventures in Greek culture ; we have to realize that that milieu and atmosphere are so far not perfectly known to us ; and finally we have to remember that he was a Jew, and how very Jewish he was.

We have only to look at the language Paul uses of idols and their sacrifices ; for the sacrifice, the mystical and sacramental meal, was of the essence of the mystery religion, its very centre and the ground of all the hopes and feelings associated with it. " I have eaten from a tambourine, I have drunk from a cymbal,

[1] Wendland, *die hell.-röm. Kultur*, p. 116.

I have become an initiate of Attis " ; so ran one snatch
of initiate song.[1] Now hear Paul. " As to eating things
offered to idols, we know that an idol is *nothing* in the
world, and that there is no God but one. Even if
there are alleged gods, whether in the sky or on earth,
for us there is one God, the Father, of whom are all
things and we unto Him. . . . Meat will not commend
us to God ; neither if we refrain from eating, are we
worse off, nor if we eat are we better." [2] This was
flat denial, and there could hardly be more abrupt
denial, of the central idea of the sacramental religions,
from which some hold he borrowed. " What do I say ?
That mea⌐ offered to an idol is anything, or that an
idol is anything ? No, but that what they sacrifice,
they sacrifice to daemons and not to God [cf. Psalm
cvi. 37] ; and I would not have you partakers (or
partners) of daemons. You cannot drink the Lord's
cup and the cup of daemons ; you cannot partake
of the Lord's table and the table of daemons." [3] Here
and elsewhere his tone is that of the Old Testament,
as many of the psalms will remind us.

I cannot help feeling that the discussion of Paul's
relations with mystery religions and their terminology
would have been different, if more of those who have
discussed it had had personal experience of the heathen
world. What was the effect of the sight and sound of
heathenism on the Jewish mind ? Round the corner
sounds the gong that beats monotonously morning
and evening in honour of Shitala, goddess of smallpox ;
day by day you see her image as you go to the University of Calcutta, you see educated men abasing
themselves before—before a doll or a devil. You see
shrines carved with legends of impurity, naked and
unashamed, indescribable ; you know quite well, and
the priests know you know, what goes on in those

---

[1] Quoted by Firmicus Maternus, 18, 1.   [2] 1 Cor. viii. 4-9.
[3] 1 Cor. x. 20, 21. It is remarkable perhaps that this is almost the
only passage where Paul uses the term " daemons."

temples—sacred prostitution flourishes in Southern India, as it did in the town of Corinth while Paul lived there two years; it was holy. It is more than possible to feel, as you look at a Hindu temple of the south, a thrill of satisfaction and sympathy with the Muslims who in God's name destroyed such places. Every time you contrast the carved idols with the beautiful texts in Arabic with which the Muhammadan adorns his mosque, you stand once more with the monotheist. That such were the feelings of the Jews in the Hellenistic world, we do not need to be told— their contempt for idols and idolaters, their hatred of them, the deep-going reaction against them, their repugnance in every fibre, need no commentary. Now let us picture a modern Muslim in India, filled with this spirit—" God's curse upon all unbelievers ! "— and he is converted to Christ; is it reason to think that, when he wishes to express the deepest things that Christ means to him, he will go to the mystical school of Chaitanya, and use the language that Chaitanya, in disorder and hysterics, used of his doll or devil ? Would he not still put it so ? If he is true to his experience, he will go to the deepest things of Islam ; he will not need to borrow from heathen mysticism ; and we know that to a Muhammadan mystic, who finds Christ, his old experience is not all foolishness.[1] If he has to render it in a popular language, he will use, so far as it is available, the terminology nearest him. The same, I think, or something like it, is the soundest account to be given of Paul ; he is a Jew captured by Christ.

We have next to look at the Jewish Dispersion, to which in most instances Paul always addressed him-

---

[1] See Duncan Black Macdonald, *Aspects of Islam*, p. 171. It has occurred to me that some reply might be made to me by saying that the Muslim converted to Christ would not need to borrow the language of Hindu mystics; he would have ready to his hand the language of the mystics of Islam. And Paul had the Old Testament.

self first. Philo of Alexandria is the outstanding figure,
but Paul (as we have seen) for some reason appears
never to have gone to Egypt—perhaps because closer
ties bound him to Cilicia and Asia, and one step north-
westward led to another. Nor is Paul much influenced
by that school. Evidence abounds for the wide
scattering of the Jews all over the Roman empire,
and indeed outside it into Babylonia ; and Judaism
became the focus of a good deal of literature—anti-
Semite [1] and patriotic—of legend, too, not less
patriotic. As we have seen in discussing the environment at Tarsus and the Gentile question, the Dispersion was bound to differ from the community in
Palestine. Perhaps as real illumination as we are
likely to get will come from such a book as Mary
Antin's *Promised Land,* a very vivid and human work—
if we may take Poland for Palestine for the moment,
and Boston (*salva reverentia*) and New York for
Corinth and Alexandria ; on the one side tradition
and tribalism, on the other liberty, a larger world, a
less exacting standard of observance, freer intercourse
with the Gentile, and yet a consciousness of Israel and
his history. The parallel between one historical
period and another can never be exact, but it may
be suggestive—" have voice for such as understand."
Wendland warns us not to under-estimate the connexion of the Dispersion and Palestine, the stiff unity
of Jewish consciousness, mixed up with questions of
pilgrimage and temple dues which were paid all over
the world. He warns us not to over-estimate the
influence of Greek philosophy.[2] If Philo gave up the
Jewish hope of Resurrection for the Greek doctrine of
Immortality, Philo is never mentioned in the Talmud.[3]
Mr Israel Abrahams tells us that the New Testament
is the best available source for knowledge of early

---

[1] Josephus, *contra Apion.*, ii. 79.
[2] Wendland, *Die hell-röm. Kultur,* p. 210.
[3] Wendland, *Die hell.-röm. Kultur,* p. 208

synagogue procedure; and that the synagogue was the real religious centre of the Judaism of the Dispersion is proved by the ease with which it survived the total destruction of the Temple and the system associated with it. Professor Kirsopp Lake suggests that Paul and Silas were not quite like missionaries in a heathen world, but more resembled Wesley or Whitefield, in going primarily to a constituency who understood them and whom they understood, Jews and proselytes. To the latter they naturally spoke with more appeal.

Amid all the religions that offered easy and emotional salvation, Judaism stood alone with the stern appeal of monotheism and morality. Here are the words of a typical man of the second century A.D., " born in the land of the Assyrians," as he says, a traveller far and wide in the Roman Empire, a student of Greek rhetoric and Greek art—for he gave attention to the great collections of it in Rome—and an initiate in various mysteries. He was shocked at the wickedness and cruelty allowed and practised in the name of religion, and "when I was by myself, I sought in what way I might learn the truth. While I was still thinking of serious things, it befel me to light on certain barbarian writings, older than the philosophic teaching of the Greeks, more divine in contrast with Greek error. And it befel me to be convinced because their style was simple, because there was an absence of artifice in the speakers, because the structure of the whole was intelligible, because it showed fore-knowledge of the future, because the precepts were remarkable, and because they taught One ruler of the universe (τῶν ὅλων τὸ μοναρχικόν). My soul was taught of God, and I understood that, while Greek literature leads to condemnation, this ends our slavery in the world and rescues us from rulers many and ten thousand tyrants." [1]

---

[1] Tatian, *ad Graecos*, 42, his birth; 35, his travels and studies, σοφιστεύσας τὰ ὑμέτερα, and the art-collections; 29, the Hebrew scriptures.

Such is the confession of Tatian, and Justin's is much the same. Justin was keen to learn about God; he tried Stoic and Peripatetic, and at last in the desert met a shrewd questioner who directed him to philosophers older than Stoic or Peripatetic, older than Plato himself, and from these he came to Christ.[1] Both men belong to the second century, but there were clearly many in the first century who were drawn in the same way to the synagogue and hung about it, proselytes in one degree or another. To men of this type the new religion of Paul had far more to offer than Judaism; it was free from the drawbacks of Jewish particularism and legalism; and when once Christianity was widely preached in the world, proselytes ceased to be made by Judaism, and at last were no longer sought or desired.[2]

Outside the circle of the synagogue and its fringe of "worshippers" were the people who played at Jewish religion as they did with other Oriental cults. The secular writers of Rome and Greece have many allusions to them. Nero's Poppaea was the most famous of them.[3] They need not delay us; they were not very serious students of religion, but their existence, their number and their occasional high place no doubt did more than secure Imperial favours for the Jews, and made it more possible for more serious persons to realize that there was such a religion and that there might be something in it.

Finally, once more we have to think of the philosophic schools, widely spread, and all of them, positive or negative, intensely individualistic. Stoic or Epicurean, it was all one; the centre was the man; he chose so and he lived so; and, if he were a Sceptic, he chose to make no choice and was perhaps even more

---

[1] *Dialogue with Trypho*, 2-8.
[2] Cf. Lake, *Earlier Epp. of Paul*, p. 33.
[3] For evidence, see B. W. Henderson, *Life and Principate of Nero*, p. 467; Merivale, *History of the Romans*, vi. p. 376.

individualistic than the rest. There was also, as we have been reminded, the school of Plutarch, wide in its scattering range, very comprehensive, thoroughly uncritical, open to believe anything and to fit everything into a loose scheme of things, provided it meant nothing in particular and could be transformed by allegory or symbol into anything the mood required. Yet, especially here, we must not forget what Mr Bernard Bosanquet pointed out,[1] that in this Alexandrine age, among these philosophies of quotation— " the successors who did not inquire concerning truth, but were overawed by the character of their teachers and the strangeness of their words and counted true each what his master taught him," [2]—gentler virtues began to find a place among men's ideals. There is more tolerance for opinion, less prejudice about race (in spite of all that was said above, but without contradicting it), more disinterested kindliness for people, more sympathy for slave and captive and woman, more love of birds and flowers. " I am a man ; nothing human can I count alien to me ! " Terence's famous saying went to the hearts of men, and the solider teaching of the Stoics gave it a philosophic warrant, showed it congenial to the universe, and inculcated it in every philosophic letter and discourse. Virgil had written and died before Paul was born ; and whenever we think of " that hard Roman world," of which a modern poet has spoken, which Tacitus drew so cleverly and Juvenal lashed with epigrams, we have to remember it was the world of Virgil, and that it loved Virgil. There is much in the famous saying of Sainte-Beuve : " la venue même du Christ n'a rien qui étonne quand on a lu Virgile." [3]

---

[1] *History of Aesthetic*, Chap. V.

[2] Justin, *Dialogue with Trypho*, 2.

[3] *Étude sur Virgile*, p. 68 ; Warde Fowler, *Religious Experience of Roman People*, p. 404, and the great W. Y. Sellar, *Virgil*, p. 371, have much the same view.

Paul wrote once that the Law was the *paidagôgos*, the trusted slave, whose duty it was to take the child to school, and that in that character it was intended to bring Israel to Christ. He recognized no such function in the poetry and philosophy of Greece— surely a testimony to the truth of the view that he had not been trained in them. But a century later Clement of Alexandria, most learned, genial, discursive and lovable of Christians, caught up his phrase and balanced it in a memorable sentence—that as the Law was the *paidagôgos* to bring the Jews to Christ, so was Philosophy the *paidagôgos* of the Greeks.[1]

Thus government, society, religious interchange, the development of individual self-consciousness, travel, intercourse, and philosophy were all combining to make the world one, to teach a more genuine humanism, and, as Paul and his followers saw, to open the door everywhere for a faith that should be one and universal.

[1] Cf. *Conflict of Religions in Early Roman Empire*, pp. 275-9; Clement of Alexandria, *Stromateis*, i. 28.

CHAPTER VII

THE CHURCH

THE earliest known form of association for religious purposes is that of the tribe or community; and it is remarked as a new feature in the history of religion when the element of personal choice becomes a factor. In the great Homeric poems there is no question but that all members of a tribe were adherents of its religion. But in the Homeric hymn to Demeter the individual is conspicuous—it is his affair whether he is initiated in the rites of Demeter, and his personal happiness beyond the grave depends on whether he will or will not accept this opportunity. When the Athenian State—one's language must not be too precise at this point—took over the general management or reorganization of the mysteries of Eleusis, instead of the old principle of birthright membership the new one of initiation was recognized; the mysteries, as Isocrates says, were opened in a spirit of liberality to mankind.[1] A new conception of religious association was thus proclaimed, personal and international rather than tribal. The date of the change is not to be precisely fixed. The period is that in which, after centuries apparently of confusion, whose history is lost to us, Greek literature springs to life again, personal and autobiographical, and proclaims for all time the new age in which—at all events where Greek thought rules—the individual is more and more the centre of real life. We need not follow the progress of the voluntary religious society in the Greek and Hellenistic world. The idea of a group, large or

[1] F. B. Jevons, *Intr. History of Religion*, pp. 358-9; Isocrates, *Panegyricus*, 28.

small, local or international, composed of individuals drawn to a particular cult for whatever reason, though not to the exclusion of other cults, was familiar far and wide. In the age of Paul perhaps the most vital and real religious life that the Graeco-Roman world has to show was in these various societies.[1] The tribal gods and the city gods remained ; their emblems were still on the coins ; the old gods and goddesses kept a great place in tradition and in popular regard till paganism fell. But their re-inforcement among more religious groups by these gods of wider range and more personal appeal was a real step forward in the development of thought.

Judaism differed, as we all know, from the other religions of the ancient world, and in various ways. Monotheism, when really alive, never has any tolerance for polytheism with its idolatry and its general loose thinking. Judaism excluded all gods except Jehovah, and with time grew more and more clear that they did not exist ; they were figments, or at best fallen angels, dolls or devils, *not* gods at all. Judaism was and remained national ; the proselyte more or less sank his nationality and became a Hebrew, as the irritation of the Gentile critic shows ; why should he live like a Jew ? In spite of Pharisee endeavours to secure proselytes, this ambition died away after the destruction of Jerusalem in A.D. 70, and the Gentiles were more and more avowedly left to any fate that God might care to assign to them ; it was His affair, perhaps He would destroy them,[2] perhaps He would not.[3]

[1] Reitzenstein, *Hell. Myst. Relig.*, p. 94, goes so far as to suggest that the whole conception of a " Church " is not Hellenistic. The suggestion is valuable, as it reminds us that the association of the earliest Christians inside Judaism was perhaps as loose as that of the Pharisees or any other group. Separation meant a new emphasis on organization.

[2] See pp. 239, 240; passages from 4 Ezra, to which may be added 4 Ezra xiii, 38.

[3] Cf. Philo, *de opific. mundi*, 61 ; Abrahams, *Pharisaism and the Gospels*, pp. 141, 149.

If the analysis, attempted in the preceding pages, be right, Paul's early uneasiness about a universal religion, with its corollary of Israel's final loss or cession of privilege and status, will help us to understand his constant surprise at the wonderful secret of God, " hidden from ages and from generations but now made manifest to His saints," [1] " which none of this world's rulers knew " [2]—the calling of the Gentiles. It is more explicitly put in Ephesians [3]—" it was in other ages not made known unto the sons of men, as it is now revealed unto his holy apostles and prophets by the Spirit, that the Gentiles should be fellow-heirs and of the same body, and partakers of his promise in Christ by the gospel." Whatever be decided about the authorship of that Epistle, in whole or in part, whatever the share of amanuensis or disciple, that idea is centrally Pauline. Paul's life was re-made by the conviction that Christ's death was a prelude of " peace to you who were afar off, and to them that were nigh." [4]

Paul was more conscious than most men of the need of the world, and more stirred than most Jews by the problem of the relation of this need to God. It seems that the Jews were in general content to do little for the moral cleansing of mankind, whatever be the historical basis for Mr Montefiore's assertion of their " most exquisite and delicate charity." In the first chapter of the letter to the Romans, Paul draws his dreadful picture of the heathen world. He would not need to be told, as some modern students are eager to tell him, that not all Gentiles were filled with all unrighteousness, fornication, wickedness, and so forth : [5] Paul knew so much. But we have to bear in mind two things—first that Paul took a more serious view of

---

[1] Col. i. 26.   [2] 1 Cor. ii. 8.   [3] Eph. iii. 5, 6.   [4] Eph. ii. 17.

[5] Deissmann, *Paul*, p. 45, warns us against relying too much on ancient literature in support of a universal charge of degeneracy. Even Tacitus (*Histories*, i. 3) admits that the age he describes produced some high examples of virtue.

K

evil than most people and had found even with "the advantages of the Jew" that righteousness in the fullest sense is an impossible task. "There is none righteous, no, not one," the psalmist had written, and Paul's experience confirmed that psalmist.[1] Nor must we forget that in a heathen world much is done openly that in a Christian society, even in a society imperfectly leavened with Christian ideas, is not done at all and is counted unnatural. Plato's dialogues show the freedom taken in certain relations now considered pathological. Nor must we forget the prevalence of slavery, with its actual horrors of cruelty, mutilation, and crucifixion, and its implicit negation of freedom, sex, and humanity. More important still, for our present purpose and generally, it is to recall that Paul traces all the filth and moral degeneracy of the world to one central cause—the lie at the heart of all pagan life—the false view of God. They did not think fit to recognize God, so God "gave them up" to what they preferred—uncleanness, violation of nature, a reprobate mind.[2]

The Gentile world was not unaware of a deluge of lawlessness that had broken over mankind, and there were many at work to try to help the world. Augustus had set an example that emperors might fitfully follow. Stoics and other popular lecturers, like Dio Chrysostom (a little later than Paul), preached reformation and self-government. After the fall of Nero, there is evidence that the world grew more sober and well-conducted under Vespasian and the great emperors who followed Domitian.[3] The world believed in moral endeavour ; but Paul, who had tried it too, realized that motive and change of nature were much more difficult problems than ordinary people guessed. It was one ground of his happiness in Christ that in

---

[1] Rom. iii. 10 ; Psalm xiv. 3.   [2] See Chap. IV., p. 83.
[3] See Merivale, *History of the Romans*, Chap. LXIV., vol. viii., p. 71.

him Paul believed the power of God was revealed for the Greek as well as for the Jew.[1] He was entrusted —and it was with joy that he realized it and spoke it— with the good news for the non-Jewish world ;[2] he was the " apostle of the Gentiles," a ministry which he " magnified."[3]

We have tried already to trace the course of his thoughts about the Gentile world, his early acquaintance, his lingering uncertainty, and at a later point the growth of his natural friendliness to Gentiles. We do not read of his having, like Peter, to overcome a taboo or some dim traditional dislike that attached to eating with Gentiles. Perhaps he had it to begin with, and in Christ it passed away, as race-prejudice must. He liked men ; and, as others have done, he found that human beings were generally very much alike — human, and also (what has escaped some observers) fundamentally spiritual. He would have accepted Augustine's saying, " Thou hast made us for Thyself, and the heart knows no rest till it rests in Thee."[4] Finding God and man so naturally congenial to each other, he felt, as is easy to see, an intense joy in God as the Author of the larger design, the salvation of all men rather than the choice of a single people. Hence the satisfaction of being the chosen agent, by whom that larger design was being brought about.

He was not the inaugurator of the mission to the Gentiles, as the records of Philip and Peter plainly show. That the Cyprian and Cyrenian Jews, scattered by the persecution in which Stephen was killed, who went as far as Antioch and preached to " Hellenists," also addressed Gentiles, seems to follow from the marked antithesis in the Greek ; but the exact sequence of events is not brought out by Luke.[5] As the story develops, Paul becomes more and more the repre-

---

[1] I Cor. i. 24. [2] Gal. ii. 7.
[3] Rom. xi. 13 ; cf. Rom. xv. 15-24.
[4] Augustine, *Confessions*, i. 1, 1. [5] Acts xi. 19-26.

sentative and protagonist of the Gentile mission, the centre of the controversy. Professor Percy Gardner asks what would have happened if the Jerusalem apostles had condemned his mission.[1] One may guess with him that very much the same would have happened as did occur at Antioch when Peter trimmed in the matter of eating with Gentiles, and that Paul would have gone on. He would not have emphasized to the Galatians the fact that he did not get his gospel from man but by revelation from Jesus Christ, if he had not meant them—and all others whom it might concern to know his plans—to realize that he was not resting on "pillars," but on Christ, whom he proposed to obey. Happily, the apostles at Jerusalem did not condemn him—strange as it must have been to them to learn from this late-comer the real universalism of their Master's teaching. The "regions beyond" meant after all no extension of their Master's mind, no departure from it, but were his real meaning. The recognition which they gave to Paul's conception of Christ's purposes was one fruit of Paul's work, but its wider significance must not be lost, when we try in our turn to recapture and to interpret the historical Jesus. If Jesus had been as Jewish as we are sometimes asked to believe, it is not likely that they would have recognized the Gentile side of the Church as they did. If we are to deal in what grammarians used to call "impossible conditions in past time," we might add another apodosis to our protasis, and say that Paul would not as a Pharisee have seen so much to quarrel with in the Christians, and so forth. But Paul's insight and the action of the apostles at Jerusalem confirm the larger interpretation of Jesus : and they encourage us to think better of the older apostles and their group than some scholars would allow.

When we come to the actual churches established

---

[1] P. Gardner, *Religious Experience of St Paul*, p. 49. See Kirsopp Lake, *Earlier Epistles*, pp. 30, 48, etc.

among the Gentiles, we are at once faced with dis-
appointment. The drawbacks of a heathen inheritance
are not easily realized in a land where Christian ideals
have at least been held up to individuals and to society
for a thousand years and more.[1] " What advantage
had the Jew ? Much, every way ! " This was true.
And the Church, drawing from the lowliest walks
of life in Hellenistic towns—slaves, small craftsmen,
small tradesmen, the illiterate and ignorant, the
classes of petty outlooks, petty ambitions and petty
souls—was handicapped by their want of background.
The English public school has been criticized for its
pagan ideals—honour, self-government, self-effacement,
esprit de corps ; if they are pagan, how Paul would have
welcomed such pagans ! His pagans had all these
great Stoic virtues to learn, and they had badly-trained
minds into the bargain. They came from the class
that believed in all the charlatans of the market-place,
the quacks who for a copper coin or two would " drive
devils out of men, and blow away diseases, and call up
the souls of heroes, and display sumptuous banquets,
and tables and sweetmeats and dainties that are not
there," the impostors with whom Celsus compared
Jesus.[2] Tertullian and Lucian both speak of these
adventurers ; and Marcus Aurelius records his
gratitude to Diognetos for teaching him to pay no
attention to such people.[3] Some of Paul's converts
no doubt did confuse Jesus with these miracle-workers
of the streets. How should they not, with their
antecedents and lack of training ? and how should not
modern converts from primitive peoples do the same ?
Was the enormous mass of magical books burnt at
Ephesus [4] the property of Paul's adherents or of his

---

[1] See Campbell Moody, *The Heathen Heart*, an illuminating and
sympathetic work on this subject—in many ways as valuable to the
student of the early Church as Reitzenstein.

[2] Celsus, quoted by Origen, *contra Celsum*, i. 68.

[3] M. Aurelius, i. 6.   [4] Acts xix. 19.

opponents ? The question needs no answer, and the
episode shows the mind and outlook of the people on
whom he had largely to depend. We have to remember
that astrology and devil-driving (with its fumigations
and incantations) are the ancestors of Astronomy and
Chemistry, and might claim—as astrology did—to be
ranked as legitimate science and not as superstition. It
is not necessary to read far into Plutarch's *Moralia* to
see the line of defence ; or, if the books of Plutarch
are too remote, some of Mrs Annie Besant's writings
may serve equally well.

Magic has never been a matter of merely intellectual
confusion ; it has always carried with it practical
imposture, and constantly the business of love philtres
and poisons. But heathenism, even apart from these,
implies low standards of morality, and here other
evidence must be sought than that of educated Chinese
and Indian students, who are not typical of the
ordinary life of their countries, and who are apt to be
on the defensive, and not unskilful at it.[1] However,
not to range into modern controversy, the character
of Paul's converts can be read in his letters to the
Corinthians, for Paul was not invited, in the name of a
hypothetical charity, as we sometimes are, to mince
matters. He told his converts quite directly, for all
his kindness and tact, what they had been and what
they were. There was moral squalor and immorality
among them ; there were quarrels very carnal, even
though they called them spiritual ; there were cliques
and lawsuits. Their disregard of ordinary conventions,
decencies and courtesies they perhaps supposed to be
Christian freedom, as others have since ; but Paul
classed it as bad manners, tactlessness,[2] and folly. Why
should a Christian woman discard a veil, in a town

[1] See p. 136.
[2] Cf. 1 Cor. x. 32, " Give no offence, to Jews or Gentiles or the
Church of God, as I try to please all men in every way, not for my
good, but for theirs."

where decent women did not, and where indecent women swarmed about temple and docks ? " All things are lawful, but not all expedient." [1] Why could they not behave like ordinary people ?—the bitter cry of Euripides four centuries earlier, when he looked at emancipated ladies. On a great many scores —" I praise you not ! " [2] That he quotes both to the Romans and to the Corinthians a maxim from the Septuagint version of Proverbs, shows how clearly it was a rule of his own, a hint often in his mind : " Provide things honest before the Lord and before men." [3] Why should their good be evil spoken of ? [4]

Tactlessness, inattention to decorum, a crude display of freedom, meant, to Paul's mind, failure to interest and to hold those to whom the Christian was definitely sent by Christ. It might also mean a bad name for the community—as in the matter of veils—and perhaps eventually danger and persecution. But, beside risks from outside and failure in winning recruits, there were dangers within the church.

The first great danger was Judaism, the story of which is written in Galatians and Acts. In essence, the controversy came to this—was the religion that centred in Jesus Christ to be a sect of Judaism ? To be a follower of Christ, must a man accept the law of Moses, and circumcision with it, and the food-laws of the Jews ? In short, was it true, as Jews had taught, that outside Israel there was no salvation, or next to none ? There is evidence for a more liberal view in Judaism, which read a spiritual meaning into circumcision. But Philo, while accepting the allegory and admitting that " the circumcision signifies the cutting away of every passion and lust, and the destruction of all godless thoughts," held that " we still are not justified in departing from the law of circumcision laid upon us," and similarly that Sabbath and festival

[1] 1 Cor. x. 23. [2] 1 Cor. xi. 22.
[3] Rom. xii. 17 ; 2 Cor. viii. 21 ; Prov. iii. 4. [4] Rom. xiv. 16.

were also to be kept in the letter as well as in the spirit.[1] The Sibylline oracles (so-called) promised the Messianic Kingdom to Gentiles who accepted the true God, forsook idols, murder, theft, and sexual uncleanness, lived a good life and were baptized, but nothing was said here of circumcision.[2] Still the point was urged by Jews and Judaizers that a convert from the Gentile world accepted Christ and Moses together. " Certain men which came down from Judaea [to Antioch] taught the brethren, and said, ' Except ye be circumcised after the manner of Moses, ye cannot be saved.' "[3] The story goes on, how Paul and Barnabas had no small contention and dispute with them, how the matter was referred to Jerusalem, and how there also " there rose up certain of the sect of the Pharisees which believed, saying that it was needful to circumcise them and to command them to keep the law of Moses." The discussion in Jerusalem it is not necessary for us to follow, nor the controversy as to what precisely happened, the enactment or recommendation and its outcome in detail. Professor Lake [4] accepts the view that the reference to " things strangled " is a gloss on the original text and that the threefold require- ment that Gentile converts should " abstain from things offered to idols, from blood [i.e., murder] and from fornication " was no compromise, but an acceptance of the Antioch party's position, and a release given to Gentile Christians. Even if we are to retain the reference to " things strangled," and however we solve the historical problems that rise, the fact remains that Jerusalem decided against circumcision, and by the decision cut off the recruitment of Judaism by the proselytes who had felt the attraction of Jewish mono- theism, Jewish ethics, and the Jewish eschatological

---

[1] Philo, *De Migratione Abrahami*, quoted by K. Lake, *Earlier Epistles of St Paul*, p. 24.
[2] *Oracula Sibyllina*, IV., 24 ff., 162 ff.   [3] Acts. xv. I ff.
[4] See Lake, *Earlier Epistles*, pp. 31 ff.

hope. From now onward the appeal of Christianity was distinct, and it was more attractive, it offered all that Judaism could offer, and a freedom that Judaism could not give. Luke, in the Acts, ascribes to Peter a leading part in the movement and in the defence, and, in spite of his fluctuation and uneasy retreat at Antioch, Paul, in the letter to the Galatians, implies that Peter belonged to the liberal side and acted generally with them. But it is fairly clear that, in the common judgment, it was Paul and not Peter who was the leader in the Gentile mission. Whoever, however many, had begun the work among Gentiles, the great campaigns of Paul, the tremendous arguments all over the Hellenistic world of Asia Minor, Macedon, and Greece, the fury of the local Jews in every place when he appealed to the Gentiles and won—all this made it plain who was the centre of the disturbance and the great menace to the existence of Judaism. "*This* is the man who teaches all men everywhere against the People and the Law and this place."[1] A variant reading in the Acts attributes to the mob at Jerusalem the cry, "Away with our enemy." It was Time's revenges indeed when the Jews of Asia Minor brought against Paul the very charges which the Cilicians and he had laid against Stephen.[2]

It is perhaps possible to trace some progress in Paul's ideas in the matter. The acceptance of Christ need not at first have implied the superfluity of circumcision ; Trypho, in the dialogue with Justin, asks whether a man may not keep the law of Moses as well as follow Christ,[3] and I have heard the same question asked in English Cambridge. Paul, in his endeavour to be " all things to all men," may have gone further on some occasions than at other times he thought well. Luke says that Paul got Timothy circumcised—Timothy,

---

[1] Acts xxi. 28. [2] Acts vi. 13.
[3] Justin, *Dialogue with Trypho*, Chaps. XLVI., XLVII.

being the son of a Jewish mother and a father who was
Greek enough to be called Greek, a Gentile.[1] But
Titus, later on, who was a Greek, Paul says, neither
Paul himself nor the Jerusalem group suggested should
be circumcised.[2]

When the storm broke in the churches of Galatia—
of South Galatia, as we must now think,[3] the Antioch,
Iconium, Lystra, and Derbe of the missionary journeys
—Paul is confronted by the undoing of his whole
work, the capture of some of his converts by a sort of
bastard Christianity, the utter relapse into paganism
of others, and he writes his Epistle. The letter bears
the marks of haste. Probably the admission made by
Theodore Roosevelt's friends, when it was suggested
that Roosevelt had been in a hurry while writing a
particular volume, would be true of Paul—" He always
was." But there are degrees of hurry, and there is
nothing like the sweep and rush in Philippians, for
instance, that we find in Galatians. This time the
issue was thought out to the end and made plain through
and through with uncompromising vigour. No doubt
the writing of it clarified Paul's own thought; it lifted
the whole controversy forward and really settled it.[4]
The Law and Christ are shown in sharp contrast as
irreconcilable alternatives ; it is to be " either or " ;
and Paul's passionate concentration of everything in
Christ was a declaration from which the Church could
never recede, whatever the human weakness of wishing
to be on both sides may at times have prompted.
The Law ? " I am dead to the law ! I am crucified
with Christ, nevertheless I live, yet not I, but Christ
liveth in me, and the life which I now live in the flesh
I live by the faith of the Son of God, who loved me
and gave himself for me." " In Jesus Christ neither

---

[1] Acts xvi. 3. [2] Gal. ii. 3.

[3] We must recognize the work here of Sir William M. Ramsay.

[4] Coming probably between the enlistment of Timothy and of
Titus, it may explain the difference of action.

circumcision avails anything nor uncircumcision."
"God forbid that I should glory, save in the cross of
our Lord Jesus Christ, by whom the world is crucified
unto me, and I unto the world." "The preaching
of the cross is to them that perish foolishness . . .
unto the Jews a stumblingblock. . . . And I determined not to know anything among you, save Jesus
Christ, and him crucified." [1]

It has been held that Paul makes no reference to a
Judaizing party at Corinth, unless, as Professor B. W.
Bacon suggests, it consisted of those who boasted, "I
am of Christ"—on the supposition that, as Christ
apparently kept the Law, they would. The explanation
is attractive. The Epistle to the Galatians did not
abolish the party; it lived on, and in later days its
descendants produced an anti-Pauline literature. But
the air was cleared, when the question was put once
and for ever: if Christ does all, what can circumcision add? Forced into a new explicitness, Paul was
explicit. When genius has decided a case, its judgment is hard for duller, shallower or timider people
to reverse. From this time onward a new line of
interpretation had to be applied to the Old Testament;
the literal law of commandments being abrogated, the
allegorical use of proof-texts, types and shadows began;
freedom was achieved, Christ was made central, and
Jewish lawgiver and prophets became his heralds, and
nothing more.[2] The Scriptures were kept, to the
great gain of mankind; the new religion had a historical background; and, though the method used
was not a sound one, the supremacy of Christ was
enhanced.

Antithetical to Jewish legalism was an antino-
mianism that parodied Christian freedom—the view,

---

[1] Gal. ii. 19, 20; v. 6; vi. 15; 1 Cor. i. 18, 23; ii. 2.
[2] See K. Lake, *Landmarks of Early Christianity*, p. 70, for the
effects of this. Also *Conflict of Religions in Early Roman Empire*,
Chap. VI.

supported by the analogy of Greek mystery religions, that when once a man's peace—or a woman's, for the prostitutes held by Isis and Cybele—was made with heaven, there was a new licence for conduct, for enjoyment without restraint and without the fear of guilt. There were other baptisms in the world, why should not Christian baptism be treated like the rest as an *opus operatum* ? [1] This magical view was to have a long life in the church. In the meantime Paul had to say, what the priests of Cybele and Isis did not feel so bound to say, that fornication was the breaking of God's law and was also disloyalty to Christ. Paul does not debate the relations of matter and spirit, the irrelevance of the two worlds to each other, spiritual to material. He brought his strong Jewish sense, inspired by his knowledge of Christ, to bear on Gentile filthiness ; and once more we realize the value of a life and a mind centred in Christ. Greeks were very clever at argument—especially the cheaper type of Greek, like the cheaper types of the emancipated everywhere ; but " ye have not so learned Christ." [2]

Paul had to deal with all sorts of crotchets, the connexion of which with religion and morals was not always obvious. There was astrology with its "weak and beggarly elements," the observance of " days and months and times and years." [3] There were curious " genealogies " [4]—schemes of principalities and powers, *plêroma* and other neuter nouns or abstracts personalized into something like deity, so vague as to be mysterious and imposing. There were dreams and fancies with more than a superficial likeness to modern theosophies ;

---

[1] Cf. K. Lake, *Earlier Epistles*, p. 46.　　　[2] Eph. iv. 20.

[3] Gal. iv. 9, 10; the Galatian days, etc., may have been Jewish, but the " elements " seem more pagan, or at least more like the generally current sham science of the day; cf. Col. ii. 8, κατὰ τὰ στοιχεῖα τοῦ κόσμου.

[4] 1 Tim. i. 4.

the theosophists at least hail the affinity. A century
later more was heard of all these things, and it is hard
for a modern man, trained on any strict lines of history
and science, to understand how anybody could ever
have attached any idea of reality to any of them.[1]
There was religious vegetarianism—not the harmless
dietetic vagary of to-day, but a vegetarianism based on
a half-belief in the transmigration of souls, and on
the fear that with fleshmeat the soul of the beast may
pass into the man. There was a similar dread or
dislike of marriage, again an idea not unconnected with
daemon-fears, and the antithesis of body and spirit.
With the last Paul clearly had some sympathy.[2] But
in all these cases, he hits the right line, and it is his
feeling for Christ that guides him. Men and women
are, of course, free to marry; Paul does not marry,
and he thinks it wiser to abstain from marriage, " as
things are "—perhaps because the Second Advent *may*
be near, perhaps because of trouble in the flesh. In
any case, his treatment of the marriage problem in
reply to the questions of the Corinthians is marked by
sense and humanity. Christianity is *not* celibacy ;
marriage, like meats, is God's device " to be received
with thanksgiving." [3] As for theosophy, and every
other notion of the ill-trained or ill-balanced mind,
Paul proceeds instinctively less by negation than by
affirmation. If men once get their affections centred
in Christ, their minds at work on the ideas of Christ,
" their thoughts into obedience to the law of Christ " [4]
—or, if all that is too hard and abstract, if they will
be content to live " along the lines of Christ " [5] and
have Christ dwelling in their hearts by love—you may

[1] A very short time with an English translation of *Pistis Sophia* will
suffice.

[2] 1 Cor. vii. 1-8.

[3] See generally 1 Cor. vi., vii., and cf. 1 Tim. iv. 3, a Pauline sentiment, whoever was the author, redactor, or editor.

[4] 2 Cor. x. 5.   [5] Col. ii. 8. ; Rom. xv. 5.

trust to their judgment; the magnet will swing to the North, if you leave it alone. This may be writing out the guidance of the Holy Spirit in very simple terms and and plain language, but it was plain language that was wanted and Paul gave it. No one could mistake his emphasis on Christ, and the test question—how such and such conduct or ideas fitted Christ (κατὰ Χριστόν) [1] —anybody could understand.

Another group in the early church remains to be considered, the people who " spoke with tongues " and were amenable to " the spirit," and the prophets generally. From the first advent of Dionysos to Greece down to John Wesley's preaching at Kingswood, and indeed later, men have been confused and perplexed by psychical phaenomena which cross the work of religion. A man is deeply moved to contrition or to acceptance of Christ, a movement primarily of the mind, stirred by thought and emotion ; and then something else breaks in, and he falls in trance, as John Wesley's hearers sometimes did. Or else, whether he loses control of his speech or gains control of another tongue, he begins to give utterance to sounds unfamiliar. This, to people who have never seen it before and whose psychology is very simple, is a perplexing thing to explain, and they fall back on the hypothesis of the intervention of a spirit. But even so the critics retain some hold of canons which they know better— if the person " possessed " is blasphemous for instance, it is an evil spirit ; otherwise it may be the Holy Spirit. There is evidence of an outcrop of such phaenomena in Corinth, and it is held that everything was being sacrificed to secure manifestations of prophecy and speech " with tongues." Paul intervened. He was not in possession of modern views of psychology, but he had sense, and he was practical. What was being effected by all this to win men for Christ ? Did the unintelligible confusion of spirit-filled gatherings

[1] Col. ii. 8.

THE CHURCH

clarify the appeal of Christ ? Was it consonant with
the gospel or with the Holy Spirit, when a man
under the influence of some spirit announced that
" Jesus was accursed " ? [1] He owns that he also spoke
with tongues [2]—a confession to which we must return
later ; but, he asks, what is the real use of it ? He
puts in the plea of edification—the real plea of getting
some foundation laid on which life can be built,
centred as ever in Christ ; and the spiritual occurrences
begin to look very irrelevant. The " tongues " might
be the " tongues of angels " [3] (he does not admit this),
but in any case love is more significant. However
mystical in temperament or in mind Paul might be,
he could not forget the work to which he was called.
Christ was to control his thoughts, and Christ did.
These confusing phaenomena are not in the gospel—
nor, we may note, in the Gospels ; they came from the
heathen world, not the Jewish. They were irrelevant
to the real work of the church ; that was their condemnation. Modern psychology confirms it by showing their more or less physical origin, their wide
diffusion among races of lower culture, and their
growing rarity with the growth of inhibition. Inhibition has a scientific sound, " the obedience of Christ "
a theological; but Paul and the men of science on
different lines have reached the same conclusion, and
the fact that they have gone on lines so different confirms their conclusion.

So soon in church history do we reach the problems
of order, discipline, and regularization. " Ye are
called to freedom," [4]—and the next thing is church
law ! Paul is faced with the problem of every liberal
government,—of Aristides and Pericles in the Athenian
Confederacy, of Oliver Cromwell face to face with
Lilburne and others, of Thomas Jefferson and his
followers confronted with the Louisiana question.

[1] 1 Cor. xii. 3.　　　　[2] 1 Cor. xiv. 18. See p. 186.
[3] 1 Cor. xiii. 1　　　　[4] Gal. v. 13.

The church is " a little self-governing republic " [1]—
so much is obvious in the Corinthian story. Can a
republic, with a real work to do, afford to be wrecked
by a handful of people who recognize nothing but the
impulse of the moment ? Must there be authority—
the crux of every church ? Controversy has raged over
the historical question of the authority in the apostolic
church, but the balance of historical opinion is to the
view, expressed by Professor Percy Gardner, that the
organization was in " a perfectly fluid state." Fifty
years after Paul's death (or a few years less) Ignatius
has an opinion or a theory about bishops which we
do not find in Paul, but even so it is not at all
established that his theory (or whatever it be called)
is on all fours with the dogma of Cyprian a century and a half later, or that either of them quite
means what their supposed followers mean to-day.
This is one case where, the word remaining the
same, historical inquiry has to ascertain its implica-
tion and its background at each stage. It is not
needful in a study of Paul to go deeply into the
controversy, and it will suffice to quote the summary
of Bishop Henson.

" Dr Lightfoot had shown that the traditional
view of Episcopacy as an Apostolical institution must
be revised in deference to the fact that it had been
developed out of the Presbyterate. Dr C. H. Turner
showed that the traditional view of Apostolic succession
was not primitive but grew out of controversy in the
fourth century. In neither case did the new theory
necessarily prohibit the traditional view, but in both
the traditional view was mitigated and stripped of its
binding authority over religious minds. . . . [Professor
A. C. Headlam] reaffirms the positions of Dr Lightfoot
and Dr Turner with learning, decision and lucidity
. . . [and] reaches the conclusion that Episcopacy is
an ecclesiastical creation, neither ordained by Christ

[1] T. M. Lindsay, *Church and Ministry*, p. 54.

nor appointed by His Apostles." [1] Professor Henry Melville Gwatkin, of Cambridge, held the same position, and this agreement among outstanding Anglican scholars may relieve us for the moment of closer argument. In any case neither episcopacy, bishops, presbyters, nor any other form or theory of church government can be said to have been central in Paul's thoughts.

The early church was very like the synagogue, as the New Testament shows us both. It could hardly have been otherwise, when it was really a group of seceders with the same tradition. The procedure seems to have been fluid as well as the government—at Corinth too fluid altogether. That hymns—rhythms of some kind—were used we know from Pliny about III A.D. [2] The Apocalypse has fragments—or perhaps the whole—of some hymns. [3] Paul himself may have echoes of them. [4] He nowhere mentions the use of the Lord's prayer, but his reference to Abba, Father, is taken to imply it. [5] Letters were read, and preaching abounded ; often many persons took part in it. [6]

It is when we come to sacraments that we reach difficulty. Professor Lake tells us that " baptism is, for St Paul and his readers, universally and unquestioningly accepted as a ' mystery ' or sacrament which works *ex opere operato*, and from the unhesitating manner in which St Paul uses this fact as a basis for argument, as if it were a point on which Christian opinion did not vary, it would seem as though this

---

[1] Hensley Henson, *Anglicanism*, p. 192.

[2] Pliny, *Epp. to Trajan*, 96, 7 ; *carmenque Christo quasi deo dicere secum invicem*. This passage, written by a Roman, a heathen and an outsider, cannot be made to serve as evidence for a belief in Christ's deity in the Bithynian church. It merely explains the practice and the type of hymn.

[3] Rev. v. 9-13 ; xi. 17 ; xv. 3.   [4] 2 Tim. ii. 11-13.

[5] T. M. Lindsay, *Church and Ministry*, p. 44 ; Rom. viii. 15 ; Gal. iv. 6.

[6] Cf. 1 Cor. xiv. 23, 26, 29.

L

sacramental teaching is central in the primitive Christianity to which the Roman Empire began to be converted." " The Catholic doctrine," he says, " is much more nearly primitive than the Protestant ; " " but," he adds, " the Catholic advocate in winning his case has proved still more : the type of doctrine which he defends is not only primitive, but pre-Christian." " The majority of the Church . . . they all accepted Christianity as a Mystery Religion, which really could do what the other Mystery Religions pretended to do." [1] Dr Lake's canon is that, to discover the central points in early Christian doctrine, we must look not at those to which Paul devotes pages of argument, but at those which he treats as the premises accepted by all Christians. Like all simple rules, this is not as simple as it looks. However, Dr Lake's contentions, partly based on the work of Reitzenstein,[2] are supported, in some degree, by a good many scholars, while others who do not go so far show the influence of this line of inquiry.

On the other hand a strong case is made against this likeness to the mystery religions,—even supposing that we really know as much as is supposed about those religions, the views they embodied and their diffusion. That likeness there was later on, is evident enough, though the likeness even there does not take us very far. In the New Testament there is language which, taken by itself, is more or less susceptible of such interpretation, but there is far more that is not. Nobody so far has alleged that Jesus held any such position, and it is assumed that the change to another basis altogether from the standpoint of Jesus was the work of Paul as much as of any one ; Paul thus becomes the man who has corrupted our religion and brought us away from Jesus. A man's language is a guide to

---

[1] Lake, *Earlier Letters of St Paul*, pp. 385, 215, 233.
[2] Professor Lake, however, warns me that he has since found Reitzenstein's quotations not too accurate.

his character, but his character is the background against which his language has to be interpreted. Paul was a Jew, and he lived first among the enemies of Jesus and then among his friends, and he is to be credited with some intelligence, some clearness, and some gift of centripetal emphasis. Can it be seriously urged that his emphasis, broad and long, is sacramental, when, as Reitzenstein admits, he never refers to his own baptism [1]—when the sacrament is for him the Lord's supper, and he does not use of it the language of the fourth gospel, never hints at " eating the flesh and drinking the blood," [2] (which was in some instances the essence of the heathen mystery meal), never but in one doubtful place [3] hints at " the belief in the marvellous virtue of sacred food, whether for weal or woe "—when he never gets near a phrase like that of Ignatius, " medicine of immortality and antidote of death "—when in setting forth to the Romans his conception of Christianity, he mentions baptism once, and the Lord's supper not at all—when he boasts for the moment to the Corinthians and thanks God that, one or two excepted, he had baptized none of them ? Is that the language of a sacramentalist, of Cyprian or of any modern disciple of Cyprian ? Why is not the sacramental position made clearer in the epistle to the Hebrews and the Apocalypse and the letters of St John—waiving the broad hint of the fourth evangelist that spirit and not flesh is what matters [4]—or in the *Didache*, or even the epistle of James ? The Epicurean in Cicero's book says ; " When we call grain Ceres and

---

[1] *Hell. Myst. Relig.*, p. 49.

[2] H. A. A. Kennedy, *Paul and Mystery Religions*, p. 270. The scholarship and the sanity of this book, and its author's real acquaintance with Paul's mind, put it in another class from Reitzenstein's loose-hung work.

[3] Does he really mean that physical disease is the result of a thoughtless sharing in the Lord's supper, 1 Cor. xi. 30 ? Is that the only necessary interpretation ? Does he nowhere else use metaphor or analogy?

[4] John vi. 63.

wine Liber, we just use a common style of speech, but
do you think that anybody is so silly as to suppose that
what he eats is God ? " [1] The commentator notes
that no ancient enemy of the church brought this
taunt against it. (What the Christians were accused
of was eating real babies.[2]) Clemen concludes that the
Lord's supper cannot be derived, even collaterally
or by way of supplement, from pagan sources ; and
that the ideas in the New Testament which are *perhaps* derived from non-Jewish sources lie on the fringe
of Christianity and do not touch its vital essence.[3]

But it is at the centre, not on the circumference, that
the issue is to be decided. Paul may argue *ad hominem*
on circumcision and baptism for the dead, but what
are his central convictions ? No one can read him for
his own sake, or with Christ in mind, and miss them.
" He that seeketh findeth "—he finds what he seeks,
as we know from the use of quotations and statistics.
But grasp the whole man and understand him ;
relevant or irrelevant, can he keep off Jesus Christ as
a personality ?—Christ who gives him guidance and
strength and everything, at night when he is by himself (to judge from our records) as often as at any other
time or in any other way, who is always for him the
figure of glory seen at the Damascus gate ; " who
loved me and gave himself for me." Dr Lake is right
enough about the pre-Christian origin, the pagan
origin, of the mystery-religion view of the gospel,
but Paul was a Jew who never lost his contempt for
idols and all concerned with them.[4] He was a man
with a mind and a nature, too spontaneous to leave

---

[1] Cicero, *de natura deorum*, iii. 16, 41, see J. B. Mayor's note.

[2] Tertullian, *Apology*, 7, 8.

[3] Clemen, *Primitive Christianity and non-Jewish Sources*, pp. 266,
372.

[4] The view that Hinduism has contributions to make to the religion
of Jesus is modern, and due to confusion of thought. Indians may very
well illumine Christ for us, but idolatry and Hinduism are on a different
footing in grammar and in fact.

any one in doubt as to what he thought most of, too fundamental, too clear to be the victim of fancies and magic, a man too genuine and too deep to miss what the Stoics and the Epicureans could see—and what his own Jews, taught by the prophets, saw perfectly well. Finally the Gospels remain to be explained : how they came to be what they are, if the products of a sacramentalist society, is not elucidated, and two of their writers were conspicuously in the Pauline circle. Whatever occasional expressions of Paul may suggest, the letters taken as a whole, the group so far as we know it from its works, the personality, the natural make of the man and his experience, suggest an outlook quite other than that of the mysteries. In a word, Reitzenstein and his followers may know more of the contemporary cults, but Luther knew Paul ; for to share a man's experience tells you more of him than the study of his contemporaries, especially if they live in another street.

But the crotchets and scandals of the church, its constitution and its sacraments, even if we are never so sure of them, do not exhaust its description ; they hardly touch its value, or its real nature. Before we leave the actual church to look at the ideal, we must come back to its members, and see what Paul has to say of them. A certain type of mind will be apt to discount the expressions of such a lover of men, and the criticism might be justified if it were not so clear in his writings that Paul had no illusions about his converts—" not many wise, not many mighty, not many noble," to quote no further. He tells the Philippian Christians, however, that they " shine like beacons in the world ; " [1] and the historian must at least concede this as to early Christians in general, on the evidence of Julian the Apostate,[2] if he will not

[1] Phil. ii. 15.
[2] Julian, Letter xlix., resting on citation of it intact by Sozomen, *Eccles. Hist.*, v. 16.

accept Paul's. Even the Corinthians developed " an insatiable passion for kindness." [1] The church bore down the opposition of the world by what used to be called holy living and holy dying. But the faculty for such life and death had not quite come by nature. Paul speaks to the Corinthians of fornicators, adulterers, sodomites, thieves, drunkards, slanderers, extortioners, and then he abruptly adds, with no hint of a feeling that anybody would gainsay it, " And such were some of you." [2]   The world from which they came he pictures in the first chapter of the Epistle to the Romans, to which we need not recur.   In that world the Christians had been " aliens from the common-wealth of Israel, strangers to the covenants of promise, without hope and without God in the universe," [3] in slavery to gods that were not gods but impostors or impositions. [4]   But all that is changed ; they have come to know God, or rather have been known by God—a characteristically Pauline correction. [5] " Beloved by God " they have been " chosen by God." [6]   Even the Corinthians, who had been so squalid—" such were some of you, but ye are washed, but ye are sanctified, but ye are justified in the name of our Lord Jesus and by the Spirit of our God." [7]   They are " partakers of the inheritance of the saints in light . . . delivered from the power of darkness, translated into the kingdom of his dear Son, redeemed in his blood " ; [8]   once far off, they are made nigh by the blood of Christ ; they are no more strangers and foreigners, but fellow-citizens with the saints and of the household of God, built on the foundation of the apostles and prophets, Jesus Christ himself being the chief corner-stone. [9]   (The

---

[1] Clement of Rome, *ad Cor.*, 2, 2.   To quote the epistle is not to decide or rule out of court the questions raised by Prof. E. T. Merrill as to Clement of Rome, in his recent volume.

[2] 1 Cor. vi. 11.   [3] Eph. ii. 12, 19.   [4] Gal. iv. 8.
[5] Gal. iv. 9 ; cf. Phil. iii. 12, 13.   [6] 1 Thess. i. 4.
[7] 1 Cor. vi. 11.   [8] Col. i. 12 ff.   [9] Eph. ii. 12, 19, 20.

absence of sacramental reference or tone in such passages may be noted in passing as very significant—still more if a pupil or amanuensis modelled or re-modelled the Ephesian epistle.) The foundation is Jesus Christ; and the men, formerly stained with every mean and filthy vice, are the temple of God, and the spirit of God dwells in them.[1]

All of this is the actual, though it sounds ideal. But it has other features still more happy. Paul had three pictures for the church—the family, the human body, and the temple of God—every one of them implying a new unity in design with great diversity of function, many members of one body, all different but all one,[2] a unity of experience, a unity of purpose, a unity in the redeeming love of God. The middle wall of partition [3] a simile taken from the temple in Jerusalem—is gone; there is love for all the saints,[4] Greek, Hellenistic, Jew, and barbarian. In fact, there are no longer Jews and Greeks at all; and the barbarians and Scythians have put on Christ and are transformed. "God's secret" is working out, visibly, in the actual. They are "all full of the Holy Spirit," and their individual powers and capacities are laid hold of, vivified and strengthened by the Spirit, and it is seen how congruous and apt all mankind are to one another in Christ.

In every epistle the ideal for believer and church is set forth, greater unity, higher character, more trained intelligence "for the full knowledge of the mystery of Christ," [5] "in full knowledge and all perception to distinguish the essential." [6] They must conduct themselves "accurately" (a rather Thucydidean adverb) and

---

[1] 1 Cor. iii. 11, 16.

[2] See 1 Cor. xii.; Rom. xii. 4-8; Eph. iv. 11.

[3] Eph. ii. 14; cf. Deissmann, *Light from Ancient East*, pp. 74, 75, with reproduction of the middle wall and its threat of death to the Gentile who passes it.

[4] Eph. i. 15; 1 Thess. i. 3.   [5] Col. ii. 2.

[6] Phil. i. 9, 10; the phrase, or part of it, in Rom. ii. 18.

worthily of their calling, in love as Christ has loved us, and as children of light.[1] They should pay tribute, taxes and all other dues, bear the burdens of the weak and (what is often harder) tolerate their fancies. It is, as Benjamin Jowett put it, "the substitution of a conception of moral growth for the mechanical theory of habits. All is freedom, and Christ is the centre of it all; and he that hath begun a good work in you, Paul is confident, will perform it unto the day of Christ." "Let your hope be a joy to you."[2]

The more closely we study Paul's conception of the church, the more clearly does it appear that he is not thinking of a reproduction of a cult-brotherhood, a *thiasos*, a mystery-group. He is moving to larger, deeper and truer ideas—moving out of Judaism, purest of all existing group-religions, into a new world, all remade by Christ. He starts, whatever the question, with the glorious Christ, whom he saw first at the Damascus gate, whom he has tested in years of trying life in city after city of the Roman world, whom, with every fresh difficulty surmounted and every fresh adventure into the regions beyond, he has found more real. Christ is not a mythical mystery-god; Paul never dreamed of such a thing; the historical Jesus belonged to another order. If we choose to find parallels, the contrasts are more patent, more numerous, more significant. "By their fruits ye shall know them," and Paul finds fruits that the mystery religions never produced and did not think of producing in their atmosphere of cash and credulity; "love, joy, peace, long-suffering, gentleness, goodness, faith, meekness, temperance—against such there is no law."[3] Nor for their production is there any law; they are the outcome of life related to a living centre of faith that works by love; personal products of a personal relation,

---

[1] Eph. v. 15; iv. 1; v. 2; v. 8.
[2] Rom. xii. 12 (Moffatt).
[3] Gal. v. 22, 23.

free, and full of the spirit of growth and exploration. Such a spirit contemporary Judaism did not produce ; still less did the friends of Plutarch and Apuleius ; " but we have the mind of Christ," said Paul,[1] and that was the real differentia.

[1] 1 Cor. ii. 16.

CHAPTER VIII

THE HUMAN PAUL

IT is a biographer's temptation, in working out the situations in which his hero (if that old-fashioned word is tolerable in this age of criticism) is placed, and the social and political forces to which he has to re-act, to lose sometimes the man himself. He will give us a picture, faithful enough, of the man's mind and nature, and the story of his formative years or his decisive moment ; and yet he may forget to all appearance that in every scene of life, in every action, the man is there. He may forget that, unless in each scene and action the character which we have seen developing is operative and in evidence, unless the great central ideas of the man are accounted for, there is a futility about the biographer's work, and he has missed his real target. It is hard to conceive of a case where the authentic man is more certainly and definitely the whole story, than when we are concerned with Paul of Tarsus. Our present affair is not biography, nor a record of travel, but portraiture, and in every chapter the first thing must be the portrait. Something of his character should have been gathered at every stage ; at this point it must be our endeavour to collect what we have gathered, and to combine it, in the hope of realizing more clearly the type of man which he represented, and (if it be not foolish to suggest it) would in some degree have represented if he had never been a Christian or even a Jew at all. The man is made by his native endowment and by his experience. Every impulse, every feeling, every unconscious motion of mind or frame, is affected by the experience. But the experience is interpreted, and in a sense made, by the reaction to it, and while it cannot be overlooked, there is something to be said for even an imperfect analysis of the man's nature, an attempt to see what impulses, what feelings, what unconscious forces moved and worked in the man who underwent so striking an experience, who was " apprehended of Christ Jesus." [1]

There are great men who, through no fault of their own, are elusive. It is a great deal easier to know the character of Plato than that of Aristotle, to be at home with Luther than with Calvin. Cicero, Charles Lamb, Horace, Augustine, reveal themselves ; and so does Paul. The difficulty in Paul for the modern student is not to seize the traits of his character, our present concern, but to realize how the whole man is possessed by Christ. Vivacity, passion, friendship many of us can in measure understand ; the heart-whole surrender, conviction, and fusion, that make Paul, lie too often outside our experience, and we are apt to leave them out of our picture or draw them amiss. Mr A. C. Bradley, in one of his Oxford lectures, said that " always we get most from the *genius* in a man of genius and not from the rest of him." [2] How easy it is, when one has not genius, to overlook it in the man who has it and to find him very like ordinary men !

There survives from antiquity a work to which scholars tend to assign a much higher historical value than it was once allowed—*The Acts of Paul and Thekla*.[3] It exists in Greek, Latin, Syriac, and Armenian. Of these Mr F. C. Conybeare tells us that the Greek text is the worst ; the Latin is better, but not so good as the Syriac ; but the Armenian text, though trans-

---

[1] Phil. iii. 12.

[2] A. C. Bradley, *Oxford Lectures on Poetry*, p. 172, on Shelley.

[3] See F. C. Conybeare, *Monuments of Early Christianity*, pp. 49-60, and translation of Armenian text that follows ; Sir W. M. Ramsay, *Christian Church in Roman Empire*, chap. xvi.

lated from the Syriac, is free from certain interpolations present in Syriac MSS. of the fifth century ; in fact, that, with one exception, all the matters conjectured by Sir William Ramsay to be second century interpolations vanish, and we have a version that may very nearly represent a first century original. In this we read how Onesiphorus goes out to meet Paul at the cross-roads ; Titus has told him what sort of a man to look for ; and by and by he sees " coming along a man of moderate stature, with curly [or crisp] hair and scanty ; crooked legs ; with blue eyes ; and large knit eyebrows ; long nose ; and he was full of the grace and pity of the Lord, sometimes having the appearance of a man, but sometimes looking like an angel." [1] The other texts omit the blue eyes ; the Syriac says they were large ; it tones down a little the crookedness of the legs, and puts it more clearly that his eyebrows met, and that it was his hair that was scanty, but it says nothing about the hair being curly. The meeting eyebrows, a modern scholar tells us, were a mark of the were-wolf ; so we have to beware lest they were added by a theological hand to link the Benjamite with his ancestor, " the ravening wolf." [2]

" This plain and unflattering account of the Apostle's personal appearance," writes Sir William Ramsay, " seems to embody a very early tradition." We have not to ignore the possibility that it was written up from Paul's description of himself, nor the certainty that there were plenty of people in Asia Minor who did not need to read his letters written to Corinth to know what he was like. " His bodily appearance," people said at Corinth, " is weakly and his speech is contemptible." [3] So Paul quotes what men said ; and, without thinking of them, he says elsewhere,[4] " we have this treasure (viz., the enlightenment of God's glory in the face of Christ) in vessels of clay." Elsewhere his

[1] Conybeare, *op. cit.*, p. 62.   [2] Gen. xlix. 27.
[3] 2 Cor. x. 10.   [4] 2 Cor. iv. 7.

body is a mere tent, in which he groans, longing for a heavenly structure quite different from it.[1] Writing to the Philippians, who did not, so far as we know, say unkind things about his looks and accents, he speaks, almost with resentment, of his " humiliating body." [2] Of frail health, of a thorn in the flesh, of some recurring disorder that degrades him (epilepsy, it is guessed), perhaps of weak eyes, he speaks in one place and another.[3] He " dies daily." [4] It seems a thoroughly sound conclusion [5] that he was very sensitive about his weakness ; it was the thing he found hardest to bear ; he felt men might " spit at it " [6]—perhaps to avert the omen.

Yet the humiliating body must have been uncommonly tough. When we read such a catalogue of adventures as he quickly runs over, in writing to the Corinthians [7]—" in labours more abundant, in stripes above measure, in prisons more frequent, in deaths oft," five inflictions of the thirty-nine stripes of the Jews, three times the Roman beating with rods, three shipwrecks, a night and a day in the sea, journeys, perils of water and land, of city and open country, brigands, traitors, " weariness and painfulness, watching, hunger, thirst, cold, nakedness " and endless worry—all or enough of it confirmed by Luke in the Acts—we can endorse the judgment that his life-work " as a mere physical performance challenges our admiration." [8]

Claudius Lysias, judging from Paul's appearance, took him to be possibly an Egyptian—not an Egyptian Jew, for he was astonished to find that Paul spoke Greek.[9] The incident is so odd, and has in the end

---

[1] 2 Cor. v. 1 ; cf. 1 Cor. xv. 53.   [2] Phil. iii. 21.
[3] Cf. 2 Cor. xii. 7 ; Gal. iv. 13, 14 (where the language is very emphatic), 15 ; and add Acts xiv. 12, where it was clear that he was no Jupiter.
[4] 1 Cor. xv. 31.   [5] B. W. Bacon, *Paul*, p. 39.   [6] Gal. iv. 14.
[7] 2 Cor. xi. 23 ff. ; cf. xii. 10 ; Rom. viii. 35 ; 1 Cor. xv. 30, 32.
[8] Deissmann, *Paul* (trn.), p. 65.   [9] Acts xxi. 38.

so little importance, that it looks very real. The very name Claudius Lysias almost precludes our thinking him a new-comer to the East, where such racial distinctions are patent at once to residents. Paul may really have looked like an Egyptian; his shaven head, if it was shaved, may have suggested the idea; but the tone of Paul's reply suggests that he did not like it. I cannot explain the point.

When we pass from Paul's appearance to his mind, we move out of the realm of conjecture. First, let us set his great gift of winning and keeping friends. "The less commonplace a man is," wrote Pascal, "the more remarkable people he will meet." Paul gathered up acquaintances and friends wherever he went. He interested men, provoked them to controversy sometimes, at other times charmed them, and won them every way. When the riot took place at Ephesus,[1] Aristarchus, the Macedonian of Thessalonica, was with him; he was with him still, when, after his captivity at Caesarea, he sailed for Rome;[2] he was with him when he wrote to the Colossians and to Philemon, one of a group that includes the evangelists Mark and Luke. The courage, that launched him on that Ephesian day into the theatre, appealed to Paul—"a Cock of the right kind," as Captain Greatheart says of Old Honest in the *Pilgrim's Progress*. But, at the same time, some of the Asiarchs, the priests of the worship of the Emperor, urged Paul not to go into the theatre; it was a friendly act, and one wonders how they came to be on such terms with him. But the same thing happens with the centurion in charge of his ship; they have not sailed far before he allows Paul to go ashore freely to see his friends and to refresh himself;[3] and, at a later point on the voyage, though he would

---

[1] Acts xix. 23 ff.   [2] Acts xxvii. 2.

[3] Acts xxvii. 3; a comparison with Acts xx. 13, where Paul prefers a land journey on foot to a not very long sail, has prompted the homely but very probable suggestion that he was not a good sailor.

not accept the old traveller's sea-lore, and was wrong,
he takes care that Paul is not killed by the soldiers ;
the other prisoners, one gathers, he was more ready to
do without—*vile damnum*, as Tiberius said. Felix too
felt Paul's charm—quite apart from base hopes, and
used to send for him and talk with him rather
frequently.[1] The long lists of men and women to
whom Paul sent greetings speak for themselves.[2]

An episode, to which he refers in writing to the
Corinthians,[3] illustrates what friendship meant to him.
" Furthermore when I came to Troas to preach
Christ's gospel, and a door was opened to me of the
Lord, I had no rest in my spirit because I found not
Titus my brother ; but I took my leave of them and
went to Macedonia." He does not idly use the phrase
of the door opened to him ; [4] and yet, in spite of the
door, in spite of the opening for the gospel, he cannot
settle down alone to preach, he needs the support
of a colleague, and he must have Titus. A few
chapters later, he describes his meeting with Titus ;
" God, who comforts the downcast, comforted us by
the coming of Titus." When Titus brings him good
news from Corinth, he is still more helped—" yes, and
so much the more overflowingly (his characteristic
περισσοτέρως, to which we must return) did we
rejoice in Titus' joy, because his soul found rest in all
of you." There is a hint of the same disposition to
be uneasy if left alone, when he writes to the Thessalonians,[5] how he had longed to hear of them, and how,

---

[1] Acts xxiv. 26, πυκνότερον.

[2] Someone has reckoned that sixty of his friends are mentioned by
Paul in his letters, and that twenty more are named by Luke. It is
not so simple to count them as might seem. I make sixty-seven
mentioned by Paul, excluding Apostles and Timothy's kindred, and a
doubtful second Gaius. I cannot make out twenty more in the Acts.

[3] 2 Cor. ii. 12, 13 ; vii. 6, 7, 13.

[4] Cf. the " great door and effectual " opened at Ephesus, 1 Cor. xvi.
9 ; and Col. iv. 3.

[5] 1 Thess. iii. 1.

when he could bear it no longer, " we thought it good to be left in Athens alone."

Other passages suggest his feeling when people are about him and are sympathetic. " You know," he tells the Galatians, " how in weakness of the flesh I preached to you the former time, and my temptation [a variant ; *your* temptation] in my flesh you did not disdain, but received me as an angel of God, as Christ Jesus. . . . If it had been possible, you would have dug out your eyes and given them to me."[1] The gratitude and the happiness that the message and the gifts of the Philippians wake in him, and the glowing and charming language in which he expresses them, show what sympathy meant to him ;—he is " initiated into doing without," but it was delightful (" I rejoiced in the Lord hugely ") that they had blossomed out into all this thought for him ; they did well in taking a share in his troubles, they had done it before, and now he has all he can want and overflows ; it is like a fragrance, and God must enjoy it as much as he does, and will meet all *their* need.[2] In particular, Paul, in his business of preaching the gospel, wants the support of men's prayers, as others have wanted it since him, and he suggests it again and again.[3] That is one of the great things, he feels, about Christ—" who also makes intercession for us." [4]

With all the obvious quickness of his temper— generally, we find, roused by crookedness or cowardice —he is eager to help men ("for whom Christ died " [5]), and he emphasizes forgiveness, gentleness, and patience —" putting up with one another and forgiving one another, if any one has a grudge against any one else ; as the Lord forgave you, so do you in your turn." [6] Why must the Corinthians have lawsuits inside the church ? Why cannot they just accept the wrong

[1] Gal. iv. 13, 14, 15.   [2] Phil. iv. 10-19.
[3] 2 Cor. i. 11 ; Col. iv. 3 ; Rom. xv. 30.   [4] Rom. viii. 34.
[5] 1 Cor. viii. 11.   [6] Col. iii. 13 ; cf. Rom. xii. 19.

done to them, and be content to be swindled ? [1] The followers of Apollos, it is thought, did what they could to embitter Paul's life,[2] but they did not succeed in making a quarrel. Paul recognizes heartily God's use of Apollos ; it is all one, " ye are Christ's and Christ is God's." He has a tolerance for weaker brethren, and suffers fools gladly, and, while he will not give way—" no ! not for an hour ! "—on a question of principle for all the Judaizers in the world, nor for Peter himself and all " the pillars," yet he will humour the crotchets of the weaker minds, and, if it will really do them any good, he is ready to eat no meat while the world stands. He has a sharp quarrel with Barnabas over Mark's desertion in Pisidia, and afterwards he is thoroughly reconciled to Mark.[3] He begs his friends to avoid annoying people,[4] and husbands not to be " cross " (or surly) with their wives.[5] His own ideals in friendship are surely to be read in his thirteenth chapter to the Corinthians.

He is a leader of men—a Garibaldi, one might almost say, in adventure, and a Socrates in thought ; he will carry his friends with him into all sorts of risks for Christ's sake, and he will emancipate their minds, not by a dialectic method, though he used that, but by winning their trust and giving them new ideas. And here a rather closer examination of his vocabulary is very illuminative.

Most great writers have their mannerisms. Thucydides has a curious fancy for recording the greatest expedition that ever sailed, the biggest disaster, the best defence on a capital charge, the most enduring counter-revolution ever effected with the smallest numbers, and other odd superlatives, almost American.[6] Cicero in his letters is noted as having a weakness

[1] I Cor. vi. 7 ; cf. I Cor. iv. 13. [2] I Cor. iii. 4, 5, 22.
[3] Acts xv. 36-40 ; Col. iv. 10 ; Philemon, 24.
[4] 2 Cor. vi. 3, προσκοπήν. [5] Col. iii. 19.
[6] See W. H. Forbes, *Thucydides I.*, Introduction, p. xxiii.

M

for diminutives and for terms with the prepositional prefix *sub-* ; it serves to qualify, to tone down, what he *suggests* rather than asserts.[1] Paul has two prepositions with which he makes great play—συν- and ὑπερ-. All three writers are highly individual men, very quick and very sensitive, who can make language do what they wish, if they have to re-model it as they write. Paul's two prepositions will have to be considered at points later on, where they bear vitally upon the subject[2]; συν- concerns us at once. Of course Greek abounds in compounds of συν-, in which any special suggestion which the preposition may have had has long been lost. We need not investigate *synagogue*, nor συντρίβω (to smash, as in Mark xiv. 3), nor kinsfolk (συγγενεῖς), nor even *sym*pathy, though these last two may or may not keep a suggestion of fellowship according to who uses them.

It is remarkable that Paul does not use anywhere the word "friend" (φίλος). "Beloved" (ἀγαπητός) is applied by him to ten persons—Timothy, Tychicus (twice), Epaphroditus, Onesimus (twice), Philemon, "Luke the beloved physician," and four less known people in Romans xvi. The general community often receives this pleasant word. Meanwhile the "brothers" occupy two columns in the concordance. But the σύν- compounds suggest even closer relations, in the case of such a man as Paul. We naturally ask what they share with him ; and above all and first comes work. Priscilla and Aquila, Urbanus, Timothy, Titus, Epaphroditus, Clement, Aristarchus, Mark, Jesus Justus, Philemon—eleven "fellow-workers" (συνεργοί) are greeted or mentioned by name, and others are indicated in the plural.[3] To a man or woman of any

---

[1] See R. Y. Tyrrell, *Cicero in His Letters*, Introduction, pp. lxxxvi., lxxxviii., " nearly every adjective and adverb in the language is intensified by the prefix *per-* and mitigated by the prefix *sub-*," verbs too.

[2] See pp. 195, 212.   [3] Phil. iv. 3.

spirit or character to be so described by one of Paul's
build and nature must have been in itself inspiration.
" Partner " (κοινωνός), though not a compound in
form, is almost a synonym, and like its derivative
" fellow-partner " (συγκοινωνεῖν, Phil. i. 7) must have
meant something to those so named. The " true
yoke-fellow " (γνήσιε Σύζυγε, if Paul is, as seems
probable, playing with the man's name) is bidden
co-operate (συλλαμβάνου) with the women who (if one
may dare coin it in English) synathletized with Paul
(συνήθλησαν)—a rather striking word ; and the verse
ends with fellow-workers unnamed—four instances
in one verse of the preposition.[1] The Philippians
are called on to be " fellow-imitators " with Paul
(συμμιμηταί),[2] and " of one soul" with him (σύμψυχοι).[3]
The Corinthians are—if a clumsy and colloquial translation may be allowed to bring out the suggestion—
" putting in joint work at prayer " for Paul,[4] and they
" are in Paul's heart to share death with and to share
life with " (συναποθανεῖν καὶ συζῆν).[5]

Paul, as we know, constantly described himself as
the slave of Christ ; then Epaphroditus and Tychicus
are his " fellow-slaves " [6] (σύνδουλος), one " beloved "
as well, and the other " brother." It is hard to
imagine language more moving for men who knew
what that service meant to Paul. Epaphroditus elsewhere is Paul's " fellow-soldier " (συστρατιώτης), and
so is the less-known Archippos.[7] And at the last,
when the dark days are come and liberty is gone, Paul
has " fellow-prisoners " (συναιχμάλωτος)—" kinsfolk,"
two of them, Andronicus and Junia, who " were in
Christ before me," [8] and perhaps, if the term is literal,
had helped to make the ferment which preceded his
conversion—Epaphroditus, again, linked by a new
bond (his fourth συν-),[9] and the loyal Macedonian

---

[1] Phil. iv. 3.   [2] Phil. iii. 17.   [3] Phil. ii. 2.
[4] 2 Cor. i. 11.   [5] 2 Cor. vii. 3.   [6] Col. i. 7 ; iv. 7.
[7] Phil. ii. 25 ; Philemon 2.   [8] Rom. xvi. 7.   [9] Philemon 23.

Aristarchus,[1] of whom, whenever he is mentioned, one regrets that we do not know more.

So far the concordance takes us ; but when from a more human point of view we try to translate it all into life, it must surely affect our estimate of Paul's character. He must have had a much more deeply affectionate and sympathetic nature than we sometimes think. " Brethren " in England is conventional and formal ; abroad, where one's fellow-believers are few and poor, it has a new value ; " beloved " is an old-world word, not often to-day used with much real meaning in common life. But look at the list of compounds—how individual they are, how full of two biographies both known to the recipient, and the greater illuminating the less ! The dearest of all ties for Paul is to find men sharing things with him. The work, the " athletic " life, the yoke, the slavery, the imitation,—these are all expressions of his relation with Jesus Christ, the very essence of life ; how much more it is to him when he finds his friends standing with him in that great loyalty ! Fond as he is of men by nature,[2] apt to fall into friendship and to enjoy men and to depend on them, these natural ties and affections have something of the infinite, something of eternity, in them, and when the ordinary relation is turned into a common devotion to Christ, the men are more to him than ever they were. To his friends in the same way the compound nouns, some of them perhaps newly made, and all newly applied, must have been full of significance. Cicero cheerily twits one of his young friends, telling him he is so vain that he would rather have Caesar ask his opinion than be " gold-plated " by Caesar ;[3] of course he would, any

---

[1] Col. iv. 10.

[2] Another Ciceronian trait. Cicero " loved young men, especially clever ones, and was apt to take an optimistic view of them." Warde Fowler, *Social Life at Rome*, p. 128.

[3] Cicero to Trebatius Testa, 53 B.C. ; *ad Fam.* vii. 13, *malle a Caesare consuli quam inaurari.*

man of spirit would ! And when Aristarchus and
Epaphroditus found the very greatest and most charming man they ever knew grappling them to his soul
by words that proclaim them of one corps and of one
college with himself, fellows in work and fellows in
suffering for the same great Chief, how did they feel ?
The wonder is rather that Demas could leave him ;
and here we may note in passing (and say no more of
Demas) how the Apostle speaks of his renunciation.
Whatever later elements critics may find in the epistles
to Timothy, or alien elements (if that would beg fewer
questions), the hand of Paul is surely there. Like
Carlyle's, according to Sterling, his signature is in every
word he writes. He is old and feeling his age, solitary
and in some anxiety as to his future, needing more than
ever support and friendship ; and Demas " has forsaken me—having loved this present world." [1] Paul
feels his going ; but above all things he grieves that a
man he loves should prefer the fugitive to the eternal
and choose not Christ but the mere present. Here
also we touch the heart of Paul, in its gentleness and its
craving for men.

Jülicher puts some relevant questions, suggested by
the complicated relations with Corinth. Had Paul, he
asks, in any very high degree the gifts of ruling men
and reading their hearts ? Was he apt to judge them
by his own standards ? Great and intense natures
do this, and misread men ; if small men, as we saw
Pascal suggesting, do not recognize greatness when
they see it, have not great men a similar habit of not
realizing how petty the run of men are ? Was Paul
never wrong when he reckoned on men seeing, and
being, with his own swiftness and sureness ? The
question itself hints his greatness. Jülicher goes
further ; was Paul rather too Jewish in outlook and
tradition to identify himself with Greek views ? Did
his abrupt changes of plan, brought about by his visions

[1] 2 Tim. iv. 10.

—or, as at Troas, by the chafing of solitude—confuse and upset his friends ? Some certainly accused him of vacillation and of impulsiveness (ἐλαφρία)—the bright quick words of Paul to the Corinthians [1] about "Yea, yea" and "Nay, nay" tell that tale. Genius in speech and action often depends on a swiftness of mind in realizing an unnoticed change in a situation that may be vital, but which commoner intelligences miss ; and such genius has the defects of its qualities, as we hardly need to be told. Alexander achieved everything by reading men swiftly and profoundly ; his very foundation was his understanding of his Macedonians ; but, when it came to Oriental state and Persian dress, he entirely misread his own countrymen. But, concludes Jülicher—to return to his criticism—the ever-infectious zeal of the enthusiast, Paul's courage and faith, his self-sacrifice and tenderness, make his influence a spell. If he had the defects of genius, he had its magic, and men followed him instinctively, ana-lysing their leader and their own motives as little as men ever do when a real leader appears. Αὐτός ἔφα.

But with so many friendships there came many claims ; there were communities in which he was involved, there were individuals who were no less a source of anxiety. To genius it must in the end be painfully clear what a faculty for going wrong the ordinary man has. Paul was in his own person the bond of unity that held some of those communities together and kept them in touch with other churches.[2] How little cohesive "saints" can be, is always a source of wonder to people who take their opinions at second hand and shape life by the proverbs and maxims of others—as if the individualizing experience of con-version and knowledge of Christ really helped to blot out personality. Even in societies without ideas, personal ambition and vanity can work disruption, and they are not unknown in churches. The churches

[1] 2 Cor. i. 17, 18.   [2] Cf. Deissmann, *St Paul*, p. 187.

and Paul's relations with them we have already discussed, but they must not be forgotten here—" that which cometh upon me daily, the care of all the churches," and the individuals in them—" who is weak, and I am not weak? who is offended, and I burn not?" Dr Strachan [1] speaks of Paul's " yearning for the stupid man "—a modern and very happy rendering of his spirit and very near his own words; the stupid man always costs a lot—in patience, if in nothing else. A pupil of genius is a stimulus when he is not a terror; bright and intelligent friends, as Paul shows, reinforce you. But " the foolish things of this world " are intolerable, if it were not for the overpowering facts that God chose them and Christ died for them. So Paul is theirs to command,—ready to explain the same thing a hundred times, to bear all things, to hope all things, to endure all things, if by any means he may save some of them from themselves and their own crotchets.

Of course, the duller and the less Christian his converts were, the more apt they were to worry him with stupidity and criticism. " After considerable experience," Mr Aldis Wright once wrote,[2] " I feel justified in saying that in most cases ignorance and conceit are the parents of conjectural emendation," and alas! they have other offspring. Ignorance and conceit produced abundant criticism of Paul[3]—he did not do many miracles,[4] nor have enough visions;[5] he was not really like an apostle;[6] he was of inexcusably mean appearance;[7] he sought to please men;[8] he did not write as he felt;[9] he tricked people with his cunning (πανοῦργος δόλῳ);[10] he was much too

[1] R. H. Strachan, *Individuality of St Paul*, p. 133.
[2] Preface to edition of Milton, p. xix.
[3] See generally K. Lake, *Earlier Epistles*, pp. 223 f.; Deissmann, *Paul*, pp. 71 f. [4] 2 Cor. xii. 11.
[5] 2 Cor. xii. 1-10. [6] 2 Cor. xi. 7-11.
[7] 2 Cor. x. 7, 10. [8] Gal. i. 10.
[9] 2 Cor. i. 13. [10] 2 Cor. xii. 16.

impulsive (as we saw already) and showed signs of being wrong in the head.[1] All these pleasant insinuations are to be gathered from his letters—when one looks for them. His defence is spirited, but it is not bitter, as with many men it would have been. But we can believe that at times he " was loaded beyond his strength, beyond hyperbole, and told himself it was the sentence of death " [2]—so much so that he had nothing between him and breakdown except God. " Without there were fights, within there were fears," [3] and then Titus turned up, or God sent him. He seems to have had other worries, beyond what we might have expected, and not all magnificent ; he was more sensitive to mockery and to criticism of his style and of his message than would have been guessed without his confession. " I was with you," he tells the Corinthians, apparently speaking of his first visit, after his Athenian experience, " in weakness and in fear and in much trembling, and my speech and my preaching were not in the persuasive language of wisdom." [4]

In all these things, as in others, he is more than conqueror. It is significant of character, that he himself is our source of knowledge for all his troubles and for all the criticism that came upon him—a sign, too, that they did not overcome him. But he himself says plainly that God delivered him, does deliver, and (he trusts and believes) will deliver him.[5] The power of God [6] is always with him ; Jesus (the Lord) assures him that " My grace is sufficient for thee," so that the hour when he is weak is exactly the time when he is strongest ; [7] and he gives thanks to God " who always makes us triumph in Christ." [8] As Luke shows us in the Acts, Paul is conscious that God sends him guidance, and, if a modern critic remarks that Paul is " not

[1] 2 Cor. v. 13.
[2] 2 Cor. i. 8, 9.
[3] 2 Cor. vii. 5.
[4] 1 Cor. ii. 3.
[5] 2 Cor. i. 10.
[6] 1 Cor. ii, 4, 5 ; 2 Cor. vi. 7 ; x. 4.
[7] 2 Cor. xii. 9.
[8] 2 Cor. ii. 14.

conscious of any co-operation of his own mind in these great leaps of faith," [1] Paul there stands with most who have known such guidance. The first condition of it is the wish to do God's will. Yet, with it all, we can understand how often he must have wished to be done with this life of fightings and fears, of criticism and strain, " to depart and to be with Christ—far better." [2]

Whether we should connect his visions and his speaking with tongues with his physical nature (if such distinctions are at all sound), and associate them with the constant strain on him, or with the movements of what might popularly be called his intellect and the workings of a passionate nature, we may avoid deciding by placing them between these two parts of our study. The whole question of visions is an intricate one, not yet fully worked out.[3] Paul was quite definite in stating that he had *seen* Jesus at the gate of Damascus. But the " certain man of Macedonia," who called him over to Europe,—did Paul see him in a dream, or awake, or between ? [4] It may be urged that it stands in the same category as the vision of Jesus, but the language would admit of a dream ; and, if Sir William Ramsay's suggestion is right that the certain Macedonian was Luke, we should have to decide that it was a dream. But at Corinth when " the Lord spoke to Paul in the night by a vision," [5]—at Jerusalem when, " on the night following, the Lord stood by him and said Be of good cheer, Paul," [6]—on the ship when " there stood by me this night the angel of God," [7] we may debate as we please between dream and other forms of vision, and reach no certainty. In such cases the psychologists tell us that it is extremely hard to be definite either way. Had the man, who saw, an instantaneous dream in the moment of waking ? It is there that time fails to be regular—it is so short and

[1] B. W. Bacon, *Paul*, p. 41.   [2] Phil. i. 23.   [3] See pp. 64-66.
[4] Acts xvi. 9.   [5] Acts xviii. 9.   [6] Acts xxiii. 11.   [7] Acts xxvii. 23.

seems so long. When Paul stood before Nero and " the Lord stood by me and put strength into me," [1] it is obvious that it was not night and that he was not asleep ; but it is not clear that he means a visible appearance of the Lord to him. On the other hand, his story of being caught up to the third heaven and hearing unutterable words,[2] coincides with the language of mystical vision, and turns the scale (with Damascus) decisively in favour of Paul also being of the company of the mystics.[3]

When he says that he " spoke with tongues " [4]—if he really means, as appears, exactly the same phaenomenon that occurred at Corinth, and is not saying (what was certainly true) that he spoke more languages than his converts who had only Greek—if we are to take it that he was himself liable to the disturbance that produces " glossolaly "—his confession is to a modern reader perplexing and uncomfortable. But his judgment flashes out in the next sentence, and whether he speaks with these unintelligible " tongues " or not, he dismisses the gift (or affliction, as we should be more apt to say) to the irrelevance which belongs to it. Tongues will cease, he says himself ; [5] and he knows with a glorious certainty what really matters. Whatever signs he may have of abnormal psychology, in judgment, clarity and sanity he is the peer of any man. As we saw in the story of the Damascus gate, whatever occurred, Paul brought it to the test of as sound judgment and as searching experiment as a whole life of verification allowed.

At this point we pass naturally to consider his habits of mind and thought. His mind, says Professor

---

[1] 2 Tim. iv. 17.   [2] 2 Cor. xii. 2.

[3] Cf. Rufus M. Jones, *Studies in Mystical Religion*, pp. 11, 12 ; " Paul was psychologically possessed of a constitution plainly adapted to experiences of an unusual sort ; . . . but . . . set slight value on extraordinary phaenomena."

[4] 1 Cor. xiv. 18.   [5] 1 Cor. xiii. 8.

Gilbert Murray,[1] " for all its vehement mysticism
and enthusiasm, has something of that clean antiseptic
quality of Minucius and the writer to Diognetus."
In an earlier chapter we noted his luminous truth-
fulness of thought ; he is as sincere and truthful with
himself, as insistent on truth in others, as the best Greek
thinkers or the Hebrew prophets. No one can read
the epistle to the Galatians with any intelligence and
fail to realize his force of character, his independence
of mind ; he did not borrow or adopt his religion from
anybody, the " pillars " really did not help him, and
he had never asked them to confirm what he knew
directly from the Lord. If he is independent of men's
judgments, he is equally plain about independence of
men's purses ; he plied a handicraft in Greece when it
was necessary, and he would again.[2] On the ship in
the storm he naturally gravitates to the front, unper-
turbed and imperturbable ; in the fair weather the
centurion might listen to the master mariner ; in the
storm Paul was in the ascendant. So it always is with
him ; if the situation is difficult, his inspired common
sense carries him straight to the real issue. At Antioch
he brings Peter abruptly face to face with the facts ;
he forces the Galatians to look squarely at the real
issue. If we are to be told to-day that he belongs
to the same sort as the adherents of the mystery
religions, it is surely said by people who have no
sense of character. If answer is needed, it lies in
his type of mind ; he is much more like Plato than
the Orphics, and intellectually not in the category
of *mystai* and initiates, the devotees of sensation
and emotion. Paul is a thinker and they were not

---

[1] *Four Stages*, p. 145. If the reader wishes to know a little more of
Minucius, he was a Latin apologist of the second or third century, a
Christian with a beautiful Latin style ; and the unnamed writer to
Diognetus was a Greek, whose little masterpiece is printed with the
Apostolic Fathers and outshines them.

[2] Acts xviii. 3 ; xx. 34 ; cf. 2 Cor. xi. 8-10.

thinkers; he is original, and they, however pious, were mere parrots.

The ancients, and not they alone, have had a way of attributing a man's thoughts to something not himself. It was a famous suggestion of Plato's—whether he was playful, ironical or serious, or all three when he suggested it—that poetry comes more or less from without to a man, it is not a matter of his thinking it out; a man who " approaches the gates of the Muses without madness," but sober and in possession of his own mind, will not produce great poetry; he will be eclipsed by the " madman," who from without has received another mind.[1] Philo, an older contemporary of Paul's, records the same sort of experience that most men have who write; sometimes he " saw clearly " what to say, but " the womb of his soul was closed "; at other times he " came empty and was suddenly full, as thoughts were imperceptibly sowed and snowed upon him from above," and, as if divinely possessed and " corybantic," he wrote, forgetful of self and place and of writing itself.[2] It is the vivid thought that startles a man, which he thus attributes to another mind. It goes with a certain quickness and sureness of perception, an almost painfully intense realization of the thing in the very colours and movements of life. As John Bunyan tells us, again and again, a man would rather be without the gift, for evil may come that way as well as good. In *Grace Abounding* he describes how his thoughts did " roar and bellow within me like masterless hell-hounds." When he describes Christian in the Valley of the Shadow of Death, he italicizes the whole passage, which he also emphasizes by special notice; fiends, he says, put blasphemies into the pilgrim's mind, which he thought were his own, and " was more put to it " than in any former trouble " even to think that he should now

[1] Plato, *Phaedrus*, 245A; *Ion*, 533-534.
[2] Philo, *de migratione Abrahami*, 7 (441M).

blaspheme him, that he loved so much before : yet
if he could have helped it, he would not have done it,"
but he did not " know from whence those blasphemies
came."
Paul tells us no such story, yet there are hints. In
one place we read of a warfare not against flesh and
blood ; he is very explicit indeed on the great war
between Christ and the powers of evil, in which he is
enlisted. Hence, when he tells the Corinthians that
his warfare is not after the flesh but mighty in God for
the reduction of strongholds, and then adds that it is
the reduction of reflexions (λογισμούς) and of every
high thing that lifts itself or is set up against the
knowledge of God, and " bringing into captivity every
thought to the obedience of Christ," [1] to those who
know something of current beliefs as to the daemon
world the passage is at once suggestive. One of his
most beautiful benedictions loses some of its value
in our Authorized Version through the translators
missing the point that he speaks of thoughts : " the
peace of God, that passeth all understanding (which
is beyond every mind), shall keep your hearts and your
thoughts in Christ Jesus." [2] Paul probably felt that his
own thoughts needed such guarding. A man who has
visions from one side will have them from the other ;
if he has guidance, if he is " told what thou must do,"
he is open to misleading too ; there will be " messengers
of Satan." [3] In a swift mind like his, the readiest
explanation of some thoughts will be the coming of
those " messengers " ; pray God, then, to keep and
control your thoughts, he says. We have to remember how he was criticized for that impulsiveness of his, to remember his quick depressions and
exaltations.
With his swiftness of mind we must connect the
sudden tangents of thought, which confuse his style
to the perplexity of the logical but illuminate the

[1] 2 Cor. x. 3-5.   [2] Phil. iv. 7.   [3] 2 Cor. xii. 7.

reader who will let him do as he pleases—always the safest way when one is reading the work of genius. For example, in a passage already noticed,[1] has he been careless of his friends in Corinth ? a Yes and No man, to one thing constant never ? As God is faithful, his word to them has not been Yes and No ; the Son of God, Christ Jesus, preached among you by us, was not Yes and No, but Yes was in him. And Paul swings off into the magnificent conception that in Christ is the Yes of all God's promises and by him comes mankind's Amen to God's work. None of it is quite relevant to the change of plan which kept him away from Corinth, but it is splendid. If the Corinthians will not forgive him now, everybody else will, and will be glad that he failed to appear at Corinth if apology can produce such illuminative irrelevance. Again, at the end of the letter to the Galatians,[2] the amanuensis lays down the pen—there must have been easier people to take down in shorthand than Paul ; and if it had to be done in longhand, the stylus would be laid down with some feeling of relief. " I, Tertius, who wrote this Epistle " [3] must have needed the pen of a ready writer. Paul picks up the pen, and plays with " the large fair hand " he writes or is going to write—and all of a sudden flashes off into some people's idea of " a large fair show " and how pleased they are with it— and then off again into one of his own most famous sentences, which forty words back, he had no vestige of an idea of writing. " God forbid that I should glory, save in the Cross of our Lord Jesus Christ, by which the world is crucified to me, and I to the world." Celsus in the second century says scornfully that every Christian of every school quoted that text. And it was written, one might say, by sheer accident ! If the Tertius of the day had held on a little longer, we should not have had it. A similar sudden tangent, about godliness after all being

[1] 2 Cor. i. 17 f.   [2] Gal. vi. 11-14.   [3] Rom. xvi. 22.

gain,[1] is one of several stylistic marks which vindicate
at least parts of the epistles to Timothy as Pauline.
Impressionable, intuitive, amazingly quick of mind,
open to doubts and tears and fears, up and down,[2]
pressed beyond belief and beyond life, and gloriously
delivered by a Saviour, whom he realizes as (one is
tempted to say) no one else ever has done—little
wonder the man was electric ; that Jews and Judaizers
hated one so swift and keen ; that matter-of-fact
Christians could never make out where he was going
or what he would do next, that Aristarchus, Epaphroditus, Luke and the rest " clave to him " through
thick and thin ; that the Church kept the letters
and got them by heart, even if it had to wait nearly
fifteen centuries for a qualified interpreter of them.

Of that interpreter he reminds us ; he and Luther
have the same mixture of tenderness and fierceness.[3]
A nature open to many appeals, swift and intense, will
be quick to understand others—quick sometimes to
misunderstand. Paul is a master of courtesy because
he does not cultivate a manner ; he likes men and
tries to put himself at their various points of view—
he will be " servant of all," a Jew to Jews, under the
law and free of the law, " weak " (which must have
been a struggle), " all things to all men to win them," [4]
for the gospel's sake. So he says, and he means it ;
but even apart from the gospel, one can guess that he
must have had charm. He has great powers of tenderness ; he thinks of himself as mother and nurse of his
friends, whose Christian life is young.[5] On the other
hand, as we saw at the beginning, he has no tolerance
for anything like falsity or injustice ; he " delivers to

---

[1] 1 Tim. vi. 6 ; the Authorized Version gets verse 5 backwards
forwards.

[2] 2 Cor. iv. 9, and passage.

[3] Deissmann, *Paul*, p. 70. A short study of Luther's letters will
confirm this.

[4] 1 Cor. ix. 19-23.   [5] Gal. iv. 19 ; 1 Thess. ii. 7.

Satan " ; [1] his enemies are " dogs " and " whited
walls." [2] He could wish them more mutilated than
they mutilate themselves, he says,[3] but we do not
believe it quite as literally as we do his words of friendship. He would relent when the fight was over, and
forgive the man and make a friend of him at the first
chance. Probably Peter and Barnabas and Mark
would all endorse this, after experience of him both
ways. It would be fair to say that every explosion,
of which we have a record, is brought about, not by
personal wrong done to himself, but by interference
with the work and liberty of Christ—a sort of reverse
of his intensity of devotion.

Like many men of genius he sees things in snatches ;
everything is lit up by a lightning flash, and one point
after another is gained, never to be lost, and the rest
have to follow or be left ; what he sees in the flash is
all-important. Such, or something like it, was in part
his intellectual growth, with hours of reasoning and
hard thinking between. When Denney wrote that
there was no time between one date and another
for a certain development in Paul, it was a lapse in the
critic. He would have admitted surely, if challenged,
that such considerations of time may be relevant to
ordinary men but are negligible with men of genius,
whose rate of development is sometimes staggering
to those who watch them. The story of John Keats
shows a development for which it might very well
have been said there was no time.

Swift thinkers have not always the balance of Paul.
His basis is experience of Christ, and whatever
thoughts flash into his head are soon brought (as we
saw) to the obedience of Christ. That service is indeed
a school of sanity. If the description of his development and character already given is true, Paul from the
first was amenable to fact ; his Jewish theories are

---

[1] 1 Cor. v. 3-5 ; 1 Tim. i. 20.
[2] Phil. iii. 2 ; Acts xxiii. 3.   [3] Gal. v. 12.

checked by the facts of Stephen's spirit and death and vision. We have seen how he talks cold, sober, Christian sense about speech with tongues, and how men complained that he did not live enough in an atmosphere of miracle. He preferred preaching Christ to people in a way that would make them think about Christ to astonishing them with Paul's gifts, natural or supernatural. There is discipline in his life ; he is initiated into the art of doing without ; into the harder art of tolerating fools and adapting himself to them. A life so hard, so full of difficulty, privation, prison and danger, must have kept any man in touch with the actual ; the risk with many men would have been of succumbing to it. But Paul is the common-sense idealist.

One point is surely worthy of notice—an omission. In all his recommendations of Christian virtues and graces to his friends, whose minds had been previously directed to Jewish or Stoic greatness, he never seems to mention courage. He is frank enough in owning to fears and discouragements of his own, and a sensitive nature is to be read in all he says or writes. The nearest he comes to mentioning courage is in writing to Timothy ; let no man despise Timothy's youth,[1] he urges ; Timothy should be " strong " ; [2] and he adds (if the reading is reliable) that " God has not given to us the spirit of cowardice (δειλίας), but of power and love and discipline." [3] If he had not said *to us*, the sentence must have hit horribly hard ; if it were not for the kind words that come with it, it would almost be cruel, as it stands. Once again, the personal touch is so strong in these two epistles, that it is very difficult to believe that " the hand of Paul " [4] is not in them. If Paul, however, as a rule does not recommend courage, two lines of explanation seem obvious. A man of his record, who

[1] 1 Tim. iv. 12.   [2] 2 Tim. ii. 1.
[3] 2 Tim. i. 7.   [4] Col. iv. 18.

N

is quite open in owning to fear, has obviously a great
deal more courage than he realizes; he simply does
not think about courage; it does not occur to him,
because it is instinctive. Or, if he does realize that
other people lack it, he sees at once that it is of no use
to talk to them about it; and he emphasizes faith.
If they once get their minds well set upon Christ,
they will forget their fears, and Christ will do for them
what they never would have achieved by courage.

After so much said of Paul's mind, a study of his
style may involve us in some repetition; here, if
anywhere, the style is the man. "The great style
(ὕψος)," says Longinus, "is the echo of a great soul." [1]
But we have to realize that he is one of the great
writers of Greece, and of the world. "Paul," said
Erasmus, "thunders and lightens and speaks sheer
flame." Luther [2] noted that "his peculiar phrase
or kind of speech is not after the manner of men,
but divine and heavenly, nor used of the Evangelists
. . . a very strange and a monstrous way of speaking,
which phrase is sweet and comfortable." Norden,
from quite another point of view, says that in Paul
"the language of the heart is born again. Since the
hymn of Cleanthes nothing so intimate, nothing so
splendid, had been written as Paul's hymn to love";
"those two hymns of love to God and love to men
(Rom. viii. 31; 1 Cor. xiii.) have given again to the
Greek language what had been lost for centuries, the
intimacy and the enthusiasm of the mystic, inspired
by his union with God. . . . How this language of
the heart must have rung into the souls of men
accustomed to the silly volubility of the sophists!
In these passages the diction of the Apostle rises to
the height of Plato's in the *Phaedrus*." [3] Norden owns

---

[1] Longinus, *On the Sublime*, 9, 2.

[2] *Commentary on Galatians*, ii. 20; fol. 83a, in the sixteenth-century
English translation.

[3] Norden, *Kunstprosa*, ii. pp. 459, 599.

honestly, as we must, that Paul is hard to understand, and he finds a Hebrew element in his Greek. That is not hard to discover.[1] Other men have caught in his style the ring of other languages, the popular, the legal,[2] the tones of the mysteries[3] and of magic[4]; but few have ever accused him of being literary. He owes more, certainly, to the Scriptures in Greek—the habit of making clauses balance and ring back, the parallelisms, the easy interchange of prose form and metre form, the massing of words without copula, familiar in Hebrew writing. But nearly everybody agrees that Paul's style is his own, the living echo of his own mind. Paul is master of the common Greek dialect spoken over the Eastern Mediterranean, a spoken and not a literary language; and in his pages it is often so near speech as to be difficult reading. He has a great range of living allusion and metaphor, not always easy for us to grasp; his words and terms come to him from the lips of men in street and market, and come back to them and to us charged with a new life and personality. The flaming individuality of his mind is all through his style, in the tangent, in the hyperbole (his own word). It may be asked whether it is only a trick of style when he piles up his superlatives—when to *perisseuo* (to abound) he prefixes *hyper-* and makes verb and adverb of the compound *hyperperisseuo*, *hyperperissôs* (to more-than-abound), and when he goes further still in heightening and says *hyperekperissou* or *hyperekperissôs*, or both. We must not digress here to his *hyper-* words, which in their way are as significant as those he makes with *syn-*; but we have to face the

---

[1] Cf. Wendland, *hell. röm. Kultur*, pp. 354-355.
[2] Cf. βεβαίωσις, ἀπολύτρωσις (seven times), χειρόγραφον, ὀφείλη, διαθήκη, and his metaphors from debt, servitude and ransom. Cf. Deissmann, *Bible Studies*, p. 107.
[3] Reitzenstein, *Hell. Myst. Relig.*, p. 51.
[4] Deissmann, *Light from the Ancient East*, p. 303.

question whether he belongs to the order of those who say " awfully " when they mean " rather." Froude said something of the kind about Bunyan ; he did not think Bunyan at all such a sinner as Bunyan did himself ; which was right ? It depends in the case of both Paul and Bunyan, whether we, who judge them, are commonplace in our outlooks or see with genius. Genius sees things in colour, where the average man sees drab ; and that is a point to remember in estimating Paul's mind from his style. The greater critics never hint a doubt of that style's utter fidelity to his mind.

We have seen how swiftly he thinks, with what tangents he sweeps from idea to idea ; and if the critic speaks of anacoluthon in the style, we shall be prepared for it. Modern writers have discovered that the employment of a stenographer may loosen style and obscure connexions of thought. Paul *talked* his letters ; if he ever wrote one of them from beginning to end with his own hand, he never wrote anything to equal the Epistle to the Hebrews for carefully thought-out design, however much we set him above the writer of that epistle in mind and outlook. He *talks* ; he yields to the inspiration of the moment ; and if his similes and allegories miss fire now and then in print, he made them effectual viva voce. Like good talkers, he indicates an idea and leaves you to develop it—and to get it fitted into what he said last and what he is going to say next—if he quite knows so long ahead. His arguments on paper, like some of those in the early chapters of Romans, are not equal to passages where he does not argue at all. In the epistle to the Galatians, his argument is a series of explosions, and every one of them tells ; it is all cumulative. It is not easy reading ; it is not strictly art ; but it is all personality. Whatever his argument is, powerful as it is in Galatians, it is not that that you chiefly remember when he is done You have been with a man of genius ; you have swept with him from peak to peak, vision to vision ; you have tried to keep pace with his moods and his subjects, indicated in the amazing vocabulary, the striking metaphors, the compressed word-pictures, popular phrase, Septuagint echo, terms of his own (which he does not always use to mean the same thing—a bad habit which common people often regret in men of genius) ; you have consorted with a man of elemental force, revelled in all the colours of God with him, mixed them (no doubt), wondered why he was not a poet and why he was so much more than any poet ; and all the time you have been growing to love more and more the greatest human being that ever followed Jesus Christ and had Christ living in him. You and he together have been adding to your experience of Christ in every tangled sentence and involved paragraph ; and you end (as Paul would have wished you to end) with the feeling that Christ is all and in all.

CHAPTER IX

THE LOVE OF CHRIST

PROBABLY most readers of the New Testament take it in the same way and read its books in the order that gives them the sequence of events—a natural and reasonable procedure. If there had been no historical Jesus, there would, in spite of certain modern theorists, have been no church. If there had been no church, Paul's Epistles would hardly have been written, and there is a certain logic in reading them after the story of his life as given by Luke. But by taking the New Testament as a whole, and in this order, the student is apt to miss at least one important feature of the story. When we realize that Paul's letters are the earliest of our documents, and that, whatever stories of Jesus were extant in speech or even in writing, none of our four Gospels was written at the time of Paul's conversion, and that Acts is probably later than any of the Synoptic Gospels and rests on authorities (as we have seen) of very different value, it becomes clear that the hardest of all periods in Church History for the historian to recover and to understand is that short interval, variously estimated between one year and six years, that lies between the Crucifixion and Paul's journey to Damascus.[1]

Every man is apt to translate the decisive moment of his experience in the light of what he subsequently sees it to have meant ; it carried such and such consequences with it undoubtedly ; then it *was* what it produced. Perhaps ; but the consequences may be in part due to conspiring causes. The peril of auto-

[1] See Chap. III., pp. 49-51.

biography is the throwing back of the developed view to a point when it was not developed, though likely to be. We have seen already—or tried to see—what it was in the early church that provoked the antagonism of Sadducee and Pharisee, and of the young Paul. We had to depend on indications, we had to use the known outlooks of schools and the later developments of Paul's mind. We concluded that he saw what the effects of the Christian movement would be, and more quickly and clearly than some of its adherents, since, for one thing, he had a quicker and a clearer mind.

But when we come to the very centre of our story, and ask, not what an opponent foresaw would be the outcome of Christian teaching about Jesus, but what that teaching actually was in the short interim under our survey, it is extremely difficult to answer. No one with any historical instinct would suggest abruptly attributing to that primitive community any body of ideas that we find at any stage of Paul's development, as shown by his epistles ; not even the earliest presentment of Christ by Paul in writing can be quite safely referred back. Paul brought to Christ a trained mind and a quick intellect—gifts apparently not to be found in the earliest group of disciples. On the other hand his predecessors had known the actual Jesus, had spoken with him and lived with him in intimacy. Neither could be expected to take over the outlook of the other.

If we ask, then, What was the Christology of those early disciples in the interim ? the answer may be another question, Had they a Christology at all ? Peter, as the Gospels show us, had recognized Jesus as the Messiah.[1] Presumably the Crucifixion shattered that conception, which in any case must have been vague. Then came the Resurrection ;—but what exactly happened, which of the accounts as given in our records, written at various later dates, or what

[1] Mark viii. 27-33.

combination of data given in those accounts, we are
to prefer—these are difficult questions and must not
now detain us. One thing is certain from the story
of the quarrel between the early church and Paul—
the disciples believed that their Master lived, though
not precisely in the form or on the terms of common
human life. It was possible once more to believe
him the Messiah ; but a great deal of re-thinking was
involved. That the little group did not consciously
do much re-thinking, and perhaps were not qualified
to do it, is reasonably probable. The Christology of
the epistle attributed to James is not conspicuous ;
the writer may be tacitly presuming more than he
writes, but his line of exhortation does not suggest a
mind of broad outlooks or deep reflection. How far
that epistle can be taken to represent the views current
among the disciples in the interim days, it is hard to
say. One may safely guess a more living enthusiasm
and a more infectious devotion to Jesus among them.
For nobody could have wished to persecute an author
so drab of mind as James ; his mild rhetoric and
humdrum good sense could have meant no danger
to any established institution ; he was no magnet to
draw men to a rising faith. We must look elsewhere.

Our two best fixed points are Stephen's speech and
Paul's avowal to the Galatians [1] that he " neither
received his gospel of man, neither was taught it, but
by the revelation of Jesus Christ." Stephen's speech,
as we have it, appears to be recast by Luke from
reminiscences of what Paul had told him of it, but it
was directed to clearing up the difficulty of Jesus'
sufferings ; so far from invalidating the possibility of
Jesus being the Messiah, they at least brought him
into line with all the great exponents and repre-
sentatives of God ; all the prophets had suffered and
been rejected. Suffering was not inconsistent with
Jesus being the Messiah. The vision of the dying

[1] Gal. i. 12.

Stephen weighed with Paul, as we saw, as possible
evidence that the story of Jesus was not closed. A
suffering Messiah might not after all be a contradiction
in terms ; and possibly Jesus was still living, and—a
considerable addition—perhaps he was in fact raised
to the right hand of God.
But there are antecedent questions for the student of
Paul as for Paul himself. What was the Messiah to
be ? and what was he to do ? So far we have only
reached one point in Paul's earlier conception of a
Messiah, and that a negative one ; the Messiah, if
Messiah there was to be, could not be supposed to
suffer. We have further to recognize that even this
negative result is reached by inference. It has to be
proved—and it will be difficult to prove—that Paul,
before his contact with the Christian movement,
thought much about the Messiah at all.

For us the idea of a Messiah is embedded in the
eventual Christian teaching ; it was almost a postulate
with those second century Apologists, who used the
Old Testament, its great age and its prophetic character,
as an argument, its texts and passages, taken often in
dreadful detachment, as an armoury. At the same
time it must be recognized that for us, as for Greeks
after 70 or 80 B.C., the name Christ is practically
a synonym for Jesus and hardly connotes anything
more. In fact, apart from Apology, the idea of a Christ
or Messiah is merged in Jesus ; or, in plainer words
and blunter, Christendom on the whole, like that old
Greek world, is not greatly interested in a Jewish
Messiah. Historical research has left it an open
question how far Judaism itself was interested in a
Messiah.

That a number of Apocalyptic writers dealt with a
future Messiah is obvious ; whether they took up the
idea from the common people or launched it among
them, it is probably impossible to say. That the idea
was widely current among the Jewish people, is not

established ; that in certain circles it was familiar is
plain from the Apocalyptic books and from Peter's
famous avowal at Caesarea Philippi.[1] What Peter, or
any other ordinary person, associated with the idea,
we hardly know, beyond the probable restoration of
the Kingdom to Israel—which Luke says was one of
the problems addressed to the risen Jesus and not
answered [2]—or the establishment of some kingdom,
perhaps Davidic. For the Kingdom was the prime
interest with the Apocalyptic writers and apparently
with the common people ; the Messiah " only appears
incidentally, in connection with the advent of the
Kingdom." [3] The writers of Apocalyptic were agreed
neither as to his origin and character, whether he were
merely human, almost divine, or pre-existent, nor as
to what exactly he was to do ; and some of them left
him out altogether.[4] The writers of *The Assumption
of Moses*, of *Wisdom*, of *Fourth Maccabees*, *Fourth
Ezra*, and *Second Baruch* ignore him. So did Philo.
A work now embodied in *Enoch* (chapters xxxvi.-lxxi.)
gives the highest pre-Christian account of the Messiah
—if the estimated date between 94 and 64 b.c. is
correct. This writer pictures the Messiah as the
Righteous One, the Elect, and the Son of Man, possessor
of Righteousness and of sevenfold gifts, of Wisdom
and of the Spirit of power ; he is the Revealer of all
things, and he will recall to life the dead who are in
Sheol and hell ; he is the Judge and slays sinners and
unrighteousness with the word of his mouth. There
is nothing about him to make men love him ; he is
no figure like the Suffering Servant. He belongs in
any case to no higher circle than that of the angels, and

---

[1] The attention of the crowds to Jesus makes nothing clear ; all
kinds of motives might outweigh *their* Messianic ideas, if they had
any—political hopes, love of novelty, all sorts of things.

[2] Acts i. 6, 7 ; Mark viii. 30, 31, show plainly how far removed
was the view of Jesus from the common idea of the Messiah.

[3] E. F. Scott, *The Kingdom and the Messiah*, p. 41.

[4] W. Morgan, *Relig. and Theol. of Paul*, p. 9.

Jewish Apocalyptic as a consequence knows nothing of worship addressed to him.[1] Canon R. H. Charles cites some twenty passages from the Epistles to show Paul's acquaintance with the book of Enoch ; and he says outright that Paul, " as we know, borrowed both phraseology and ideas from many quarters ; from the Greek poets ; from the apocryphal writings, as the Book of Wisdom ; from the lost Revelation of Elias—1 Cor. ii. 9, according to Origen, and Eph. v. 14, according to Epiphanius. We shall find that he was well acquainted with and used 1 Enoch." [2] The proof of acquaintance however depends on the quality as well as on the quantity of the parallels, and many of Canon Charles' parallels are frankly very slight. On evidence as good it is suggested that Horace, in his second *Epode*, borrowed from Virgil's *Culex*, and that Virgil returned the compliment and borrowed from the second *Epode* when he wrote his first *Georgic*—all on the strength of common features of country life described.[3] That Paul had the same general outlooks as the writers of the Apocalyptic books [4]—their pessimism as to the world, their conceptions of a daemon war with God, of another world and a great Assize—is another thing. Even if Canon Charles' parallels are real, it is not proved that Paul, before his conversion, was supremely or at all interested in a Messiah. In spite of Enoch, there were still very commonplace elements in the Messianic hope. When we are told that the transformation of the Messiah to a heavenly being, created before the sun and stars and kept by God till the fated hour, a being who shall descend again on the clouds and judge the nations,

---

[1] William Morgan, *Paul*, pp. 46, 47 ; E. F. Scott, *Kingdom and Messiah*, p. 44. Contrast Heb. i. 4.

[2] R. H. Charles, *Book of Enoch* (1 *Enoch*), p. xcix.

[3] Tenney Frank, *Vergil, A Biography*, p. 142. Prof. Frank (pp. 56, 136) thinks Philodemus of Gadara knew about the Messiah, and may have told Virgil.

[4] See Chap. X., p. 232.

was laid hold of by Christians at an early stage, we can agree. Perhaps already in the interim they were preaching of Jesus as " exalted to the Messianic throne, and of his speedy descent to judge the world and bring in the Kingdom " ; and we can understand Paul resenting it. But that does not imply that he had himself any very definite ideas about the Messiah, or about any Messiah. It all depends on evidence as to himself, as to his group, as to Gamaliel, none of which is available. We are driven back to the issues, already discussed, which disturbed him and drove him into conflict with the primitive Church. Quite conceivably it was this conflict which first made him think seriously of the Messiah at all. A man may be long familiar with an idea—aware, at least, of the attention paid to it by others—before he really looks into it himself.

Paul at all events did not proceed from books to a recognition of Jesus—by assessing his claims to a Messiahship, the marks of which Paul had previously determined. Books, of course, formed a part of his training, directly and indirectly, consciously and unconsciously—the Old Testament and Isaiah far more than any Apocalyptic books known to us. But such ideas as he had so acquired on Israel, Israel's future, the Messiah and God's purposes, were challenged, as we saw, by the new outlooks suggested by the Christian movement, and shattered at last by the shocks of Stephen's speech, Stephen's death and vision, and his own experience outside Damascus. There he was definitely convinced of the continuity of the crucified Jesus with the glorified Jesus—they were one and the same. Whatever he had got from books or men about the Messiah, whatever he now began to find had been said of Messiah or of Suffering Servant, gained a new interest and was submitted to a fresh examination ; it was tested by the vision at Damascus and in the light of the experience that followed it. Some of the predictions or hopes relating to the

Messiah obviously went overboard ; some, like his Davidic descent,[1] were retained—they were quite neutral matters now and of little or no consequence, but not obviously wrong. Other conceptions—and here might be classed those of Enoch, if we were really sure that Paul knew them—were of more value. But it was the experience that guaranteed the forecast ; Paul found out for himself and did not depend on Enoch ; Jesus was his authority. He never alludes to the patriarch or to his book,[2] so far was he from quoting him as he does the Old Testament and the book of Wisdom ; and his picture of Jesus goes far beyond Enoch's account of the Messiah ; morally it is nearer the Suffering Servant.

If a modern reader, who dabbles in Psychology, as we all do nowadays, asks what was the source of the vision, or what gave the suggestion that led to it, the answer is clear and certain. Paul's mind had been concentrated on the historical Jesus, whom his followers declared to have risen from the dead. If it is remarked that in his letters Paul says little of historical events in the earthly life of Jesus, and dwells upon the cross and the resurrection and on his continued life and helpfulness, the inference is not that he was unaware of that earthly life or that he dismissed it as trivial. His whole conversion centred on the struggle to determine who that crucified Galilean really was. Everything turned, not on a proposition taken from a book, but on the valuing of a historical person. The actual Jesus was the precipitating cause of the vision— whether we say that the risen Lord of his own volition showed himself to Paul, or whether we put it that Paul's mind, working upon real and supposed facts,

---

[1] I find it hard to assert on the authority of such passages as Mark x. 47, xi. 10, that Jesus definitely accepted the ascription of the title Son of David, in view of Mark xii. 35-37.

[2] It takes a brilliant and very questionable piece of emendation to get Enoch into 1 Peter iii. 19.   Jude 14 is a definite allusion.

and working with desperate energy, got them distinguished finally in one tremendous moment and knew henceforth the great certainty.

There followed, as we have seen, the relation of his new knowledge to the rest of his knowledge. We may certainly say that the struggle which a modern man with some knowledge of the mind and its habits might have in determining the value of the vision, Paul would not have—or not in the same way. Satan could transform himself into an angel of light, he held ; [1] and the question rises, Was there no dark hour in the early months or years after his illumination, when he asked himself if he had been deceived by Satan ? If it was possible to be " disobedient to the heavenly vision," [2] was it not possible to be sceptical of it ? Paul is not ignorant of Satan's devices,[3] and we can believe that he could have listened to Bunyan's story in *Grace Abounding* and the *Pilgrim's Progress* with more sympathy and more knowledge than some critics. How should we assume that supreme gifts exempt a man from supreme temptation, when in our common experience the enlarging circle of light involves an enlarging series of points of contact with darkness ? How was Paul to *know* ? It is easy to say, There was the vision ; but visions may grow dim with years. What was to guarantee this vision ? So far our answer has been that the vision was tested in obedience. Whatever differences in phrase and in conceptions of the spiritual world, whatever divergence as to purpose and design in the Universe and the ways of discovering these, may divide the ancient and the modern, we have to remember that in these we have only the tools which the mind uses, the modes in which it works. The fundamental fact is that then as now the mind did work, and was stimulated to work by evidence, and that, whatever changes the centuries have brought, life and its reactions on the soul are much the same.

[1] 2 Cor. xi. 14. [2] Acts xxvi. 19. [3] 2 Cor. ii. 11.

To the modern much that we find in ancient books and ancient ways is bizarre and odd ; but when we meet a real mind at work, we are more impressed by the kinship than by our own progress. Barnabas and Cyprian are old and odd ; Plato and Pericles are amazingly modern ; mind belongs to every age.

When we analyse the content of Paul's conception of Christ—or, let us say now, of Jesus Christ—what we find may be grouped, roughly and with some over-lapping, in two classes, to which a third one, of deduc-tions, must be added. We have, first, a great mass of ideas as to Christ's pre-existence and his relation to the Father, where, as we should indeed expect, there is a certain degree of indistinctness. Paul rests here on the teaching of his people, on Wisdom-literature, on Apocalyptic, on inference. It is hard to make one fabric of all he gives us—partly, no doubt, because he develops his views, as we saw, with years, and does so with the unevenness of so swift a genius ; partly because, as Matthew Arnold pointed out and Clement of Alexandria suggested long before him,[1] Paul has not and cannot have exact knowledge of what he speaks, and has further no vocabulary at all adequate to what he wants to say ; he is " throwing out " suggestions to bring us to some divination of the reality, which, like Moses in the old story,[2] he sees in part, through a glass and darkly.[3] In the second place, we have another kind of testimony, the record of a life of prayer, and endeavour, and (Paul would say) answer to prayer—a story of personal dealings with Christ and of experience. To these we must add the influence of all Jesus said and did to transform the conception of the Messiah.[4] In the third place, we have Paul's accounts, or explanations, of what he believed and what he had experienced ; and these are couched in very various language. In one place he will tell us

[1] See p. 90.   [2] Exod. xxxiii. 17-23.
[3] 1 Cor. xiii. 9, 12.   [4] Mark viii. 30, 31.

that God appointed Jesus as a ἱλαστήριον and he steps outside our language and our ideas. The term comes twice in the New Testament,[1] and where Paul used it the English translators rendered it " a propitiation," while in Hebrews they translated it " the mercyseat." When, on the other hand, Paul tells us that " God was in Christ, reconciling the world unto himself," he makes a much more intelligible and universal proposition, and therefore comes a great deal closer to our hearts. Even so his statement is not very easy to grasp, partly because of the difficulty of the subject, partly because of our habits of using unexamined preconceptions and of bringing to bear on the statement views of God which are compound and often not in all their factors Christian.

Paul started his Christian life at the Damascus Gate, and his Christian thinking starts at the same point ; he begins with Jesus in glory. We do not as a rule start there, with our canons of thought. Luther told his friends to " begin at the wounds of Christ," to " begin where Christ himself began," viz., the earthly life ; but Luther lived in another age. Paul made a different start from most of us, for the suffering of Jesus had been his difficulty ; it is hardly ours. When once that problem was solved for him, and, with it, the question of the resurrection, by the vision of Christ in glory, his course was clear—a course of amazing light and of transcendent happiness. He can never get away from the wonder of it—that such a Being should choose to suffer, and that Paul should be in his mind. " The Son of God loved me and gave himself for me," [2] is the keynote of all his thinking. Here Luther helps us, and a word or two from his commentary will bring out Paul's attitude ; the two men are together here. " Christ, therefore, in very deed is a lover of those which are in trouble and anguish, in sin and death, and such a lover as gave

---

[1] Rom. iii. 25 ; Heb. ix. 5.   [2] Gal. ii. 20.

himself for us. . . . Read, therefore, with great vehemency these words *Me* and *for me*. . . . For what are all things which are in heaven and earth in comparison with the Son of God, Christ Jesus, my Lord and Saviour, who loved me and gave himself for me ? " [1] Nothing could be more in the vein of Paul. We may add other similar utterances of Paul—he " gave himself for our sins " [2] (not the most immediately lucid of Paul's sentences as it stands) ; since the weakness of the Law was that it did not provide for the frailty of the flesh, " God sent his own Son in the likeness of sinful flesh " ; [3] he came, and " became poor," [4] " emptied himself," [5] and was crucified. " I determined not to know anything among you," writes Paul to the Corinthians, " save Jesus as Christ, and him crucified " [6]—which was indeed to begin with the wounds of Christ. Those wounds which had been Paul's trouble before have now become his confidence. It is easy to string together the passages to illustrate how central the incarnation and the death of the Heavenly Christ are for Paul ; but it is not so easy to realize what such thoughts mean, when they are to a man the supreme reality and the supreme motive. Something stands between most of us and the understanding of Paul. There is a warmth, a colour, a personality, in Paul's pictures of Christ, in striking contrast with the dim and doctrinaire figures of even the best Apocalyptist, and no less with the figure that we see across long and low planes of History, dimmed with the vagueness of our misty general conceptions.

Everything is vivid and personal with Paul here. " The love of Christ constraineth us," [7] he says ; " the

---

[1] Luther, *Commentary on Galatians, ad loc.*
[2] Gal. i. 4 ; the texts waver between ὑπὲρ and περὶ, and neither can be translated abruptly or without reference to other passages.
[3] Rom. viii. 3. [4] 2 Cor. viii. 9. [5] Phil. ii. 7-8.
[6] 1 Cor. ii. 2. [7] 2 Cor. v. 14.

Lord is near " ; [1] " Christ may dwell in your hearts " ; [2]
" to me to live is Christ " ; [3] " Christ liveth in me." [4]
In Christ he finds consolation, loving comfort, a
sympathetic spirit, kindness and compassion [5]—" for
Christ," as Luther comments, " is everlasting peace,
consolation, righteousness and life." The riches of
Christ are unsearchable,[6] his love passes knowledge ; [7]
—and there a great many of Paul's followers in all
ages have left the matter. Not so Paul. The modern
man of science, face to face with a Nature which
he may call unsearchable, and, in its intricacy of
wonder, beyond knowledge, does not leave things
alone ; he presses on to his goal, if it is always the
more remote the nearer he comes to it ; he is caught
up in his subject and must know the utmost of it ; he
is full of it and realizes how little he has grasped its
fullness ; he is absorbed in it and lives in it. This
is true ; and those who do not realize it do not
understand the appeal and fascination of science. The
reader, who knows the New Testament, will have seen
that I have been using the terms and phrases of Paul
himself in this description. Then let us picture a man
as intensely absorbed as the modern man of science,
but absorbed in the wonder and variety of Christ—
not in the detail of the laws of growth and reproduction and structure of things physical, but in the
infinite intricacies of God's relation through Christ
with all varieties of racial and individual experience ;
he contemplates not only experience but possibility ;
explores the complexity of man's nature and gifts,
and the unfathomed purposes and kindnesses of God,
the whole creation in birth-pangs ; and he conceives
that everything God has so far done of wonder and
goodness is to be eclipsed in fresh revelations. " O
the depth of the riches both of the wisdom and knowledge of God ! " [8] " Who hath known the mind of

[1] Phil. iv. 5.   [2] Eph. iii. 17.   [3] Phil. i. 21.   [4] Gal. ii. 20.
[5] Phil. ii. 1.   [6] Eph. iii. 8.   [7] Eph. iii. 19.   [8] Rom. xi. 33.

the Lord, that he may instruct him ? But we have
the mind of Christ." [1] The common run of Christian
people accept a faith once delivered to the saints—
and it becomes a formula. Paul came, as he tells us,
face to face with Jesus Christ, and gave the rest of his
life to exploring him, to enjoying the zest of search
and the joy of discovery. He lives that he may " win
Christ."

The secrets of personality are only to be made out
and known in one way—by identification and surrender.
In literature little can be done with criticism on
other lines. Readers must first devote themselves, as
Carlyle said, " to study honestly some earnest, deep-
minded, truth-loving Man, to work their way into his
manner of thought, till they see the world with his
eyes, feel as he felt and judge as he judged, neither
believing, nor denying, till they can in some measure
so feel and judge." [2] Among the qualities necessary
for real understanding Carlyle sets " lovingness " ; [3]
and it is here that most of us break down as critics in
literature and still more in religion. Another thinker,
nearer our own day, Edward Caird, Master of Balliol,
bids us begin by accepting what we read of the man
we would understand and reserve criticism till later.
Here again we break down as critics. But Paul loved
Christ and accepted him, and deliberately aimed at
identification with him. That Paul's chief interest in
life was to do what he was called and created to do
—to preach the Son of God among the heathen [4]—is
plain ; " Woe is me if I preach not the gospel ! " [5]
But he has another ambition, not obviously connected with evangelization, a more personal hope,
" that I may know him and the fellowship of his
sufferings " ; [6] that, if anything be wanting in the
shame and suffering that Jesus bore,[7] he may experi-

[1] 1 Cor. ii. 16.   [2] Essay on *Novalis*, p. 50.
[3] Essay on *Mirabeau*.   [4] Gal. i. 15, 16.
[5] 1 Cor. ix. 16.   [6] Phil. iii. 10.   [7] Col. i. 24.

ence that himself ; that he and his Saviour may know
and share between them the whole story of human
suffering. If he uses the phrase " in Christ " again
and again,[1] it does not exhaust his meaning to say that
Christ is, as it were, the air or element in which he
moves and has his being, true as that is. Quite apart
from Christ within him as a factor, there is the more
objective Christ with whom he can speak and act,
and with whom he can share all experiences.

We have seen how he makes compound nouns with
the preposition *syn-* to describe his relations with his
friends.[2] To describe his relations with Jesus he has a
similar series of verbs :—" I have been crucified with
Christ " ; [3] " becoming conformed with his death " ; [4]
" buried with Christ and risen with him " ; [5] " God
made us alive with Christ " ; [6] " if we have died
with Christ, we believe that we shall also live with
him " [7]—a pair of verbs that he uses elsewhere of his
friends ; [8] and finally the preposition three times in
one verse—" heirs of God and joint-heirs with Christ,
if so be that we suffer with him, that we may be also
glorified together," [9] and again in yet another place,
where, if Paul was not writing himself, his disciple
or amanuensis re-captured his phrase, " dead in sins
He quickened us with Christ, raised us with Christ,
seated us in heavenly places with Christ." [10]

Metaphor or mysticism, or whatever the term we
may prefer to apply to this remarkable series of words
and ideas, we may notice that the church to-day does
little with them or with the man whose experience
they represent. Perhaps, in an age of science and
analysis, language that is not prosaic and literal lacks
meaning for us. The idea of identification with

---

[1] It is stated, variously, to come 160 or 240 times in his Epistles.
[2] See Chap. VIII., p. 178.
[3] Gal. ii. 20.   [4] Phil. iii. 10 ; cf. Rom. viii. 29.
[5] Rom. vi. 4.   [6] Eph. ii. 5.   [7] Rom. vi. 8.
[8] 2 Cor. vii. 3.   [9] Rom. viii. 17.   [10] Eph. ii. 5-6.

Christ is carried further than we go. It could hardly be carried beyond this point, unless we are to use the language of mystery religions and of some extravagant experiments in Christian speech, and pretend that we can " be deified into Apathy and become Monadic." [1] " Deification " has not made itself at home in Christian thinking, though not for want of trial ; and it is to be remembered, when we are told of the influence of the mysteries on Paul, that he did not use this form of speech ; a Jew hardly could. Further, in all these utterances he never alludes to his baptism or to any sacrament.[2] But taking what he did say, and realizing how little it expresses the current attitude of Christians toward Christ to-day, we have to admit that Paul has an experience of Christ that lies outside our range, and that till we have some closer acquaintance with it it will hardly be becoming for us to pronounce on what he found in Christ.

Very often heathen mysticism left the initiate with no impulse to a higher morality—perhaps as often with a nature more apt than before, in its reaction, to be the prey of vague emotions and immoral desires. It is to be noticed that Paul's identification with Christ is always associated with ethics and duty, with thought and reason—" we have the mind of Christ " ; [3] " we are ambitious to be acceptable to him." [4] Everything must be " according to Christ," [5] and in these words he at once sets the standard of conduct higher than any other teacher in that world.

" According to Christ," on the lines of Christ—determined, no doubt, by the records of the earthly life of Jesus, though Paul does not in his letters linger over details or episodes of that life, but drives straight for the central fact—" the Son of God loved me and

---

[1] Clement of Alexandria, in an unhappy moment.

[2] He nowhere alludes to his baptism, to the Lord's Supper only in other connexions. Cf. p. 163.

[3] 1 Cor. ii. 16.   [4] 2 Cor. v. 9.   [5] Rom. xv. 5 ; Col. ii. 8.

gave himself for me." [1] A life according to a Christ
of those dimensions and of that kindness will be right.
The same conception gives the motive. " The love
of Christ constraineth us." [2] In human history the
great motives have been the high conception, the
great example, and the deep personal attachment,
and Paul's sentence covers all three. The constant
dwelling of the mind and the imagination upon the
new view of God—that wider range of sympathy than
any religious teacher had ever dared teach men to
expect from God ; the spectacle of the Son of God
becoming poor, emptying himself, taking the form of a
slave and dying a slave's death, paying " so costly and
dear a price " [3] for Paul's salvation ; and the perpetual
and recurrent sense of having been thought worth
so much, of having been loved so intensely and chosen
so individually—these are the factors that make Paul's
life.

Gratitude—passionate self-giving in thankfulness
and overpowering sense of obligation—is the " necessity
laid " [4] on Paul. He is " a debtor " [5] to Greek and
barbarian, to every man for whom Christ died ; and
whether the debt is best paid by preaching in Rome,[6]
or by being a vegetarian [7] or by undergoing everything
that came,[8] he will discharge the debt and in no wise
omit it. But it is more than debt, it is privilege—
" by the grace of God I am what I am " ; [9] " to me
who am less than the least of all saints is that grace (or
privilege) given that I should preach among the Gentiles
the unsearchable riches of Christ." [10] Grace is a theological term by now, almost a legal technicality. But
the historian at least will remember that Paul wrote

---

[1] Gal. ii. 20.   [2] 2 Cor. v. 14.
[3] Luther's words, cf. 1 Cor. vi. 20.   [4] 1 Cor. ix. 16.
[5] Rom. i. 14.   [6] Rom. i. 15.
[7] 1 Cor. viii. 13.   [8] 2 Cor. xi. 23-29.   [9] 1 Cor. xv. 10.
[10] Eph. iii. 8.; the super-superlative ἐλαχιστοτέρῳ is a phrase so
closely in keeping with Paul's *hyper* words that it suggests that the
amanuensis wrote at dictation at this point if he did not elsewhere.

before the great developments of Christian theology;
that Augustine borrows Paul's language (and in Latin),
not Paul the words of Augustine; that the use of the
word is an innovation of Paul's, and that in his speech
it is, as it was in ordinary Greek vocabulary, a peculiarly
personal word. Paul takes the word, a word of charm
in any case, and uses it as an epitome of all he saw in
Christ and received from Christ; and, in case we
make it technical, a phrase in Ephesians stands to
remind us to bring it back to Paul's meaning—" grace
on the scale of Christ's giving." [1]
Not only the motive and impulse, but the power to
live the life " according to Christ," Paul finds in
Christ. Christ is the power of God for men's salvation.[2] The life of the Stoic was one of constant effort
at self-repression and self-mastery, and the modern
Christian's is very often not much better. Paul, of
course, " presses to the mark," and speaks of " working
out our own salvation," of working more abundantly
than others; but these phrases, suggestive of effort,
do not give his central note, which is not Stoic, and
is quite unlike our modern tone. " Thanks (χάρις)
be unto God, who always causes us to triumph in
Christ and manifests the sweetness (fragrance) of the
knowledge of himself by our means everywhere"; [3]
" Thanks (χάρις) be unto God who gives us the
victory through our Lord Jesus Christ! . . . your
labour (κόπος, toil and hard work) is not in vain in
the Lord." [4] Paul goes beyond victory and uses
one of his *hyper* words in a famous and beautiful
passage: " Who shall separate us from the love of
Christ? shall tribulation? or distress? or persecution? or famine? or nakedness? or peril? or sword?
. . . Nay, in all *these* things we are more than conquerors"; and he goes on to survey things of more
moment than these—semi-spiritual beings included,

[1] Eph. iv. 7.   [2] I Cor. i. 24.
[3] 2 Cor. ii. 14; compare also 2 Cor. ix. 15.   [4] I Cor. xv. 57, 58.

life, death, angels, principalities, powers—and sweeps
them all aside ; not they can separate us from the love
of God in Christ.[1] With these passages we should
associate others where his mind runs on glory—Where
the spirit of the Lord is, there is liberty, and it means
our transformation from glory to glory ; [2] whom Christ
calls, he in the end glorifies ; [3] and he will at the last
not only glorify us but " change our humiliating body
to be like his glorious body "—a *parergon* as it were of
that transfiguring power, in virtue of which he " sub-
dues all things to himself." [4] So " finally, my brethren,
rejoice in the Lord " ; [5] " ye are Christ's, and Christ
is God's." [6] " The evidence of joy," asks Matthew
Arnold,[7] " who has rendered like Paul ? " " Let any
one," says Dr William Morgan, " compare the
benevolence of the gods of the Oriental cults with
the love which Paul adores in Christ, and he will
hardly escape the feeling that the gulf between them
is that between the mythical and the historical." [8]

When we pass on to consider how Paul conceived
of the relation between God and Christ, one or two
cautions are necessary. First, we have to remember
that all we have of his writing is a collection of letters.
One or two of them may run, like Romans, to the
length and something of the care of a treatise ; but
they are all primarily occasional, called out by situations or by questions. We have to remember that he
is dealing with a problem the perplexities of which
are not yet all exhausted, a problem where certainty
would seem to depend on completer knowledge than
is yet available for us. We have to remember that we
do not in any real sense know the Christology of the
group of Christians whom Paul found ; but we may
be sure of this at least—from a comparison of Paul's
own writings and from the study of Church History—

---

[1] Rom. viii. 35-39.   [2] 2 Cor. iii. 18.   [3] Rom. viii. 30.
[4] Phil. iii. 21.   [5] Phil. iii. 1.   [6] 1 Cor. iii. 23.
[7] *Literature and Dogma*, p. 260.   [8] W. Morgan, *Paul*, p. 40.

that that earliest Christology, whatever it was, was not Nicene and could not be. We have to remember that, if it was not Nicene, it was not necessarily wrong nor necessarily right ; that it may have contained the Nicene solution in germ, and also have been susceptible of other developments. In short, we have to remember what is perfectly obvious—that Paul was a pioneer, investigating what, upon the most orthodox and Nicene hypothesis, Jesus could not well have explained to his followers, and what, so far as the historical evidence available serves, he did not explain.

We must recall the fixed points with which we have in any case to start. Paul was a Jew, with the monotheism of a Jew and a Jew's dislike for anything that impinged or seemed to impinge on monotheism. He was face to face with apparently spiritual phaenomena, the explanation of which was not clear even in Wesley's time—viz., speaking with tongues, the descent of the Holy Spirit, and what people have called miracles, some attributing them directly to God, others using the mediary processes of suggestion and so forth to explain them.[1] Paul, again, was convinced that he had seen the glorified Jesus face to face. Finally, in his own life, in things more serious than the sudden and startling healing of diseases, he had come into contact with what he could only call the power of God. His categories, his modes of thought, his Psychology, and his general outlook on the universe were not ours, and there is no return to them possible for us. Such terms as spiritual, evolution, eschatological, suggestion, remind us at once of the changes in vocabulary that the centuries have brought and the changes of preconception which they imply. The term God ought to remind us of this equally, but it

---

[1] It may be noted that, until we can finally and accurately distinguish between natural and supernatural, the use of the word *miracle*, whether as a general term or with reference to a particular case, may be premature.

does not as a rule, and there lies our difficulty. For us it is charged (though we may be unaware of it) with a vast medley of unrelated or ill-related contributions derived from various strata of the Old Testament (prophetic, pre-prophetic, and legalistic), from Greek philosophy of every school from Plato to Plotinus, from primitive animism and from modern science, from Roman law and from the teaching of Jesus. The first step to an understanding of Paul's views, or the views of the church at any stage, is to unlearn enough of our own certainty to be able to see and to feel as clearly as we can the mind of the man or the period we are studying. Here such a prolonged and intricate investigation is not possible ; all that can be done is to give a few indications with a baldness of outline, that, taken aright, may be of use, and, taken amiss, will lead at once to inaccuracy.

Paul's language lends colour to the view that he identifies the source of spiritual manifestations in his early church with the Spirit, and the Spirit with Jesus himself.[1] Nicene Christianity got the Spirit differentiated from Jesus ; but that was at a much later date. What the modern church makes of the Spirit, when it is not merely reciting quotations, it is hard to say ; very little, might be the answer, if we were truthful. One great theologian of our day, at any rate, says bluntly that no original work has been done by the church upon the Holy Spirit since the days of the Apostles. Let the reader try if he can to make a real distinction between God and the Spirit of God, as men of that age thought they could. Is there any statement of divine action on the world or divine relation to the world of men, where we could use the one expression and not the other ? " Ye are not in the flesh, but in the Spirit, if the Spirit of God dwelleth in you. But if any man have not the Spirit of Christ he is none of his. And if Christ is in you, the body is

---

[1] See discussion of W. Morgan, *Paul*, pp. 24-26.

dead because of sin, but the Spirit is life because of righteousness. But if the Spirit of him that raised up Jesus from the dead dwelleth in you, he that raised up Christ Jesus from the dead shall quicken also your mortal bodies through his Spirit that dwelleth in you." [1] No Greek of the Classical day could have written a sentence so entangled and so perplexing. We are familiar in medieval theology and hymnody with almost algebraic balancing of terms in different senses, as in the hymn from J. H. Newman's *Gerontius*. Paul is obviously doing nothing of the kind. The Spirit is here at once and equally the Spirit of God and of Christ, as elsewhere ; [2] and the indwelling of the Spirit thus doubly described is also the indwelling of Christ. (A modern attempt to get rid of the difficulty by giving " Spirit " of Christ a small letter would not be true to the Greek ; that idea is conveyed by Paul as " the mind of Christ "). Elsewhere Paul says explicitly : " The Lord is the Spirit, and where the Spirit of the Lord is, there is liberty." [3] The Spirit and the Risen Christ are for him practically indistinguishable—the source of the new life, the earnest of God's intentions for us, the hope of glory, the origin of the graces of love, joy, peace and the rest. The indwelling Christ seems to leave nothing distinctive for the Spirit to do or to be. Once more we have to recall the extreme vagueness and fluidity of the conception of Spirit in that age. We can see how no one speaking in the Spirit could conceivably call Jesus accursed.[4]

In the next place, Paul does not in explicit description equate God and Christ. " Christ is given a place inferior to God, and his work as Mediator and Reconciler is eventually traced to the Father as originative cause." [5] God sent forth His Son ; [6]— spared not His own Son ; [7]—it pleased the Father

---

[1] Rom. viii. 9-11.   [2] Gal. iv. 6.   [3] 2 Cor. iii. 17.
[4] 1 Cor. xii. 3.   [5] H. R. Mackintosh, *Person of Christ*, p. 71.
[6] Gal. iv. 4.   [7] Rom. viii. 32.

that in him all fulness should dwell ; [1]—Christ, being in the form of God, did not think it a prize to be caught at, to be equal with God, but God has highly exalted him and given him a name above every name ; [2]— Christ is God's ; [3]—and the head of Christ is God, as the head of the woman is the man.[4] Finally, there is the strange verse in the Resurrection chapter, to which verse we have not the key : " Then shall the Son also himself be subjected to him that did subject all things unto him, that God may be all in all." [5]

Yet at the same time, when it comes to the work of Christ in the present-day world, Paul assigns to Christ the same functions as to God and the same attributes,[6] and transfers to Christ words used in the Old Testament of God. He derives his apostolate from God or from Christ.[7] His favourite term for Christ, " the Lord," was a Septuagint name for God—a more significant fact than its use by contemporary pagans for their gods. Every knee is to bow to Jehovah, says the second Isaiah ; to Christ Jesus, says Paul, and says it twice.[8] To Christ he transfers the words of Joel : " Whosoever shall call on the name of the Lord shall be saved." [9] He describes believers as those who call on the name of the Lord Jesus [10]—a recognition that men did actually address prayer to Jesus, and surely an acceptance of their practice, though it is pointed out that the usual expression among New Testament writers is that prayer is addressed to God in Christ's name. To clinch this, we have the famous passage of the " thorn in the flesh " : [11] " For this thing I besought the Lord thrice, that it might depart from me. And he said

---

[1] Col. i. 19. [2] Phil. ii. 6, 9.
[3] 1 Cor. iii. 23. [4] 1 Cor. xi. 3.
[5] 1 Cor. xv. 28. [6] See W. Morgan, *Paul*, pp. 43 ff.
[7] Compare Gal. i. 15, and 2 Cor. v. 18 (God's call), with 2 Cor. x. 8, xiii. 10 (the Lord).
[8] Isa. xlv. 23 ; Phil. ii. 10 ; Rom. xiv. 11.
[9] Rom. x. 13 ; Joel ii. 32.
[10] W. Morgan, *Paul*, pp. 44, 45. [11] 2 Cor. xii. 8 ff.

unto me, My grace is sufficient for thee; for my strength is made perfect in weakness." The sentences that follow show plainly who " the Lord " is. " Most gladly therefore will I rather glory in my infirmities, that the power of Christ may rest upon me. Therefore I take pleasure in infirmities, in reproaches, in necessities, in persecutions, in distresses for Christ's sake."

Of the three points which we have noticed, this identification of function and attribute is much the most significant, especially in view of the short interval of time between the crucifixion and Paul's writing. The historian will ask how it came about; the philosopher will ask what is its validity or what is its value. At the centre of it all was the reconciliation with God—" God was in Christ reconciling the world to himself "; the peace with God—" therefore being justified by faith, we have peace with God " ; [1] the new creation, the new life, and the new evidence of power. If we might borrow a modern word from another field, the power of God, God Himself, was liberated in Christ. All this was nothing without God. Paul, like ourselves in being without a key to all the mysteries of personality, proceeded from Jesus to God, and found no difference in mind or nature. Whatever may be said on the technical side of Theology—particularly where our conceptions are insufficiently analysed and remain compound and indistinct—there is a strong defence for Paul's movement of mind. He finds God and Christ equivalent in function; he finds love (not a vague general benevolence, but a personal attachment to the individual) the moving principle of Christ and God; he sees the world shaken by a new power in the preaching of Christ; and he goes forward to a practical conclusion, which those will count invalid

---

[1] Rom. v. 1; the indicative is surely confirmed against the subjunctive, in this passage, even if scholars will not allow us to use the constant thought of Paul, by verse 10, " we were reconciled."

who have not his experience and who are content with preconceptions. The Christian church, perhaps before him, certainly after him, has accepted that conclusion, and where it has used that conclusion in life and action, it has had again the evidence that Paul had— fresh experience of power and the happiness of resting upon a real love at the heart of things. Where it has modified that conclusion, its appeal to mankind, its belief in God, and its own power of work and happiness, have flagged. Such evidence demands of course to be tested, as does all genuine evidence on matters of vital import ; our deductions from it need perpetual examination. But what underlies the facts of Christian experience ? After all the love of Christ still constrains men, and the conclusion is hard to resist that God was in Christ reconciling the world to Himself.

CHAPTER X

THE CONSUMMATION

OF late years a new and intenser study has been given
to Apocalyptic writers and to their ideas ; and, as
happens when a new subject absorbs attention, very
different opinions are held as to the part played by
these writers in shaping religious thought in their day
and, more particularly, their influence upon the whole
Christian movement and upon Jesus himself. On the
one hand, we are shown a Jesus very much on a level
with the average mind of his day—and, one is tempted
to say, not quite on a level with the average intelligence
of our own day, still less of Plato's day,—and we are
told we must repeat Paul's experience and know
Christ after the flesh no more ; the historical Jesus is
no longer to be very much of a help to us.[1] On the
other hand, we are told that the best thing we can do
with the Apocalyptic writers is to forget them. In
most controversies of the kind there is a middle way—
very often several middle ways, some of which may
mean nothing and one of which may lead us aright.
" If in this life only we have hope in Christ, we are
of all men most miserable," said Paul.[2] Some forward
look is involved in any serious attempt to make one
universe of God's doings. But we might not be much
less miserable, if we were tied down to the feeble fore-
casts and the tribal conceptions of God offered to us
by Jewish Apocalyptic. In any case, whatever other
canons are valid, it is surely certain that it is the worst of
bad criticism to attribute one man's ideas to another,

[1] See Schweitzer, *Quest of Historical Jesus*, p. 399.
[2] 1 Cor. xv. 19.

when one of the pair is commonplace and the other a genius ; the sin against sense is not to be forgiven on the plea that both used the same words. Words, in spite of dictionaries, never mean the same thing. The observation of Heraclitus that " All is flux," that we never step into the same river twice, applies to words also.

We are told that " with both feet Paul stands on primitive Apocalyptic ground. . . . In Apocalyptic his preaching of redemption has, in part at least, its background." [1] He thinks, we are told, in terms of two worlds ; he stands in the old and evil age, and looks with eager longing to the new, pessimistic about the old, hopeful as to the new. Nature, all of it, is involved in sin and ruined by it ; all have sinned ; in the flesh there is nothing good ; and Nature groans in concert with man's ruin. This is an age of death, itself the outcome of man's sin. Round man are daemon powers at war with God—though in truth this particular belief has no special connexion with Apocalyptic, as the belief in spirits is world-wide and in most regions they are considered to be generally evil. Eventually God is to win, Satan is to be cast underfoot, and a new era is to begin. And all this, so far from being philosophic, belongs not to the domain of reasoned thought, but of mythology. The war, the daemons, the Messiah, the world-catastrophe—it is all mythological drama.

Perhaps this is all true, and yet not all the truth. Perhaps the gifted writer, whom I have been quoting, has forgotten what Plato says about his Myths. [2] It will not be a sufficient retort that Plato knew his Myths to be Myths,—not myths in our common English sense ; and that Paul took his to be Gospel truth. " I do not mean to affirm that the description, which I have given of the soul and her mansions, is exactly true

---

[1] See W. Morgan, *Paul*, pp. 11-15.
[2] Plato, *Phaedo*, 114 (Jowett).

—a man of sense ought hardly to say that. But I do say that inasmuch as the soul is shown to be immortal, he may venture to think not improperly or unworthily, that something of the kind is true." So says Plato. Let us imagine Paul confronted with the quiet judgments of some scholars of our day, of another type from those so far quoted. One tells us—and him—that " it does not appear that any one of the attempts to bring the teachings of St Paul into perfect harmony is altogether successful. The likelihood is that he had not attained to the goal of his thinking on this subject." [1] Another says it is " impossible to get a systematic scheme of eschatology out of Paul." [2] A third says that " Paul has no eschatology . . . he has never approached the subject in a systematic fashion," he does not give us material for a scheme nor attempt to reach such a construction himself.[3] What would Paul have said ? Can any one have entered into Paul's mind and nature, or read the letter to the Philippians [4] with any intelligence, and not feel that Paul would have laughed and admitted the indictment, that he would have quoted the *Phaedo* if he had known it, and that he would have swept clear of pictures and scenes, and emphasized the exceeding greatness of Christ's power, and perhaps struck off a new expression of his conviction that " He must reign " ? [5] Let his background have been Apocalyptic—two worlds, the present evil world, the good age to come, cataclysm, catastrophe, judgment—the daemon-world of every animist into the bargain—he talks experience, and the Apocalyptic writers guess-work; they dream ; he has lived and has his feet on something solider than any world of theirs.

[1] Leckie, *World to Come*, p. 181.
[2] Stevens, *Theology of New Testament*, p. 482.
[3] H. A. A. Kennedy, *Paul and Last Things*, p. 21.
[4] Phil. iii. 12-16.
[5] 1 Cor. xv. 25.

P

Professor Kennedy [1] offers us a key to the discussion when he points out that men represent the Last Things to their minds by pictures, which stamp themselves on the imagination; the pictures are outgrown in thought, but being pictures they haunt the imagination and remain, rough working instruments of thought, while their content, their value and significance are undergoing change, till at last they mean something quite different. Paul starts with his contemporaries, hears the same sort of account of the things of God and History, perhaps reads some of the same books, uses the same language ; but, once more, genius and experience make all the difference.

Paul was confronted with the same problem as the Apocalyptic writers. There are ages when things go well with the world — or, to be more exact, with nations,—or, at least, with those classes in the nations who write the books and who shape the thoughts, never (it should be added) without some relation to the general feeling of their own people and perhaps others. Then one world suffices—" the world went very well then." There are other ages of breakdown, some of which may be compared (the comparison is made by Paul and the fourth Gospel [2]) to a scene of child-birth ; will the mother live—or that civilization survive, that is the nidus of real life ? Or will the mother die, and nothing survive but the child—a new start, with all to learn at the old cost, a waste terrible to the mind of any who understands ? Is all to be washed away that man has built upon the floodbanks ? Is all in vain ? Is there to be perceptible again any principle of right in human things—and triumphant ? The easy dogma of natural, inevitable and effortless Progress, is quite modern,[3] as Professor Bury has

---

[1] *Paul and Last Things*, p. 36.
[2] John xvi. 21 ; cf. Rom. viii. 22.
[3] Perhaps it is not now widely held outside the United States, that home of lost causes, forsaken beliefs and impossible loyalties.

shown ;[1] it is due to confusion of ideas ; it omits important factors ; it forgets that History denies one of its main elements, for progress has never been effortless ; it forgets the sheer devil in the human heart. It is easy to talk of the swing of the pendulum, to say cheerily that things will right themselves. There are the histories of long ages to be read, when things did not right themselves. It is just as possible for a human society continuously to decline as continuously to advance.[2] There is no known guarantee in Nature, or in human nature, that a positive end of folly and degeneracy must some day be reached. Optimists may hold that a bottomless pit must have a bottom somewhere ; the question is, has it ? And there is yet another question, Would that bottom be a sound foundation for a regenerated society, for the City of God or any modern equivalent of it ?

When such thoughts come over the thinking portion of a people, something must be found once more to inspire effort. The Apocalyptists—to their credit, and in spite of their triviality and tiresomeness—recognized that the Prophets were right, and that there is still God in the world—or, perhaps, rather, outside it, but still in the scheme of things. Then, as Jeremiah saw,[3] God is not to be permanently baffled by human folly and wickedness ; He has probably more shots in His locker than He tells us, another card in His hand which we have forgotten. (The Greek poet Sophocles at least suggests that God's dice always fall favourably for His game.) If He puts His hand to the human race, depend upon it He has a purpose, which nothing will stop Him carrying through. If we can discover that purpose, and work for it, nothing we do can be in vain ; or, if human forces against us are too strong, then God Himself will step

---

[1] In his book, *The Idea of Progress*, 1920.
[2] As for instance in many states of Latin America.
[3] Jer. xxxi. 31.

in and close the game ; one way or other, the arm of
the Lord will be revealed. He is not tied down to one
world as we are ; He who made this world can make as
many more worlds as He needs to mature His purpose.
He has only to speak, and it is done.

It has been suggested that Apocalyptic gives us a
Jewish philosophy of history,[1] a Semitic philosophy of
religion [2]—" an attempt to see the world steadily and
to see it whole, to unify the physical world, the moral
world, and the political world, the world, that is,
of the national destiny of God's chosen people." [3]
This is well put—it is such a philosophy of history as
is possible with one intractable reservation ; nationalist
dogma ran through all. For this reservation there was
a twofold apology no doubt, resting on dogma and
in a degree on experience. Apocalyptic, in short,
as Professor Burkitt says of one apocalypse, " like so
many things that come down to us from the Jews, is
a strange mixture of hope and despair, of prejudice
and insight." [4] No consistent account of History, past
and future, can be made of the data of the various
writers of Apocalypses ; they were not bound to any
particular general outline, they were not exponents
of any standardized doctrine ; if they are related, it
is by borrowing and adaptation. Nor is it always
easy to make a unity of what a single writer gives us,
even when it is definitely certain that a book as we
receive it is really the work of one author and not,
like *Enoch*, pieced together out of fragments of various
books. Certainty, definition of outline, agreement
are hard enough for historians to achieve with docu-

---

[1] F. C. Burkitt, *Jewish and Christian Apocalypses*, p. 7, referring
to *Daniel* in particular.
[2] R. H. Charles, *Eschatology*, p. 182.
[3] F. C. Burkitt, *op. cit.*, p. 21, of *Enoch*.
[4] F. C. Burkitt, *op. cit.*, 39, of the *Assumption of Moses*. Cf. R. T.
Herford, *The Pharisees*, p. 191, " Apocalyptic uses the words of hope
but its message is despair, despair of all human means for establishing
the Kindgom of God on earth. . . ."

ments and evidence before them ; for prophets who
rest on intuition, inference, dogma and sheer fancy,
they are obviously impossible.

Some of their data the Apocalyptic writers draw
from the Prophets—" the day of the Lord," for
instance, as a crucial and central factor in all history,
God's universal sway and survey, the conception of
some final adjustment of world and fact to God's
ideals, and sometimes of a Servant of the Lord who in
some way may be instrumental in God's final triumph.
These ancient contributions of the Prophets to the
picture include, it would appear, no clear reference
to the individual man, no message of light for him.[1]
Yet the individual could not be kept out, and in time
he made himself felt in all Apocalyptic forecast. What
was morality, if there were no individual in God's
scheme of things ? Men of light minds may still talk
of national morality and corporate thinking, but
behind such conceptions and more real is the man who
is moral and who thinks, or the man who is not interested in morality or thought.   Even the Prophets had
to deal with the individual ; whatever they say of the
nation, they were confronted by the man whose father
had eaten sour grapes ; would his own teeth be set on
edge ? Jeremiah, in his most famous passsage, looked
clear past the nation to the day when every individual
man would know the Lord and have the Lord's words
written in his heart and need no brother to tell him
to obey them ; it would be a New Covenant indeed.[2]
The early church was quick to see how the prophecy
could be used, and here at least their use of the Old
Testament was not independent of its meaning.

When all the world had justice done to it, it was
clear to the Israelite that Israel's day would come ;
there would be a Kingdom of Israel all over the world,
brought in by an anointed Servant of God, perhaps
of David's line—though the Maccabaeans, who seemed

[1] R. H. Charles, *Eschatology*, p. 178.   [2] Jer. xxxi. 31.

to promise the fulfilment of this prophecy, were not
Davidic, but perhaps (more vaguely) of the order of
Melchizedek.[1] But what became of the dead Israelite,
who had all his life looked for the coming of this
Kingdom—was he to be disappointed ? No ! he
was to come in ; and he came in and brought confusion
with him. He was presumably not lost,—he was in
some way so far immortal—he would need a body,
however, for the Kingdom, and he would receive it ;
there would be Resurrection. But one individual
can never be treated alone ; admit one case and ten
thousand appeals follow. Here is the Kingdom of
the Messiah,[2] an earthly Paradise, in which the return-
ing dead share, endowed with new bodies receptive
of mundane joys ; and all the ten thousand appeals
have to be settled. So there is obviously a Last
Judgment and cases are heard and decided—and, of
course, with absolute Justice. Not *all* Israelites, but
good Israelites are admitted. The just alone shall rise,
some said. Others drew a more fair conclusion—all
men shall rise and all men shall be judged ; which
in the end must imply that there is no particular
Kingdom of Israel. The attempts at a mundane Kingdom all miscarried ; and after all it was perhaps a little
ludicrous—at least to people conversant with Greek
ideas, this earthly Kingdom full of people with new
bodies. The Kingdom became spiritualized in some
way, and its standard features were all in turn slurred
over or lost ; perhaps there would be a temporary
Kingdom on earth to be followed by Judgment and
Heaven. But now the thing became purely spiritual,
and universal ; it was to be in heaven, no new bodies
were needed, immortal spirits were enough, or by way

---

[1] Psalm cx.
[2] For what follows see W. Fairweather, *Background of the Gospels*,
Chap. VII. ; J. H. Leckie, *World to Come*, Chaps. II. and III. ;
W. Morgan, *Paul*, Chap. I. ; H. A. A. Kennedy, *Paul and Last
Things*, pp. 59-76.

of compromise living and dead alike should receive spiritual bodies. Thus Resurrection yields to Immortality, the Jewish to the Greek idea. In heaven it could hardly be a Davidic Kingdom ; so David's son has a tendency to be eliminated ; and in fact, if it be, really and fundamentally, Immortality, it is hard to see what part or duties can be assigned to any Anointed One—unless perhaps he eventually judge quick and dead ; but if good and bad are distributed to their proper spheres at death—and even these are (in the judgment of some) interim spheres—the Messiah's functions seem very limited. Consequently, as we have seen, the Messiah drops out of some of the books altogether ; and a bodily resurrection logically drops out too—the *Book of Jubilees, Wisdom* and Philo ignore it. In short, the ethical predominates over the national interest, and a universal doctrine of Immortality really makes all the old apparatus mere lumber.

But theological lumber is as hard to get rid of as any lumber ; association may endear an old doctrine, or an old expression of a doctrine, as deeply and as surely as it will a piece of old furniture, a personal relic. " Only a woman's hair " Swift had written on a little packet found after his death in his desk ; was it worth keeping ? Perhaps not, for anybody else. Perhaps the forms, in which one's father expressed the beliefs on which his character was founded, may come to look old and inadequate ; but for his son, whatever expression he might personally prefer, the old formula, the old words, carry something of the man he knew ; and he will not readily respond to the cry, " New lamps for old." In the Arabian tale it was the new wife who responded to it and made the fatal exchange.

What attention, if any, Paul paid to Apocalyptic books before his conversion, we do not know. It is quite clear, as said already,[1] that they did not for him stand at all on a level with the Canonical books. It

---

[1] See Chap. IX., p. 205.

is easier to suppose that he was familiar with some doctrine of Immortality or Resurrection than it would be to maintain the opposite ; it is obvious. But this does not imply either knowledge of particular books or any particular theory. Once again, his views owe more to the vision of the Risen Jesus than to any book, and the conclusion seems clear that behind all his pictures of another world is the glimpse he had of it on the road to Damascus. That is his starting-point, and anything derived from books or teachers must thereafter be adjusted to what he had himself experienced. Then he begins to frame his own scheme of Last Things, his own philosophy of history and of religion. In the centre of it all is the Incarnation of the Son of God with his Crucifixion and Resurrection —not conjectural points, not removed to a greater or less distance from this present age, but actual events that came under the eyes of men and women still living. What became of the conjectural schemes then of Apocalyptists ? When these amazing facts of God's love of the world—of God's love of Paul—are thrust before a man's eyes, they must become the prime facts of any philosophy of religion or history that he shapes for himself. If certain features of Apocalyptic remain —the badness of the present age, does one really need to go to Apocalyptic to be told that an age that crucified Jesus is not ideal ? Immortality—can Apocalyptic supplement or confirm the Damascus vision ? The transformation of the age—when Paul has experienced it in himself and seen it in his friends and in his churches ? All that Apocalyptic has really to contribute is the Second Coming of Christ ; and to a man for whom the cleavage between right and wrong was more drastic than for any Apocalyptist, for whom any end to things but the utmost victory of Christ was unthinkable, it must sooner or later have been clear that whatever steps remained to complete that victory Christ would take. The form or picture was perhaps suggested by Apocalyptic ; the value of it came from elsewhere. The content of all that he says comes from Christ. Here as elsewhere he might plead for the newness of spirit as against the oldness of the letter.[1] It is not clear how far Paul was influenced in things eschatological by the teaching of Jesus. A good deal is said in the Gospels—and a good deal more is made of it by some readers—which might imply that Jesus shared the Apocalyptic view. As we have seen, it is urged that Jesus held that view so centrally as to make him unserviceable for the religious life of to-day.[2] But Matthew Arnold's dictum of long ago is still unrefuted ; Jesus was above his reporters. Paul, coming into the Christian community without their personal experience of the Master on earth, was naturally dependent on their reports. His early preaching did contain a reference to the return of Jesus and apparently an early return. He wrote explicitly of it to the Thessalonians. " If we believe that Jesus died and rose again, even so them also which sleep in Jesus will God bring with him. For this we say unto you by the word of the Lord, that we which are alive and remain unto the coming of the Lord shall not precede them which are asleep. For the Lord himself shall descend from Heaven with a shout, with the voice of the archangel, and with the trump of God ; and the dead in Christ shall rise first. Then we which are alive and remain shall be caught up together with them in the clouds to meet the Lord in the air ; and so shall we be ever with the Lord." [3] It is not needful here to discuss the difficult question of the relations of the two epistles to the Thessalonians ; both appear to be genuine, and they seem to be contemporary. In the second, there is an added touch : [4]

[1] Rom. vii. 6.   [2] See page 223.   [3] 1 Thess. iv. 14-17.
[4] 2 Thess. i. 7-10 ; for the quotations see Appendix to Westcott and Hort.

" The Lord Jesus shall be revealed from heaven with his mighty angels, in flaming fire taking vengeance on them that know not God and that obey not the gospel of our Lord Jesus Christ, who shall be punished with everlasting destruction from the presence of the Lord and from the glory of his power, when he shall come to be glorified in his saints and to be admired in all them that believe." The passage is a curious mosaic of small phrases from different parts of the Septuagint.

Probably nothing in Paul is so thoroughly typical of the mind of his contemporary Christians as the picture given in these two passages. It is significant that he does not repeat it in later letters. The whole tone of his mind more and more impresses an attentive reader with the feeling that the Thessalonian passages are somehow not the real Paul [1]—certainly not the ultimate Paul. If the passages came in Jude's epistle, they would give no surprise. Paul does not give up the return of Christ, but he seems with time to have felt it to be of less immediate interest ; and he discards the Old Testament picture language.

A comparison and a contrast will make this clear. To the Romans he writes of the reward of the good and patient in eternal life, and of the " indignation and wrath, tribulation and anguish " predestined for those who fight against truth.[2] Jesus and Plato had said as much. The stress is on the sheer facts of the case and their bearing on morality and honesty : " God will judge the secrets of men by Jesus Christ." [3] We have seen already how intimate a thought, how deep a conviction, of Paul's this certainty of judgment had been from the beginning, how vital a factor in that upheaval which led to his conversion. " We must all be exhibited before the judgment seat of Christ," is a thought which he never lost. But the tone is not that of the letters to the Thessalonians ; the note

[1] I do not mean that they are interpolations.
[2] Rom. ii. 7-9.
[3] Rom. ii. 16.

is deeper. In the chapter which he writes to the
Corinthians he might have repeated the earlier picture ;
it is noticeable that he does not, and it is worth while
to ask why. He says emphatically that flesh and blood
cannot inherit the Kingdom of God, nor corruption
incorruption ; the heavenly body will be different
somehow from the earthly—it will be spiritual, and
there he leaves its description ; and he continues :
" Behold, I show you a mystery ; We shall not all
sleep (*i.e.* we shall none of us sleep), but we shall be
changed, in a moment, in the twinkling of an eye, at
the last trump. For the trumpet shall sound, and
the dead shall be raised incorruptible and we shall be
changed." Death has lost its sting, the grave will lose
its victory ; " but thanks be to God which giveth us
the victory through our Lord Jesus Christ." [1]   There
is a distinct change in handling ; he is laying more
emphasis on the fundamental and is less interested in
the manner.[2] Perhaps he is less certain that the picture
is as true as it might be ; he is surely clearer that it is
not after all of first importance. It is further suggested [3]
that he found preoccupation with the Second Coming
and its phaenomena to militate against that concentration on life and reality which is one part of a Christian's
essential business for God. He believed in people
working ; he told the Thessalonians so at the time.[4]
They may be going to live to see the Lord come on the
clouds ; they had better go about their daily duties.
Once more it is a preference for sense and for the
fundamental. Meantime he has comfort for those
anxious about what they supposed to be the fatally
premature departure of their loved ones ; they were

[1] 1 Cor. xv. 43-57.
[2] Cf. H. A. A. Kennedy, *Paul and Last Things*, p. 196, " an almost
complete lack of scenery " in Paul's presentment of the Second Coming,
in contrast with Apocalyptic writers.
[3] Hastings Rashdall, *Conscience and Christ*, p. 209.
[4] 2 Thess. iii. 6-14.

safe with God; he believes in the soul and its
immortality, whatever his view of resurrection.

The discussion so far shows us what we have seen in
other regions of our study—a Paul who inherits ideas,
who responds to the preconceptions of his environment,
but who more and more bases himself on experience.
Men had the picture of the Messiah on the clouds as
they had that of a reigning Israel. Paul has faced a
living Christ; and in a life, which did not grow slacker
but intenser, he has tested the life of Christ—does he
live, does he reign, has he the power, does he achieve?
Paul is loyal to the fact discovered in all the experiments he records.[1] He does not discard all he has
inherited; perhaps he believed to the end what he
told the Thessalonians, that Christ would come on the
clouds and we should meet him in the air, just as from
affection he held on to the idea that Israel has still
some function of importance in God's universe. But
his great convictions are far more closely in touch with
the experience of the Church in all ages; Israel *may*
have a part to play, though that has grown less likely
with the centuries; the Second Coming *may* take the
form that ancient dreamers gave it; perhaps—but
one thing admits of no perhaps: " He must reign." [2]
The words sum up the real eschatology of Paul, and
they are the fruit of his experience.

He is as convinced as any Apocalyptic writer that
God does not improvise. God had a plan, which God
kept to Himself till the hour came—a plan which
embraced everything and everybody that God had
ever thought of, a plan with no gaps and no after-
thoughts. So much was bound up even with the
Greek conception of a vague Providence; how much
more with the God who has been made known by a
Hosea, a Jeremiah, a second Isaiah—Whose nature has
been shown by Jesus ? " Before the foundation of the
world " God foresaw and foreordained its story—and

---

[1] E.g. 2 Cor. xi. 23 ff.   [2] I Cor. xv. 25.

chose His agents,[1] Paul among them. To people who have no clear notion at all what they are doing in the world, Paul's conviction that God " set him apart, from his mother's womb " [2] is of course unintelligible. It is a conviction that other men have shared before and after Paul, from Jeremiah onwards ; [3] and if Paul and Paul's outlooks are to be understood, that conviction must be recognized as central. Many impulsive people have felt the same thing, and there has been some conspicuous contrast between their belief and the ends they proposed, or the character with which they thought of doing things, or the effect they produced in the world—a contrast so strong that it has been clear to quieter minds that God never chose such persons and never harboured such purposes. But Paul is one of the men against whom such criticism cannot be brought. His certainty that God has a plan for the universe rests not merely on Jewish dogma about God, a deduction from a syllogism about omniscience, but on a consciousness that God had a plan for Paul, not of Paul's choice or devising, which was carried through all against Paul's initial wishes, and was justified. We also have to admit with History before us that this conviction of Paul has been justified by the experience of nineteen centuries.

We start then with Paul's belief in a plan of God's for the world—" that nothing walks with aimless feet "—with his belief, much like that of Jeremiah,[4] that Israel, for all Israel's waywardness and folly, will never really succeed in wrecking God's plan—no, nor Satan nor any other prince of the power of the air, nor any combination of principalities and powers, even if evil men, getting worse and worse,[5] coppersmiths [6] and emperors,[7] join with them. Paul may be in bonds, " but the Word of God is no prisoner." [8] If he is

[1] Eph. i. 4.   [2] Gal. i. 15.   [3] Jer. i.
[4] Jer. xxxi. 31.   [5] 2 Tim. iii. 13.   [6] 2 Tim. iv. 14.
[7] 2 Tim. iv. 17.   [8] 2 Tim. ii. 9 ; cf. Isa. lv. 11.

asked for his evidence, it begins with the ludicrous failure of the spiritual and social leaders of Israel, reinforced by a young man from Tarsus in Cilicia, to stamp out the church of Christ when it was a mere handful of trivial people in Jerusalem, when (to a historian looking back) its theology was elementary and contradictory and doomed to collapse at the first touch of Jewish learning or of Greek thought. The rest of his evidence was of the same kind—a mass of experience that no man could have foretold, all shot through with one note of incredible triumph—$\acute{v}\pi\epsilon\rho\nu\iota\kappa\hat{\omega}\mu\epsilon\nu$,[1] all full of proof of the presence of God in His power and His wisdom. Jewish Apocalyptic has nothing of the kind to offer—nothing even distantly like it, except the struggling survival of Judaism.

Paul inherited the spiritual experience of Israel, and he is right in emphasizing the immense value of it ; he had read the story of patriarch and prophet with keener eyes and a more responsive heart than any Apocalyptist—with the eyes and the heart of genius, and none of them can claim anything beyond mediocrity. His Christian experience showed him that the thread, which they believed somehow to run through history, was indubitably there, and of far stronger texture than any of them could have guessed ; they had never tried to snap it, they had never been bound and tied up with it, as he had. He was the heir of the prophets, and he *knew*, in virtue both of genius and experience. He inherited the prophetic sense of God, as we saw from the beginning of our study—the realization of God's righteousness and attention and power ; and he tested what he inherited and made it his own. There was indeed a vital force running through all history, and nothing that the prophets had read in the nature of God was lost. All was confirmed and developed in Jesus Christ and brought to a tremendous and splendid certainty. The Crucifixion

[1] Rom. viii. 37.

had proved to be the confirmation of all, the evidence
of triumph ; God's character was known now and His
great plan was being revealed.

The crowning sorrow of every prophet, the problem
of every apocalyptist, was Israel's rejection of God,
of God's ideas and of God's law, with the awful narrow-
ing down of God's triumph that it involved. God
would indeed win the victory over the devil and his
angels, but a Pyrrhic victory ; He would come out
of the fray conqueror with a mere handful of His
forces ; they were few who should be saved, a remnant,
and the vast masses of mankind that were to have been
his auxiliaries were the hopeless prey of Satan, swept
into Gehenna with their captor, lost to God. " Now
I see," we read in Fourth Ezra, " that the coming age
shall bring delight to few but torment to many." [1]
The Apocalyptist pleads that the Most High is called
compassionate, gracious, long-suffering, and forgiving ;
and the reply comes, " This age the Most High has
made for many, but the age to come for few. . . .
Many have been created, but few shall be saved." [2]
" I saw and spared some with great difficulty, and
saved me a grape out of a cluster, and a plant out of
a great forest. Perish then the multitude which has
been born in vain ; but let my grape be preserved
and my plant which with much labour I have perfected." [3]   It is suggested that the nations (except a
few individuals [4]) deliberately rejected the Law of
God ; [5] " they even affirmed that the Most High
exists not." [6]   If, as is evident, it is hard for a man to
understand God's doings, " how should it be possible
for a mortal in a corruptible world to understand the
ways of the Incorruptible ? " [7]   " It would have been
better," reflects the Apocalyptist, " that we had never
been created than having come (into the world) to

---

[1] 4 Ezra vii. 47.   [2] 4 Ezra viii. 3.   [3] 4 Ezra vii. 21, 22.
[4] 4 Ezra iii. 36.   [5] 4 Ezra vii. 23, 24.   [6] 4 Ezra vii. 23.
[7] 4 Ezra iv. 11.

live in sins and to suffer, and not to know why we
suffer." [1] " If then with a light word thou shalt
destroy him, who with such infinite labour has been
fashioned by thy command, to what purpose was he
made ? But now I will say : Concerning man in
general (*i.e.* the Gentile world) thou knowest best,"
and he turns to the question of Israel, which is a little
more compassable.[2] Things have not turned out as
the Almighty had wished—" The Most High willed
not that men should come to destruction ; but they—
His creatures—have themselves defiled the Name of
Him that made them, and have proved themselves
ungrateful to Him who prepared life for them. Therefore my judgment is now nigh at hand." [3] " I will
not concern myself," so the word of God is suppoesd
to say, " about the creation of those who have sinned,
or their death, judgment, or perdition " ; [4] God will
concentrate His mind on the few righteous, and Ezra
is advised to do the same. " Do thou rather think of
thine own case, and of them who are like thyself search
out the glory. For for you is opened Paradise, planted
the tree of life, the future Age prepared, plenteousness
made ready, a City builded, a Rest appointed, good
works established, wisdom preconstituted ; the (evil)
root is sealed up from you, infirmity from your path
extinguished, and Death is hidden, Hades fled away,
Corruption forgotten, sorrows passed away ; and in
the end the treasures of immortality are made manifest.
Therefore ask no more concerning the multitude of
them that perish." [5] Even intercession for them is
forbidden.[6] So the mass of mankind are lost ; the
thoughtful Jew dismisses the matter—God knows
about it, no one else can understand it ; and God—
God did not wish it and won't think about it either ;
" perish then the multitude that was born in vain ! "

[1] 4 Ezra iv. 12. [2] 4 Ezra viii. 14-16.
[3] 4 Ezra viii. 60, 61. [4] 4 Ezra viii. 38.
[5] 4 Ezra viii. 51-55. [6] 4 Ezra vii. 102-105

But if for the Apocalyptist God's victory is so miserably limited that God Himself cannot think of it, for the Apostle there was another prospect. He had, if our reconstruction is right, loved the Gentiles from boyhood; he had never quite shared the Jew's " ready and not unwilling consignment of the non-believer and the non-Jew to perdition and gloom " ; [1] he had shared the Apocalyptist's perplexity, and " suddenly there shined round about him a light from heaven." " By revelation he made known to me the mystery which in other ages was not made known to the sons of men, as it is now revealed unto his holy apostles and prophets by the Spirit, that the Gentiles should be fellow-heirs and of the same body, and partakers of his promise in Christ by the gospel,—whereof I was made a minister." [2] The horrible cloud has rolled away, and " God hath shined in our hearts." [3] He has known in himself the joy of reconciliation with God, he has peace with God himself, and to him the unspeakable trust is given of preaching in all the Gentile world that God was in Christ reconciling the whole world to Himself. Was he the victim of delusion ? Then what was the meaning of the Christian church— the most glorious evidence of the power of God at work in the world, delivered from the power of darkness and translated into the Kingdom of His dear Son,[4] who loved the church and gave himself for it ? [5] The church may have every defect that we have noted, on Paul's observation, among the Corinthians ; it may be as futile and self-centred as we see it to-day ; but it is better than what it replaces—and that surely is an apocalyptic sign in itself ; and it carries in its heart the conviction that it must be " according to Christ," which is another sign of yet more significance ; and, in any case, it has proved that God's heart is large

[1] C. G. Montefiore, *Judaism and St Paul*, p. 56.
[2] Eph. iii. 5-7.   [3] 2 Cor. iv. 6.
[4] Col. i. 12, 13.   [5] Eph. v. 25.

Q

enough to contain mankind, and that is the best omen of all.

So, putting on one side the outward lineaments of a figure on the clouds, surrounded by others in strange and unexpected form, we have in Paul's writing and Paul's conviction a new and more glorious Apocalyptic, founded upon fact—founded on the renewal of Paul's own nature, on his peace with God, on God's visible and demonstrated call of the Gentiles, on the passing away of old problems in a great light, on the moral change from darkness to light, from death to life, of men all over the world, on the infectious gladness of the redeemed, and on fresh evidence every day of Christ's power to save. And what would be the end of it ? Could there be any end but one—the capture of the whole world for Jesus Christ and immortal life ? Could there be any limit to what God will do for Christ and in Christ, " the image of the invisible God, the firstborn of all creation ; for by him were all things created . . . and for him ; and he is before all things and by him all things consist. And he is the head of the body, the church ; who is the beginning, the firstborn from the dead, that in all things he might have the pre-eminence. For it pleased the Father that in him should all fulness dwell, and having made peace through the blood of his cross, by him to reconcile all things unto himself, whether things in earth, or things in heaven." [1] There is no limit to this reconciliation till all are reconciled, that Christ may be all and in all. Let the reader turn to the glowing and comprehensive pictures of the letters to the Colossians and the Ephesians, to the great prophecy of the final conquest of death (concentrating here on the great conception and not wandering off on the detail), to the eighth chapter of the letter to the Romans ; let him realize that all this is based on experience of the love of Christ and the power of God ;

[1] Col. i. 15-20.

and, if here and there the phrase is borrowed, will he not feel that the Apostle knows of what he speaks and draws a picture worthy of God ? The love of Christ constrains us to the belief that he must reign ; that the Son of God, who loved me and gave himself for me, will pursue his work of reconciliation till he is indeed all and in all.

INDEX OF BIBLICAL PASSAGES

GENERAL INDEX